Tea with Thomas Boston

"The Scottish Presbyterians of the seventeenth and eighteenth centuries—saturated as they were in the doctrine and piety of their Covenanter forefathers—were staunch allies of the English Puritan tradition, and proved, over the course of history, to be more stalwart in their defense and proclamation of the Westminster Standards than even the Puritans of Old and New England. Thomas Boston was no exception. A central figure in the Marrow Controversy, he defended Christian assurance and the free offer of the gospel with a passion. Combining rich biblical doctrine and warm, experiential piety, Dr. Chun Tse provides a taste of Boston's commentaries and sermons on the Westminster Shorter Catechism that is ideal for personal devotions, small group studies, and Sunday school lessons. Here is a treasure trove of Reformed catechesis, repackaged most delightfully for a fresh church audience. Enjoy your 'teatime' with Thomas Boston!"

—**JOEL R. BEEKE**, Chancellor, Puritan Reformed
Theological Seminary, Grand Rapids, Michigan

"Chun Tse has done the church a blessed favor by making the beautiful theology of Thomas Boston easily accessible to contemporary audiences through clear, profound daily readings based on all 107 questions and answers in the Westminster Shorter Catechism. By combining the best of Boston's catechetical instruction with Bible texts, application questions, and prayer prompts, Dr. Tse provides doctrinal insight for the Christian mind and spiritual refreshment for the believer's soul."

—**PHILIP RYKEN**, President, Wheaton College, Wheaton, Illinois

"This volume feeds the soul with the theological and pastoral insights of Thomas Boston, in a format which is accessible to all. A voice from the past speaks again for the present believer, and it is as powerful now as it was for his original flock. Dr. Tse is to be thanked for this labor of love and his commitment to the arresting idea of taking the most appropriate tea available in the company of Thomas Boston."

—**ALISON JACK**, Professor of Bible and Literature,
School of Divinity, University of Edinburgh

"Over the years I have tried to read for myself, and recommend for others, mini systematic theologies to grasp a comprehensive view of the Christian faith. And now I have just found my new favorite: *Tea with Thomas Boston*. It is not because I love tea. In fact, I do not drink tea or coffee. (Sorry, Dr. Tse!) Rather, this book has become my new recommended mini systematic theology because of Thomas Boston, a pastor-theologian I have come truly to appreciate in recent years. Thomas Boston is one of those theologians who gives you the whole Christ in the whole of Scripture, with memorable illustrations (see his 'covenant chariots' sent from heaven to earth to take us to heaven), and in pastorally applicable ways. The Westminster Shorter Catechism provides one of the most clear, concise, and comprehensive summaries of the Christian faith; and now, thanks to the efforts of Chun Tse, we have a most able teacher to guide us through it—the venerable Thomas Boston. So, sit back and, with a cup of tea in hand (if so inclined), drink in the riches of the Christian faith."

—**JONATHAN GIBSON**, Professor of Biblical and Systematic Theology, Westminster Theological Seminary, Philadelphia

"Loose leaf tea can, at first, seem rather dried up and uninspiring, but when it's given time to brew and infuse it can revive and refresh. Tse does just this as he intriguingly draws out the riches of Thomas Boston's commentary on the Shorter Catechism. This creative guide for individuals, families, and other groups encourages prayerful and scriptural reflection on the questions and answers of this catechism, helping draw out life-giving refreshment."

—**MARTYN C. COWAN**, Director of Postgraduate Research, Union Theological College, Belfast

"Chun Tse has given us a real gem—a solid devotional text based on Thomas Boston's sermons and notes on the Westminster Shorter Catechism. Divided into ninety-one devotional readings, we have instruction in the great doctrines of the Reformed faith, as well as literature which stirs the heart and strengthens faith. What more could a reader want?

—**KIM RIDDLEBARGER**, author of *A Case for Amillennialism*

"Thomas Boston (1676–1732) is one of the best-known figures in Scottish Church history, but most Christians today know relatively little of what he taught. *Tea with Thomas Boston* serves as a helpful summary of, and introduction to, Boston's theology. Dr. Chun Tse—an expert on Boston—has distilled his teaching on the Westminster Shorter Catechism into an accessible, devotional format that contemporary Christians will find spiritually instructive and edifying."

—**Russell Newton**, Academic Dean, The Faith Mission Bible College, Edinburgh

"This creative devotional breathes new life into Thomas Boston's insights on the Westminster Shorter Catechism, making his theological and practical wisdom accessible to modern readers. The *Tea with Thomas Boston* format creates a unique learning experience inviting you to join the great pastor in his theological study. Each devotion weaves Boston's exposition with thoughtful discussion questions that can be used for small group contexts. For those unfamiliar with Boston's writings, this book serves as a helpful introduction to one of Scotland's most gifted theologians. Dr. Tse helps us, through Boston's study, to cultivate a deeper love for Christ underneath a trusted guide."

—**Cory Brock**, Minister, St Columba's Free Church of Scotland, Edinburgh

"Christians need not only to retrieve sound doctrine; we also need the wisdom to know how to retrieve and apply Christian theology today. For this, Dr. Tse has accomplished two great things. First, he summarized the theology of a Reformed pastor with a heart for God and the church. Secondly, he invites us to meditate (through questions) on what we have learned to consider, then how we can apply it in our contexts. This is perfect to study with your friends!"

—**Israel José Guerrero Leiva**, Minister, Cornerstone Free Church, Edinburgh

"This devotional helps readers step back in time and sense what it was like for the beloved minister of Ettrick to visit their home and catechize them over a cup of tea. The daily readings present Boston's views on the Shorter Catechism in a way that makes deep doctrine accessible to all readers. Much of Boston's large corpus of writings still needs republishing for twenty-first century readers, and Chun Tse has provided a much-needed devotional and reader-friendly contribution to this task. Those who may be intimidated to read Boston's more lengthy works will find *Tea with Thomas Boston* an enjoyable and edifying read."

—**Ray Burbank**, Associate Pastor, Charlotte Chapel, Edinburgh

Tea with Thomas Boston

Devotionals on the Westminster Shorter Catechism

CHUN TSE

Foreword by Sinclair Ferguson

WIPF & STOCK · Eugene, Oregon

TEA WITH THOMAS BOSTON
Devotionals on the Westminster Shorter Catechism

Copyright © 2025 Chun Tse. All rights reserved. Except for brief quotations in critical publications or reviews, no part of this book may be reproduced in any manner without prior written permission from the publisher. Write: Permissions, Wipf and Stock Publishers, 199 W. 8th Ave., Suite 3, Eugene, OR 97401.

Wipf & Stock
An Imprint of Wipf and Stock Publishers
199 W. 8th Ave., Suite 3
Eugene, OR 97401

www.wipfandstock.com

PAPERBACK ISBN: 979-8-3852-4743-1
HARDCOVER ISBN: 979-8-3852-4744-8
EBOOK ISBN: 979-8-3852-4745-5

VERSION NUMBER 10/13/25

I would like to sit at Jonathan Edwards's feet, to learn what is true religion, and at Thomas Boston's, to learn how I am to get it.

Prof. John Duncan (1796—1870),
Chair of Hebrew and Oriental Languages,
New College, University of Edinburgh

Contents

Foreword by Sinclair Ferguson | xi
Preface | xvii
The Significance of the Westminster Shorter Catechism | xxi
A Brief Biography of Thomas Boston | xxv

PART 1: MAN'S CHIEF END AND SCRIPTURES (Q1—Q3)

Day 1: Man's Chief End and Happiness (Q1) | 3
Day 2: The Divine Authority and Utility of the Scriptures (Q2) | 6
Day 3: The Scope of the Scriptures (Q3) | 9
Day 4: The Diligent Study and Search of the Scriptures (Q3) | 12

PART 2: GOD, CREATION, AND PROVIDENCE (Q4—Q12)

Day 5: God and His Perfections (Q4) | 17
Day 6: The Unity of God (Q5) | 20
Day 7: The Holy Trinity (Q6) | 23
Day 8: The Decrees of God (Q7, Q8) | 26
Day 9: The Work of Creation (Q9) | 29
Day 10: The Creation of Man (Q10) | 32
Day 11: The Providence of God (Q11) | 35
Day 12: The Covenant of Works (Q12) | 38

PART 3: MAN AND SIN (Q13—Q19)

Day 13: The Fall of Our First Parents (Q13) | 43
Day 14: Sin in General (Q14) | 46
Day 15: The First Sin in Particular (Q15) | 49
Day 16: Our Fall in Adam (Q16, Q17) | 52
Day 17: The Sinfulness of Man's Natural State (Q18) | 55
Day 18: The Miseries of Man's Natural State (Q19) | 58

Part 4: Christ and Redemption (Q20—Q28)

Day 19: Election to Everlasting Life (Q20) | 63
Day 20: The Covenant of Grace (Q20) | 66
Day 21: Christ the Only Redeemer of God's Elect (Q21) | 69
Day 22: Christ's Incarnation (Q22) | 72
Day 23: Christ's Offices in General (Q23) | 75
Day 24: Christ's Prophetical Office (Q24) | 78
Day 25: Christ's Priestly Office (Q25) | 81
Day 26: Christ's Kingly Office (Q26) | 84
Day 27: Christ's Humiliation (Q27) | 87
Day 28: Christ's Exaltation (Q28) | 90

Part 5: Spirit and Salvation (Q29—Q38)

Day 29: The Application of Redemption (Q29) | 95
Day 30: Union with Christ (Q30) | 98
Day 31: Effectual Calling (Q31) | 101
Day 32: The Benefits of Effectual Calling (Q32) | 104
Day 33: Justification (Q33) | 107
Day 34: Adoption (Q34) | 110
Day 35: Sanctification (Q35) | 113
Day 36: Union with Christ the Only Way to Sanctification (Q35) | 116
Day 37: The Benefits Flowing from Justification,
    Adoption, and Sanctification (Q36) | 119
Day 38: Increase of Grace and Perseverance (Q36) | 122
Day 39: The Benefits Which Believers Receive at Death (Q37) | 125
Day 40: The Benefits at the Resurrection (Q38) | 128

Part 6: The Ten Commandments (Q39—Q84)

Day 41: The Duty Which God Requires of Man (Q39) | 133
Day 42: The Moral Law, the Rule of Man's Obedience (Q40) | 136
Day 43: The Moral Law Summarily Comprehended in
    the Ten Commandments (Q41) | 139
Day 44: Love to God and Our Neighbor, the Sum of
    the Ten Commandments (Q42) | 142
Day 45: The Preface to the Ten Commandments (Q43, Q44) | 145
Day 46: The First Commandment (1) (Q45, Q46) | 148
Day 47: The First Commandment (2) (Q47, Q48) | 151
Day 48: The Second Commandment (1) (Q49, Q50) | 154
Day 49: The Second Commandment (2) (Q51, Q52) | 157
Day 50: The Third Commandment (1) (Q53, Q54) | 160

Day 51: The Third Commandment (2) (Q55, Q56) | 163
Day 52: The Fourth Commandment (1) (Q57, Q58, Q59) | 166
Day 53: The Fourth Commandment (2) (Q60, Q61, Q62) | 169
Day 54: The Fifth Commandment (1) (Q63, Q64) | 172
Day 55: The Fifth Commandment (2) (Q65, Q66) | 175
Day 56: The Sixth Commandment (1) (Q67, Q68) | 178
Day 57: The Sixth Commandment (2) (Q69) | 181
Day 58: The Seventh Commandment (1) (Q70, Q71) | 184
Day 59: The Seventh Commandment (2) (Q72) | 187
Day 60: The Eighth Commandment (1) (Q73, Q74) | 190
Day 61: The Eighth Commandment (2) (Q75) | 193
Day 62: The Ninth Commandment (1) (Q76, Q77) | 196
Day 63: The Ninth Commandment (2) (Q78) | 199
Day 64: The Tenth Commandment (1) (Q79, Q80) | 202
Day 65: The Tenth Commandment (2) (Q81) | 205
Day 66: Man's Inability to Keep the Law Perfectly (Q82) | 208
Day 67: Sin in Its Aggravations (Q83) | 211
Day 68: The Desert of Sin (Q84) | 214

PART 7: FAITH AND REPENTANCE (Q85—Q87)

Day 69: The Means of Salvation in General (Q85) | 219
Day 70: Faith in Jesus Christ (Q86) | 222
Day 71: Repentance unto Life (Q87) | 225

PART 8: THE WORD, SACRAMENTS, AND PRAYER (Q88—Q107)

Day 72: Christ's Ordinances in General (Q88) | 231
Day 73: How the Word Is Made Effectual to Salvation (Q89) | 234
Day 74: How the Word Is to Be Read and Heard (Q90) | 237
Day 75: How the Sacraments Become Effectual
  Means of Salvation (Q91) | 240
Day 76: The Nature and Number of the Sacraments (Q92, Q93) | 243
Day 77: The Nature of Baptism (Q94, Q95) | 246
Day 78: The Nature of the Lord's Supper (Q96) | 249
Day 79: The Worthy Receiving of the Lord's Supper (Q97) | 252
Day 80: The Necessity of Self-Examination Considered (Q97) | 255
Day 81: The Nature of Prayer (Q98) | 258
Day 82: A Discourse on Secret Prayer (Q98) | 261
Day 83: The Rule of Direction in Prayer (Q99) | 264
Day 84: The Preface of the Lord's Prayer (Q100) | 267
Day 85: The First Petition (Q101) | 270

Day 86: The Second Petition (Q102) | 273
Day 87: The Third Petition (Q103) | 276
Day 88: The Fourth Petition (Q104) | 279
Day 89: The Fifth Petition (Q105) | 282
Day 90: The Sixth Petition (Q106) | 285
Day 91: The Conclusion of the Lord's Prayer (Q107) | 288

Appendix: Thomas Boston's Personal Covenants | 291
Bibliography | 295

Foreword

IMAGINE FOR A MOMENT that as you sort through your mail, automatically discarding most of it, you notice a return name and address you do not immediately recognize. "Do we know a Dr. Tse?" you ask nobody in particular while opening the envelope. An invitation card falls out:

You are invited

by

Dr. Chun Tse

to

TEA WITH THOMAS BOSTON

Ettrick,

Selkirkshire, Scotland

RSVP to Dr. Chun Tse at your earliest convenience

*A driver will meet you at Glasgow Airport
and explain details on the journey*

A voice from the kitchen responds, "I have always wanted to go to Scotland. This sounds like an adventure. Let's go!" And despite the fact that you know neither Dr. Tse nor Thomas Boston, and you cannot find Ettrick on a map of the world, this is just the excuse you needed.

Two months later you arrive at Glasgow Airport. If you have never driven on the left-hand side of the road, sitting in the right-hand side driver's seat, in a stick-shift automobile, encountering numerous traffic circles just trying to exit the airport, you will probably be glad to have me as your driver to Ettrick. I can explain more on the way before I entrust you to the expert guidance of Dr. Tse.

You might have thought it would be better to fly into Edinburgh. But I suggest you visit the capital city later (and then perhaps go on to St. Andrews for a day or two). Plus, I want to drive you on the Kingston Bridge over the River Clyde and through the city and then in a southerly direction, because there are a few landmarks you might be interested to see.

As we pass through the city, over on the right is Glasgow Cathedral. Here the great English Congregationalist theologian, John Owen (some think he was the *greatest* theologian England ever produced), once debated church government against the Scottish Presbyterians. And behind the cathedral—can you see a statue on the high point of the city necropolis, looking over the city? That's John Knox. Will God ever do such a work of reformation again in Scotland?

I wish there were time to show you where John Paton, the Scottish missionary to the New Hebrides (Vanuatu), served as a city evangelist, and where he studied theology and medicine, and the church where Dr. Andrew Bonar preached, and the areas where Thomas Chalmers served as parish minister. And if there were more time, we could take some detours as we leave the city, because we will not be too far from the family home of William Chalmers Burns, the young instrument of spiritual awakening in 19th-century Scotland and later missionary to China and friend of Hudson Taylor. And it would be fascinating to take some diversions from the main road to visit some famous Covenanter sites, including the scene of the Battle of Bothwell Bridge. With a little more time we could pay a visit to the Kirk o' Shotts, where the young John Livingstone preached and it was believed around five hundred people were converted. Or we could go to Blantyre, the birthplace of the missionary and explorer David Livingstone. But we have an appointment, so we must make our way south on the M74 motorway.

And so, more than an hour later, we turn off the motorway, on to the meandering "B roads" that will eventually take us to Ettrick. I am not the world's greatest driver, but I suspect you will be glad not to be driving yourself (the "B" in "B roads" is self-explanatory). First, we will be on the B7076, then on to the B723, and finally on to the B709 up through the Ettrick Forest with Ettrick Water alongside us.

Then, eventually we will reach the turn off for the small village of Ettrick. If we have a few minutes to spare, I will show you the church and old manse. Neither of these buildings dates back to the 1700s. You might think that is an irrelevant detail. After all, Dr. Tse invited you to "tea with Thomas Boston." But you do know that Boston himself won't be there, don't you? I am sorry if I assumed you would have looked him up in the *Dictionary of National Biography* or on the web. I probably should have told you as we left the airport: we can only visit Boston's grave. He died in 1732.

I apologize profusely if you didn't know this. Dr. Tse did not mean to deceive you by his invitation. I should have mentioned this when we met. But whether you knew this or not, I have my own reasons—good ones!—for wanting you to make the journey to Ettrick.

One is that otherwise you would probably not think about visiting this part of Scotland (and to tell the truth, I hoped you might like to go on further to visit Anwoth, where Samuel Rutherford was minister). But more than anything else I wanted you to see where one of the most influential, faithful, and fruitful ministers in the history of the Scottish Church (and perhaps any church) lived, loved, and laboured.

To everyone, apart from those who live in this area, Ettrick is situated in what we Scots sometimes call "the Back of Beyond." Today there are probably fewer than a couple of hundred residents. But seeing this place with your own eyes will, I think, underline some of the spiritual lessons Thomas Boston's life and ministry can teach us.

The first is that it is not so much *where* you serve, the size of a place or its prominence, that matters. It is *who and what you are* and *how* you serve the Lord wherever he places you. For we all live under his sovereign and wise superintendence and providence. He—not we—is the One who chooses our sphere of service.

Second, the best servants of Christ are those who can say, like Boston (and his fellow-countryman of the next century, Robert Murray M'Cheyne), "As to myself, I have no ambitions"—except that their lives and service will make Christ known and point people to him, wherever he sets them down.

And then, third, those who thus serve the Lord can touch the world from anywhere in it. In the far-off British colonies of the 18th century, no less a figure than Jonathan Edwards wrote that Boston was a great theologian. His books have made a lasting impact on countless thousands of his fellow Christians down through the years, most notably his *Memoirs*, his *Human Nature in Its Fourfold State*, his *Crook in the Lot*, and his famous "Notes" on *The Marrow of Modern Divinity*. These works are still being published and eagerly read today.

This last-named book (his explanatory notes on it are probably better than the book itself!) helped Boston to a richer understanding of the fulness and freeness of God's grace in Jesus Christ. Those who heard him preach noticed a distinct "tincture" in his preaching—a Christ-fulness and Christ-richness that was all-pervasive in his ministry of the word and attracted people to the Saviour.

That special "tincture" is not something that can be taught in a theological seminary. But it is something every minister should want and every congregation should pray that their minister will have. In Boston's case it was observed and experienced by people in this out-of-the-way place where he immersed himself in profound study of God's word, deep devotion to Christ, and love for his congregation—and where he experienced the anointing grace of the Holy Spirit.

Here too, in Ettrick, Boston needed and tasted the comfort of his heavenly Father. And he was a man who needed that. For six of his beloved children pre-deceased him; his wife, Katherine Brown (with whom he was in love from the moment he saw her), suffered from an agonizing mental disturbance; and Boston himself had his share of personal affliction and opposition to his ministry.

One evening many years ago (I must have been twenty-two at the time, so the memory has lingered long), I was invited with some fellow students to have supper with one of my theology professors. He was kindly disposed towards me, and during the evening turned to me as though remembering something he meant to do. "Sinclair," he said, "I have something that I think will interest you." Disappearing into his study he soon reappeared. He put into my hands a small but thick notebook, each page dense with writing. "Interest" me? I was profoundly moved. For what he placed in my hands was one of Thomas Boston's sermon manuscript books. As with his New England contemporary Jonathan Edwards, paper was a scarce commodity for Boston. Every available space on the page was used.

Protestants do not believe there is any sacred or sanctifying power in the "relics" of the saints. But we treasure possessions of those we have loved and honoured. So although I cannot claim to have taken tea with Thomas Boston, I did feel that I was holding in my hands a cup containing something much more refreshing—sermons in which he described the grace of Christ and expressed the truth of the gospel that had come alive to him and that he longed to communicate: that all who are spiritually thirsty can come to the waters that flow from Christ and drink freely, and those who have no money can buy and eat, and enjoy wine and milk, without money and without price, since Christ in all his saving and keeping fulness is offered to them and is able to save them "to the uttermost" (Isa 55:1; Heb 7:25).

Dr. Tse has prepared a similar experience for you. It may not be either as unexpected or moving as mine was. But what you will find in these pages is an invitation to listen to Boston teach you as though you were sitting drinking a cup of fine tea with him and he was answering your questions. I hope you will find his company as helpful as I and many others have.

But I must no longer detain you. For Dr. Tse is waiting to show you his book *Tea with Thomas Boston*. Unlike myself (although I am an admirer of Boston), he is an expert on him. He has lovingly and carefully selected some very refreshing teas for you to enjoy. For in these pages you will find some of the actual teaching on the Christian faith that Thomas Boston gave to his congregation in far-away, long-ago, and little-known Ettrick. I hope you will enjoy it and find that it will help you grow in grace and in the knowledge of our Lord Jesus Christ.

But now, here is Dr. Tse. Thank you for allowing me to bring you (at least in imagination) to Ettrick for *Tea with Thomas Boston*. Sip slowly and often!

Sinclair B. Ferguson

Preface

> Knowledge is a necessary foundation of faith and holiness; and where ignorance reigns in the mind, there is confusion in the heart and life.
>
> THOMAS BOSTON (1676–1732)

THESE PROFOUND WORDS, WRITTEN at the outset of Thomas Boston's commentary on the Westminster Shorter Catechism,[1] reflect the emphasis on integrating theology and practice characteristic of the eminent Scottish theologian-pastor. His life and works testified to the belief that genuine faith and true holiness are rooted in a deep understanding of God's Word.

Thomas Boston was no ordinary theologian; he was primarily a preacher and a shepherd of souls. Concerning his sermons, the late J. I. Packer characterized them as demonstrating "a dazzling mastery of the text and teaching of the Bible; a profound knowledge of the human heart; great thoroughness and clarity in exposition; great skill in applicatory searching of the conscience; and a pervasive sense of the wonder and glory of God's grace in Christ to such perverse sinners as ourselves."[2]

Although Boston attended the School of Divinity at the University of Edinburgh for just one semester in the spring of 1695, God honed his theological acumen in the crucible of ministry and personal afflictions.[3] Unlike

---

1. Boston, *Works*, 1:9. Boston's commentary on the Shorter Catechism, comprising the first two volumes of his *Whole Works*, is formally called *An Illustration of the Doctrines of the Christian Religion with Respect to Faith and Practice, Upon the Plan of the Assembly's Shorter Catechism, Comprehending a Complete Body of Divinity*.

2. Packer, *Puritan Portraits*, 117.

3. Boston was no stranger to life's hardships. He endured the unimaginable pain of losing six of his ten children in infancy. Throughout his life, he also struggled with poor

some academic theologians, whose primary audience is seminary students or fellow scholars, Boston's chief concern was not abstract theological discourse but the real salvation, assurance, and holiness of the people of Simprin and Ettrick, whom God entrusted to him. For this reason, in addition to preaching weekly sermons, he also held weekly catechetical sessions with his parishioners, teaching all 107 questions and answers of the Westminster Shorter Catechism twice a year.[4]

The concept of this book came from my personal experience. After learning about Thomas Boston through Dr. Sinclair Ferguson's book *The Whole Christ*,[5] I found Boston so intriguing that I took my family from the US to Scotland to embark on a doctoral study of his theology of assurance at the University of Edinburgh. Having recently published my dissertation for an academic audience,[6] I have been struck by the pressing need to make Boston's invaluable insights accessible to a broader audience. Many have heard of Boston as a devout scholar-pastor, but few have had the privilege of immersing themselves in his extensive writings.[7] Some might be familiar with the title of Boston's most influential work, *Human Nature in Its Fourfold State*,[8] while others may be familiar with his portrayal as a "Scottish Puritan."[9] For most, however, the scope of Boston's extant writings remains largely unexplored. An idea then dawned on me: why not introduce people to Thomas Boston via a devotional on his notes on the Shorter Catechism?

This book aims to accomplish just that! I have reimagined and distilled Boston's commentary and sermons on the Shorter Catechism—originally extending over 1400 pages[10]—into ninety-one concise daily devotionals,

---

health. In addition, his wife suffered from chronic (mental) illness and was bedridden during the last ten years of Boston's life.

4. The word *catechism* refers to oral instruction on the basic truths of Christianity in a question-and-answer format. For more on the history and significance of the Westminster Shorter Catechism, see the chapter following this preface: "The Significance of the Westminster Shorter Catechism."

5. Ferguson, *Whole Christ*.

6. Tse, *Marrow of Certainty*.

7. In 2022, twenty-eight previously unpublished sermons of Boston, spanning over four hundred pages, were printed in *Scattered and Kept: Twenty-Eight Lost Sermons of Rev. Thomas Boston* (see bibliography). Together with *The Whole Works of Thomas Boston*, the extant published works of Boston exceed eight thousand pages.

8. First published in 1720 with the full title *Human Nature in Its Fourfold State of Primitive Integrity, Entire Depravity, Begun Recovery, and Consummate Happiness or Misery*, recorded in Boston, *Works*, 8:9–375. It is the most published work in the entire history of Scottish theology, according to Torrance, *Scottish Theology*, 220.

9. Beeke and Pederson, *Meet the Puritans*, 653–67.

10. Boston, *Works*, 1:9–660; 2:5–645; 7:9–143.

each occupying just two to three pages. These devotionals, as theological as they are pastoral, are organized into the following eight parts:

1: Man's Chief End and Scriptures (Q1—Q3)

2: God, Creation, and Providence (Q4—Q12)

3: Man and Sin (Q13—Q19)

4: Christ and Redemption (Q20—Q28)

5: Spirit and Salvation (Q29—Q38)

6: The Ten Commandments (Q39—Q84)

7: Faith and Repentance (Q85—Q87)

8: The Word, Sacraments, and Prayer (Q88—Q107)

Parts 1 to 5 cover what humanity is to believe about God, while Parts 6 to 8 address what God requires of us. These terse questions and answers from the Shorter Catechism, first published in 1647, have stood the test of time, serving as a distinguished guide for deepening believers' understanding of the central tenets of the Christian faith.

In addition to presenting the question and answer from the Shorter Catechism paired with Boston's exposition, each devotional is enriched with a title and biblical reference(s)[11] taken directly from Boston that correspond to the catechetical question(s). To help readers tap into Boston's insights firsthand, I have included direct quotations, illustrations, and Bible verses from his writings within each unit. To foster deeper meditation, each devotion concludes with a section called "Tea with Thomas Boston," which includes five reflection and discussion questions, an introduction to a tea matched with the content of the devotion, a personal prayer, and a pungent quote from Boston capturing the essence of the respective theological topic. You may view this devotional as if Boston were sitting across from you, personally catechizing you during your morning or afternoon teatime, engaging in a heart-to-heart conversation about the Christian faith.

Apart from individual and family use, this book can be easily integrated into a church setting, as the ninety-one units align perfectly with a thirteen-week Sunday school class or small group study. To support these purposes, I have included ample Bible references throughout both the content and the reflection and discussion questions, which parents can use for family devotionals and church leaders can utilize for discipleship and group study. I have also included, following this preface, a chapter on the significance of

---

11. Unless otherwise stated, I have changed the Bible verses from the original KJV to ESV.

the Westminster Shorter Catechism and a brief biography of Thomas Boston, as well as two of Boston's personal covenants in the appendix.

I wish to thank Dr. Sinclair Ferguson not only for introducing me to Thomas Boston but also for graciously writing the, if I may say, one-of-a-kind foreword to this devotional, which is as intriguing and inspirational as it is delightful to read. I am also grateful for the endorsements of Drs. Joel Beeke, Philip Ryken, Alison Jack, Jonathan Gibson, Martyn Cowan, Kim Riddlebarger, Russell Newton, Cory Brock, Israel José Guerrero Leiva, and Ray Burbank. John Hughes deserves special thanks for his many suggestions and his help with this book. I appreciate Dr. Colin Godwin for his support of this project. My heartfelt thanks go to my wife, Wing Sze, for suggesting the inclusion of a different tea for each devotional and to my daughter Charis for researching the various types of tea. I also thank my daughters Shulamite and Eden for brainstorming different titles for this book—and especially Eden for finalizing the current title, *Tea with Thomas Boston*.

I pray that this book will lead you on a spiritually refreshing journey through the enduring Shorter Catechism, offering an intimate glimpse into the heart and mind of Thomas Boston, described as "one of the most remarkable and godly ministers to grace the church of Christ since the days of the apostles."[12] May these devotionals, inspired by the insights of the Pastor at Ettrick,[13] lead you to a renewed encounter with God's Word and a more profound experience of faith, assurance, and spiritual growth in your Christian walk.

Now, enjoy a cup of tea with Thomas Boston!

Chun Tse
Hong Kong
September 2025

---

12. Ian Hamilton, President of Westminster Seminary UK, spoke those words in "Thomas Boston's Memorable Last Words," 17.

13. This is a title given by Watson, *Pastor of Ettrick*.

The Significance of the Westminster Shorter Catechism

> Even if the youngsters do not understand all the questions and answers in the Westminster Assembly's Catechism, yet, abiding in their memories, it will be of infinite service when the time of understanding comes, to have known those very excellent, wise, and judicious definitions of the things of God.
>
> CHARLES HADDON SPURGEON (1834–92),
> PASTOR AT METROPOLITAN TABERNACLE, LONDON

CHARLES SPURGEON, OFTEN CALLED the "Prince of Preachers," spoke these words to his congregation in the sermon "A Promise for Us and for Our Children," delivered at the Metropolitan Tabernacle in London on April 10, 1864, expressing his deep appreciation for the importance of the Westminster Shorter Catechism. The significance of the Shorter Catechism is also evident in Thomas Boston's parish at Ettrick, where one of the requirements for first-time participants in the Lord's Supper was to answer affirmatively to the question, "Do you believe in the doctrine of the Shorter Catechism?"[1]

Benjamin B. Warfield (1886–1902), often referred to as the "Lion of Princeton"[2] for his staunch defense of biblical inerrancy and Reformed theology during a time when higher criticism and liberal theology were gaining traction, provided the following anecdote in response to the question: What is the indelible mark of the Shorter Catechism?

---

1. Tse, *The Marrow of Certainty*, 253.
2. Riddlebarger, *The Lion of Princeton*, 4.

During a time of violent unrest, a U.S. Army officer noticed a man whose calm and confident demeanor stood out amidst the chaos. After they passed each other, both turned around, and the man asked the officer, "What is the chief end of man?" The officer responded, "Man's chief end is to glorify God and to enjoy him forever." The man replied, "I knew you were a Shorter Catechism boy by your looks!" The officer smiled and said, "That was just what I was thinking of you." Benjamin Warfield then concludes: It is worth while to be a Shorter Catechism boy. They grow to be men. And better than that, they are exceedingly apt to grow to be men of God. So apt, that we cannot afford to have them miss the chance of it. "Train up a child in the way he should go, and even when he is old he will not depart from it."[3]

Unfamiliar to many in the modern church, the term *catechism*—named after the Greek word κατηχέω (*katecheo*), meaning oral instruction—is a teaching tool that presents core Christian beliefs in a question-and-answer format. Its purpose is to instruct believers, particularly the young and those new to the faith, in the fundamental doctrines of Christianity.[4] While the practice of catechizing dates back to the early church, Martin Luther popularized it during the Reformation.[5] It has been widely used throughout the centuries across various Christian traditions because it promotes understanding, facilitates memorization, and provides a structured approach to teaching and learning.

The creation of the Westminster Shorter Catechism was deeply rooted in the religious and political turmoil of seventeenth-century England. The English Civil War had created a period of instability, generating an intense desire among many for a more Reformed and unified approach to the practice of Christianity in the British Isles. In adherence to the Solemn League

---

3. This story is recorded in *Is the Shorter Catechism Worthwhile?* by Benjamin B. Warfield: https://www.westminsterconfession.org/resources/confessional-standards/is-the-shorter-catechism-worthwhile/

4. The practice of catechism is not restricted to Christianity. The Jewish tradition developed the Passover Haggadah, which involves the annual ritual of retelling the exodus story during a meal. The term "Haggadah" means "to tell." During the Passover seder, children are instructed to ask four questions: (1) How is this night different from all other nights? On all other nights, we eat both leavened and unleavened bread; why do we eat only unleavened bread tonight? (2) On all other nights, we can eat any vegetable; why do we eat only bitter herbs tonight? (3) On all other nights, we are not required to dip our vegetables even once; why do we dip them twice tonight? (4) On all other nights, we eat our meals in any way; why do we sit around the table in a ceremonial manner tonight? The seder leader then answers each of these questions in turn. Goldberg, *Passover Haggadah*, 8–9.

5. Kapic and Lugt, *Pocket Dictionary of the Reformed Tradition*, 31.

and Covenant—a 1643 agreement between the English Parliament and the Scottish Covenanters to unite against King Charles I and establish Presbyterianism in England—the English Long Parliament appointed the Westminster Assembly to reform the Church of England. The Assembly's mission was to oppose tyranny and Catholicism by aligning the faith and practice of the Church of England more closely with the Presbyterian Church of Scotland and other Reformed churches.[6]

The Assembly convened from July 1643 to February 1648 and drew together some of the most learned biblical scholars, theologians, and pastors from various constituents of England and Scotland. They, commonly called the Westminster divines, produced documents that sought to unify the doctrine and practice of Protestant churches across England, Scotland, and Ireland.[7] These documents, the Westminster Standards,[8] include the Directory for Public Worship (1644), the Form of Presbyterian Church Government (1645), the Westminster Confession of Faith (1646) and the accompanying Westminster Shorter Catechism (1647) and Westminster Larger Catechism (1647). Unlike the Larger Catechism intended for clergy and adults, the Assembly designed the Shorter Catechism to instruct children and new Christians.

The Shorter Catechism is a concise yet thorough summary of the Christian faith. It consists of 107 questions and answers covering Christianity's main points, beginning with the purpose and predicament of humanity and concluding with an exploration of the sacraments and the Lord's Prayer. The Catechism's first question is undoubtedly its most famous: "What is the chief end of man?" The answer, "Man's chief end is to glorify God and to enjoy him forever," encapsulates the central aim of the Christian life and sets the tone for the entire Catechism. This answer testifies that doctrine is for doxology.

The theology of the Shorter Catechism and the Westminster Standards was heavily influenced by Reformed theology, notably the teachings of the French theologian and reformer John Calvin (1509–1564). The Catechism's emphasis on the authority of Scripture, the sovereignty of God, the depravity of humanity, the centrality of Christ's work in atonement, and the application of redemption through the Holy Spirit provides a solid theological foundation for understanding the gospel, which is the basis for engaging the Ten Commandments, the sacraments, and the Lord's Prayer. By

---

6. Torrance, "Strengths and Weaknesses of the Westminster Theology," 41.

7. Gerstner, et al., *A Guide to the Westminster Confession of Faith*, vii.

8. For the historical and theological aspects of the Westminster Standards, see Fesko, *The Theology of the Westminster Standards*.

systematically teaching these core doctrines of Christianity, the Catechism informs the mind, shapes the heart, and directs the will. It helps believers grasp the Bible's overarching message and apply its teachings to daily lives.

While designed with a younger audience in mind, the Shorter Catechism is by no means simplistic and shallow.[9] It addresses complex theological issues in a way that is both theologically robust and accessible, making it an invaluable resource for lifelong learning and spiritual growth. The Catechism's question-and-answer format and concise content encourage memorization, which helps believers internalize critical biblical truths and recall them in times of need. The structured nature of the Catechism provides a clear framework for understanding the Christian faith, making it easier to grasp the coherence and unity of Scripture.

The Westminster Shorter Catechism is a potent tool for Christian education that has stood the test of time. Completed in 1647, the Scottish Parliament promptly approved it in 1648, and it, along with the Westminster Confession of Faith and the Westminster Larger Catechism, remains a standard for preaching and teaching, especially in Presbyterian and Reformed churches worldwide. David Fergusson, the Regius Professor of Divinity at the University of Cambridge, calls the Shorter Catechism "the most important Reformed confession in the English-speaking world."[10]

In an age marked by biblical and theological illiteracy, when unbelievers often possess a deeper understanding of why they reject Jesus than Christians comprehend why they believe him, the Shorter Catechism's concise and theologically rich content remains a vital spiritual diet for those seeking to deepen their knowledge of God and his Word.[11] Whether used in personal devotion, a family setting, or a church, the Shorter Catechism—explained in this book by the pious and learned Thomas Boston, whom J. I. Packer described as having "a first-class mind, a retentive memory, and a way with words"[12]—provides a solid foundation for a lifetime of worship and discipleship.

---

9. Greenwald, "'Written for Children'": https://journal.rts.edu/article/written-for-children-the-westminster-shorter-catechisms-unhelpful-reputation/

10. From David Fergusson's endorsement of J. V. Fesko's book, *The Theology of the Westminster Standards*.

11. For arguments on why historical creeds, confessions, and catechisms are pertinent and essential to the modern church, see Trueman, *The Creedal Imperative*, 159–90.

12. Packer, *Puritan Portraits*, 96.

A Brief Biography of Thomas Boston

> It would be difficult to name a man who has a higher claim to an honourable place in the Christian biography of Scotland in the eighteenth century than Thomas Boston of Ettrick.
>
> Andrew Thomson (1814–1901) Biographer of Thomas Boston and Minister of Broughton Place United Presbyterian Kirk, Edinburgh

Thomas Boston was born on March 17, 1676, in Duns, a town in Scotland near the English border. His early years were marked by the persecution of Presbyterians due to the religious and political turmoil during the reign of King Charles II. One memorable event from Boston's childhood was his accompanying his father, who was imprisoned for refusing to conform to Episcopacy, highlighting the family's commitment to their Presbyterian faith.

From a young age, Boston exhibited a keen interest in learning. Around 1684–85, at the age of eight or nine, he enrolled in the grammar school in Duns, where he received year-round instruction with a strong emphasis on mastering Latin, the language of instruction at universities during that time. Boston and his fellow students were required to speak Latin inside and outside the classroom. Boston's studious nature and innate seriousness set him apart from his peers, allowing him to focus intently on his education.

Boston's linguistic talents became evident during his time at grammar school. By the age of thirteen, he had learned Greek and could translate Latin texts into English without needing a dictionary. He also learned Dutch and French, later enabling him to reference foreign sources in his writings.

Moreover, Boston's commitment to learning led him to become an expert in Hebrew, a language he would later describe as his "darling study."

In the late summer of 1687, Boston's father took him to Newton of Whitsome, about four miles from Duns, to hear a sermon by Henry Erskine, the father of Ebenezer and Ralph Erskine, who would later become allies with Boston in ministry. Boston found the message of Henry Erskine, a Presbyterian preacher who had suffered for his faith, profoundly impactful, especially compared to the Episcopal sermons he had previously encountered. Under Erskine's evangelistic preaching, Boston experienced a personal conversion at the tender age of eleven.

Boston graduated from grammar school in November 1689 at the age of thirteen. Financial constraints, however, delayed his plan to pursue university education in the spring of 1690. Still, he remained determined and intensively prepared for his academic journey. By December 1691, seeing an improvement in his family's financial situation, Boston's father arranged for him to be examined in the Greek New Testament by Mr. Herbert Kennedy, a regent at the University of Edinburgh. Boston excelled in the examination, surpassing his peers and securing a place in Kennedy's second-year logic class. This accomplishment enabled him to shorten his college study by a full year.

On January 13, 1692, at almost sixteen, Thomas Boston enrolled at the University of Edinburgh. His academic pursuits were well-grounded, and he diligently attended lectures for four years that covered a broad range of subjects, including Greek, logic, ethics, and physics.

Despite his academic success, Boston faced financial hardship and lived a modest and reclusive life during college. He rarely left his private room, focusing his energies on studying. This lifestyle took a toll on his health, leading to frequent bouts of fainting and other health issues in the years that followed.

Boston graduated from the University of Edinburgh at eighteen on July 9, 1694. His courses encompassed logic, metaphysics, ethics, and general physics. After college, Boston's next step in preparing for Christian ministry was to enter Divinity School. In January 1695, he enrolled in the School of Divinity at Edinburgh to further his theological studies. Unfortunately, due to limited financial resources, Boston chose to pursue practical training in theology rather than completing his studies at the Divinity School, which he only attended for one semester. He hoped to secure employment by teaching in a parish school or tutoring a pupil from a wealthy family while under a Presbytery's care. This alternative path allowed him to gain valuable teaching experience.

Boston secured two short-term teaching positions after leaving the Divinity School in 1695. After a series of twists and turns in his career, Boston eventually accepted an invitation to apply for a preaching license in his native Presbytery in Duns. He became a probational preacher on June 15, 1697, at twenty-one. During a two-year probational period, he preached itinerantly at local churches, further honing his skills and gaining practical experience.

During this period, Boston also proposed marriage to Katharine Brown, whom he described as "a woman of great worth."[1] At the age of 22, he also authored a well-circulated treatise on evangelism titled *A Soliloquy on the Art of Man-Fishing*.[2] Soon after, Boston received a call to the parish of Simprin and was ordained there on September 21, 1699. Simprin was a small congregation whose members, in Boston's view, were religiously ignorant. Some had professed faith throughout their lives but showed minimal evidence of salvation. Boston's approach to addressing this situation was to preach from 2 Corinthians 13:5, urging the congregation to "Examine yourselves, whether ye be in the faith; prove your own selves."

While Simprin marked the early years of Boston's ministry, the Ettrick parish became his primary pastoral field in 1707, where he would spend the last twenty-five years of his life. His initial decade in Ettrick posed considerable pastoral challenges, and Boston responded by implementing a systematic preaching scheme. His goals were to emphasize the congregation's need for Christ and establish the basics of practical religion. To achieve the first goal, starting in May 1708, Boston launched a famous sermon series on the "fourfold state," the second of which—man's natural state in sin—had been preached in a rudimentary form at Simprin over eight years earlier.[3] As for the second goal, from October 1709 to September of the following year, Boston preached on the doctrines of the Shorter Catechism. Unlike most Scottish ministers who conducted catechetical sessions annually, Boston made it a practice to catechize the entire parish twice a year.

After three years of intensive preaching, catechizing, and pastoral visitations at Ettrick, Boston initiated the annual sacrament of the Lord's Supper on July 16, 1710. By this time, the spiritual progress, primarily due to preaching the "fourfold state," had become increasingly evident. However,

---

1. Boston lavished high praise on her: "whom I therefore passionately loved, and inwardly honoured; a stately, beautiful, and comely personage, truly pious, and fearing the Lord; of an evenly temper, patient in our common tribulations, and under her personal distresses; a woman of bright natural parts, an uucommon stock of prudence; of a quick and lively apprehension, in things she applied herself to; great presence of mind in surprising incidents; sagacious and acute in discerning the qualities of persons." Boston, *Works*, 12:144–45.

2. J. I. Packer describes this book as "a masterpiece on ministry, worthy to stand on the same shelf as Baxter's *Reformed Pastor*." Packer, *Puritan Portraits*, 96.

3. For an analysis of the theology of the *Fourfold State*, see Ryken, *Thomas Boston as Preacher of the Fourfold State*.

amidst his pastoral duties and ministerial challenges, Boston's personal life was marked by tragic family losses. Since his marriage to Katharine Brown in July 1700, six of their ten children had died by March 1716, with the youngest only two months old. Moreover, just six weeks into their marriage, his wife became chronically ill and had to be confined to bed during the last ten years of Boston's life.

The early 18th century brought the Marrow Controversy to the forefront of Scottish theology, impacting Boston's ministry significantly.[4] This theological debate centered around the republication of Edward Fisher's book *The Marrow of Modern Divinity*.[5] In a conversational format involving four characters, Fisher discussed the nature of the gospel, assurance, and the relationship between repentance and faith. The General Assembly's decision to condemn the *Marrow* in 1720 triggered further debates, leading Boston and other ministers to protest this decision and defend the teachings of the *Marrow*. Boston viewed the republication of the *Marrow* as providential, as it helped him grapple with theological issues he had long wrestled with, including the question of assurance.

Boston's health began to deteriorate sharply in the last quarter of 1729. He experienced a range of physical ailments, including shaking of the head, legs, and the entire body, along with issues with his teeth and eyes. Given his frail condition, Boston turned to personal covenanting, reaffirming his commitment to God and pleading for God's faithfulness to the covenant.[6] Boston engaged in extended confessions and self-examination. He reviewed each period of his life and acknowledged his sinfulness, yet he also found solace in God's goodness and longsuffering. Boston's deep theological convictions were evident as he pleaded God's covenant and gospel promises, affirming his certainty of salvation.[7] Despite his unwavering certainty, Boston felt compelled to gather "evidence for heaven" through self-examination. These marks of salvation included belief in the gospel, trust in the covenant of grace, hatred of sin, hope of heaven, love for God's law, confidence in salvation, and victory over besetting sins.

---

4. For a succinct account of the history and theological issues involved in the Marrow Controversy, see Macleod, *From the Marrow Men to the Moderates*, 59–112. For the contemporary significance of the controversy, see Ferguson's *The Whole Christ*. For a most detailed analysis of the Marrow Controversy, see Lachman, *The Marrow Controversy 1718–1723*.

5. For an analysis of the theology of this book and Boston's interpretation of it, see Tse, *The Marrow of Certainty*, 81–119.

6. Consult the Appendix for two personal covenants of Boston.

7. In 1729, Boston wrote a second personal covenant with God.

As his condition worsened, Boston continued to engage in pastoral care and attended public worship when he could. On April 2 and 9, 1732, too frail to preach at the Ettrick church, Boston preached his last two sermons from his study window, titled "The Necessity of Self-Examination Considered." Despite his failing health, he displayed remarkable composure and spoke on the assurance of salvation with a passion characteristic of his ministry.

Thomas Boston passed to glory on May 20, 1732. His life, marked by fervent devotion, deep theological insight, and unwavering commitment to his congregation, continues influencing theologians and ministers today. His written works, particularly *Human Nature in Its Fourfold State*, *The Crook in the Lot*, *A Soliloquy on the Art of Man-Fishing*, and his *Memoirs*, have endured as classics of Scottish theology, offering valuable insights into Christian doctrines and practical piety. His more theologically oriented works, *A View to the Covenant of Works*,[8] *A View to the Covenant of Grace*,[9] the notes on *The Marrow of Modern Divinity*,[10] *Miscellaneous Questions*,[11] and *An Illustration of the Doctrines of the Christian Religion*[12] on which this devotional is founded, remain masterful in their grasp of covenant theology and the principles of the Christian faith.[13]

---

8. Boston, *Works*, 11:171–339.
9. Boston, *Works*, 8:379–604.
10. Boston, *Works*, 7:143–388.
11. Boston, *Works*, 6:11–220.
12. Boston, *Works*, 1:9–660; 2:5–645; 7:9–143.
13. For an intellectual biography of Thomas Boston, see Tse, *The Marrow of Certainty*, 33–80, 263–64. For a more detailed biography and theology of Boston, see Macleod, *From the Marrow Men to the Moderates*, 1–112. For Boston's general theology, see McGowan, *The Federal Theology of Thomas Boston*.

PART 1

Man's Chief End and Scriptures
(Q1—Q3)

Day 1

Man's Chief End and Happiness

Q1. *What is the chief end of man?*
A. Man's chief end is to glorify God and to enjoy him forever.

So, whether you eat or drink, or whatever you do, do all to the glory of God.
1 CORINTHIANS 10:31

Whom have I in heaven but you? And there is nothing on earth that I desire besides you. My flesh and my heart may fail, but God is the strength of my heart and my portion forever.
PSALM 73:25–26

IN RESPONSE TO THIS renowned question and answer from the Shorter Catechism, Thomas Boston distinguishes between man's paramount purpose—glorifying God—and his ultimate source of fulfillment—enjoying God forever. He stresses that God, being infinitely glorious, can only be glorified declaratively. While inanimate objects declare God's glory objectively (Ps 19:1), humanity does so actively—by the heart (understanding, will, and affection; 1 Cor 6:20), the lips (Ps 50:23), and life's conduct (Matt 5:16).

Glorifying God is not just humanity's end but its chief end—the highest aim of existence. Humans serve other purposes, like exercising dominion or multiplying, but these are "subordinate ends to his glory." For example, if eating and drinking serve only bodily nourishment rather than God's glory, they fail to align with our primary purpose. Likewise, while we seek salvation, we must not treat God's glory as a means to an end; rather, salvation should be pursued to glorify God.

Every aspect of life—natural actions (eating, sleeping; Zech 7:6), civil actions (working, buying/selling; Eph 6:7), and religious actions (prayer, worship)—should glorify God. Without this intent, our deeds cannot truly please him. Though we cannot consciously direct every action to God's glory, Boston encourages a habitual orientation toward magnifying him, aligning with his word and will.

Believers enjoy God imperfectly on earth through union and communion with him. The former is "a special saving interest in him, whereby God is their God by covenant," while the latter is "a participation of the benefits of that saving relation." Perfect enjoyment occurs only in heaven—seeing God as he is (1 John 3:2), dwelling in his presence (Ps 16:11), experiencing full union with him (Rev 21:3), and receiving everlasting joy and satisfaction (Matt 25:21).

Boston highlights a definite order: believers cannot truly glorify God unless they regard him as their "chief good and supreme happiness." At the same time, glorifying God precedes enjoying him—the path to enjoyment is through the duty of glorification. As he puts it, "Holiness on earth must necessarily go before felicity in heaven" (Heb 12:14).

For Boston, glorifying and enjoying God serve as criteria for evaluating doctrines and practices. Teachings that honor God should be embraced, while those that dishonor him, elevate the creature, or diminish grace are not from God.

Finally, since "there is no glorifying of the Father without the Son, 1 John 2:23, and no enjoying of God but through him," Boston links the catechism's first question to Christ's absolute necessity. As the sole mediator, Christ alone enables us to glorify and enjoy God.

TEA WITH THOMAS BOSTON

1. In what areas of your life have your actions prioritized creation over glorifying God? Can a person have more than one chief end? (1 Cor 10:31; Isa 43:7; Ps 73:25–26)
2. Can atheists or followers of other religions glorify God? How is glorifying God in Christianity different from other religions? (John 14:6; 1 John 2:23; Acts 4:12)
3. How does holiness lead to enjoying God, and what hinders this pursuit? (Heb 12:14; 1 Pet 1:15–16; Rom 6:22)
4. What daily habits help you glorify God? (1 Thess 5:16–18; Col 3:17; Rom 12:1)
5. How can we teach children or new believers to glorify and enjoy God? (Deut 6:6–7; Matt 19:14; Prov 22:6)

Jasmine green tea is a fragrant and calming green tea infused with jasmine blossoms, symbolizing the uplifting joy of glorifying and enjoying God.

Heavenly Father, transform my heart and align my life with your glory so that I may seek and find joy in you until perfect communion in heaven. Amen.

"God is the fountain of our being; and therefore, seeing we are *of* him, we should be *to* him."[1]

---

1. Boston, *Works*, 1:14 (1:9–18; 7:9–10).

Day 2

The Divine Authority and Utility of the Scriptures

> Q2. *What rule has God given to direct us how we may glorify and enjoy him?*
>
> A. The word of God, which is contained in the Scriptures of the Old and New Testaments, is the only rule to direct us how we may glorify and enjoy him.

All Scripture is breathed out by God and profitable for teaching, for reproof, for correction, and for training in righteousness.

2 TIMOTHY 3:16

SCRIPTURE IS NECESSARY BECAUSE, argues Thomas Boston, although God's works of creation and providence manifest God's goodness, wisdom, and power, leaving men inexcusable (Rom 1:20, 2:14–15), "they are not sufficient to show us either how we should glorify or how we may enjoy God, and so are not sufficient to give that knowledge of God and of his will that is necessary for salvation." Scripture is also essential for the better propagation of truth. As Boston puts it, "The apostles could not with their voice teach all nations, but by their writings they could."

Boston interprets "the Old and New Testaments" as the covenant of grace, a testamentary covenant without proper conditions upon us. Christ, the Testator, confirmed the covenant with his death, and the Holy Spirit drew the testament and dictated it to the human authors. The Old and New Testaments share the same substance—"Jesus Christ is the testator; eternal life is the legacy; sinners of mankind are the legatees; and faith in Jesus Christ is the way of claiming and obtaining the legacy." They differ in clarity, with the Old Testament being more obscure and the New Testament providing clearer revelation. The Old Testament ends with prophecies of Christ and John the Baptist (Mal 4), while the New Testament begins with the fulfillment of those prophecies through their coming. Boston compares the Scriptures of both Testaments to the cherubim in the most holy place, whose wings stretched out and touched one another.

Scripture is the word of God because the Holy Spirit is its principal author. The Spirit inspired and guided the human writers. Boston affirms the infallibility and inerrancy of Scripture: "By this inspiration all of them were infallibly guided, so as they were put beyond all possibility of erring. And this inspiration was extended not only to the things themselves expressed, but to the words wherein they were expressed, though agreeable to the natural style and manner of each writer (2 Pet 1:21; Ps 45:1)."

Boston asserts that Scripture's authority comes solely from God, not from the church. The church is built upon Scripture (Eph 2:20), not the other way around. The foundation of Scripture is doctrinal, based on the teachings of the prophets and apostles. If Scripture's authority depended on the church, our faith would rest on fallible human testimony. Scripture is self-attesting, not requiring the church's endorsement. Furthermore, Scripture's clarity is not dependent on the church's interpretation, which is fallible.

To understand Spirit-inspired Scripture, Boston emphasizes the necessity of the Spirit's illumination due to humanity's depravity. He encourages fervent prayer for the Holy Spirit's enlightenment, warning that without it, "we will remain in the dark, and the word will be but a dead letter to us."

TEA WITH THOMAS BOSTON

1. Why is Scripture the only rule for glorifying and enjoying him? In what areas of your life have you struggled to submit to its authority? (2 Tim 3:16–17; Matt 15:3–6; Col 2:20–23)

2. Do you trust Scripture's inerrancy, despite lost manuscripts? What are the consequences of denying its infallibility? (Matt 5:18; John 17:17; 2 Pet 1:20–21)

3. Why are creation and providence insufficient for salvation knowledge? (Rom 1:19–20; Ps 19:1–4; 1 Cor 2:9–10)

4. What challenges arise in interpreting Scripture, and how can we address them? (1 Cor 2:14; John 16:13; Luke 24:45)

5. How can we teach children and new believers the importance of Scripture? (Josh 1:8; 2 Tim 3:14–15; Ps 119:105)

Earl Grey is a black tea infused with bergamot oil, offering a fragrant, citrusy flavor that symbolizes the clarity and wisdom of God's word, guiding us to glorify and enjoy him.

Heavenly Father, thank you for your word; by your grace and the Spirit's illumination, shape my heart, mind, and life to glorify and enjoy you. Amen.

"There can be no faith nor knowledge of Christ but by revelation."[1]

---

1. Boston, *Works*, 1:25 (1:19–41, 7:10–11).

Day 3

The Scope of the Scriptures

Q3. *What do the Scriptures principally teach?*

A. The Scriptures principally teach what man is to believe concerning God and what duty God requires of man.

Follow the pattern of the sound words that you have heard from me, in the faith and love that are in Christ Jesus.

2 TIMOTHY 1:13

THE CHARACTER OF SCRIPTURE, as Paul illustrates, is doctrine—sound in itself and in its effects, possessing a soul-healing virtue (Ezek 47:9). The essence of Scripture centers on faith (revealing what we are to believe) and love (indicating what we are to do; John 14:15). Our duty to Scripture is to "follow the pattern of the sound words," holding fast to it and not flinching from it.

Scripture primarily teaches, as Thomas Boston succinctly summarizes, faith and obedience. Faith concerns belief about God—his nature, the divine persons, his decrees, and their execution in creation and providence. Obedience pertains to duties owed to God due to his authority, motivated by love and gratitude. Faith and obedience are closely linked because genuine faith is always followed by obedience, and true obedience flows from faith.

The close relationship between faith and obedience means that faith is the foundation for obedience (Titus 3:8). Knowing what to believe comes before knowing how to act. This sequence mirrors the structure of the

Ten Commandments, which begin with "I am the LORD your God, who brought you out of the land of Egypt, out of the house of slavery" (Exod 20:2). These words, Boston notes, represent the essence of the covenant of grace. The subsequent commandments are based on God's prior sovereign grace and love. Boston observes that Paul's epistles follow a similar pattern, explaining the doctrine of faith first, followed by moral duties. In today's language, the "imperatives" follow the "indicatives."

Being skilled in biblical languages, as well as Latin, Dutch, and French, Boston believes that knowledge of Hebrew and Greek is crucial for a proper understanding of Scripture, as these "original tongues are the best commentaries on Scripture." However, he also values "the commentaries of godly and learned writers." Furthermore, a mindset focused on godliness can serve as an excellent commentary. Boston warns against a "carnal, earthly, and fleshly mind" that blinds the heart and renders one "utterly unfit for searching the scriptures."

Having experienced ecclesiastical controversies, Boston held a dim view of "decrees of councils, opinions of ancient writers, doctrines of men, and private spirits" as judges of religious matters. Reason alone cannot serve this purpose, as unregenerate reason is blind in spiritual matters (1 Cor 2:14) and fallible (Rom 3:4). Reason must humble itself before Scripture and accept God's judgment (2 Cor 10:4–5). The ultimate authority for settling religious disputes, according to Boston, is the Spirit of God speaking through Scripture.

True religion, Boston argues, must be practical, rooted in faith, and evidenced through obedience. Faith must be demonstrated by obedience to God's commands, as outlined in his infallible word. Since the Bible is the sole guide for faith and obedience, we must thoroughly explore it to shape our understanding of God and salvation, rejecting anything contrary to it.

TEA WITH THOMAS BOSTON

1. Why must knowing come before doing, and in which areas of your life does your faith need to align more with obedience? (Rom 10:17; Jas 2:17; Heb 11:1)

2. Do doctrines divide or build up? What are the primary and secondary doctrines in the Bible? (1 Tim 1:10–11; Eph 4:4–6; Rom 14:1)

3. How can you distinguish true from false religions? (Jas 1:27; Matt 7:15–23; 1 John 4:1)

4. How should theological disagreements be resolved by the Spirit through Scripture? (Acts 15:1–21; 2 Tim 2:24–26; 1 Cor 1:10)

5. How can we teach children and new believers to cultivate a godly mindset when reading the Bible? (Rom 12:2; Ps 119:11; Col 3:16)

Oolong is a partially fermented tea with a complex, balanced flavor, reflecting the harmony of faith and obedience taught in Scripture.

Heavenly Father, thank you for Scripture as the guide to faith and obedience; grant me wisdom to study it, accept its authority, and live faithfully in obedience. Amen.

"Faith is the loadstone of obedience, and obedience the touchstone of faith."[1]

---

1. Boston, *Works*, 1:44 (1:42–56, 7:11–12).

Day 4

The Diligent Study and Search of the Scriptures

> Q3. *What do the Scriptures principally teach?*
>
> A. The Scriptures principally teach what man is to believe concerning God and what duty God requires of man.

Seek and read from the book of the LORD: Not one of these shall be missing; none shall be without her mate. For the mouth of the LORD has commanded, and his Spirit has gathered them.

ISAIAH 34:16

THE PROPHET ISAIAH URGED those who doubted God's end-time judgment to *seek* and *read* from "the book of the LORD," God's divine revelation. Seeking implies diligent inquiry, and reading, rather than just hearing, leaves a deeper impression. Thomas Boston asserts, "The eye often leaves a deeper impression than the ear." In the preceding verses, God declares that fearsome creatures will inhabit the lands of his enemies, and "none of them or their mates will be absent" because "the LORD has commanded" it, and "his Spirit will ensure its fulfillment."

Boston explains that seeking Scripture implies that humans have strayed from the right path and need guidance (Ps 119:176). Without it, they are prone to wander further. This need arises because humans have "lost the sharpness of our sight in spiritual things in Adam." Furthermore, Scripture's depths are so profound that it is "wherein an elephant may swim." God commands this pursuit for our benefit, and a humble heart will find treasures in these wells of salvation.

Scripture, as God's most excellent visible work (Ps 138:2), is "the best of books," containing "the oracles of God" (Rom 3:2), "the heavenly laws" (Ps 19:7), "Christ's testament and final will" (1 Cor 11:25), "the scepter of God's kingdom" (Ps 110:2), "the conduit of grace," and "the price of Christ's blood." It is "a light for the blind" (Ps 19:8), "a means of awakening the spiritually dormant" (Song 7:9), "a sword for the Christian soldier" (Eph 6:17), "a counselor" in doubt (Ps 119:24), "a comforter" in sorrow (Ps 119:49–50), and "a remedy for all spiritual ailments" (Prov 4:22).

Boston offers nine practical suggestions for studying Scripture:

1. Read Regularly—establish a routine to familiarize yourself with the *entire* Bible. A systematic plan benefits spiritual growth more than random reading.
2. Meditate on Key Passages—highlight verses that resonate with your life, struggles, or joys, revisiting them often.
3. Compare Scripture with Scripture—cross-reference unclear passages (2 Pet 1:20). Marginal notes can help. Remember, both Testaments point to Christ.
4. Read with Reverence—approach Scripture with awe, focusing on "the words, their meanings, and the divine authority of Scripture" (1 Thess 2:13).
5. Apply What You Read—"Be doers of the word, and not hearers only" (Jas 1:22). Read with a heart ready to obey.
6. Pray for Illumination—seek the Spirit's guidance for a "saving understanding of Scripture" (1 Cor 2:11).
7. Avoid a Worldly Mindset—earthly distractions "eclipse the divine light of Scripture."
8. Live a Godly Life—"A spiritually disciplined life greatly enhances one's understanding of Scripture."
9. Practice What You Learn—"To him who has, more will be given" (Matt 13:12). Obedience deepens understanding.

By diligently seeking and applying Scripture, believers grow in faith, wisdom, and godliness, discovering its hidden treasures.

TEA WITH THOMAS BOSTON

1. What distractions hinder your Bible reading, and how can we develop a regular reading habit? (Isa 28:10; 2 Tim 2:15; Ps 1:1–6)

2. How can you read Scripture for worship and transformation, not just knowledge? (Jas 1:22; John 15:7–8; Ps 119:11)

3. How can you defend the Bible as the ultimate source of truth and highlight its uniqueness? (John 17:17; 2 Pet 1:20–21; Ps 119:160)

4. How has Scripture been a light, counselor, or comforter in your life? (Ps 119:105; Rom 15:4; 2 Cor 1:3–4)

5. How can parents and church leaders instill a love for Scripture in children and new believers? What practical steps encourage their study? (Ps 78:4; 2 Tim 3:14–15; Col 3:16)

 Gyokuro is a shade-grown Japanese green tea prized for its rich, umami depth and careful cultivation—symbolizing the reverent, diligent pursuit of Scripture.

 Heavenly Father, illuminate my heart through your word, help me develop regular reading habits, and grant me strength as I apply your teachings to my life. Amen.

 "If the world beautified with sun, moon, and stars, be as a precious ring, the Bible is the diamond in the ring."[1]

---

1. Boston, *Works*, 1:70 (1:56–76).

PART 2

God, Creation, and Providence

(Q4—Q12)

Day 5

God and His Perfections

Q4. *What is God?*

A. God is a Spirit, infinite, eternal, and unchangeable in his being, wisdom, power, holiness, justice, goodness, and truth.

God is a Spirit: and they that worship him must worship him in spirit and in truth.

JOHN 4:24 (KJV)

THOMAS BOSTON DISTINGUISHES BETWEEN God's incommunicable attributes (such as infinity, eternity, and unchangeableness) and communicable attributes (such as wisdom, power, holiness, justice, goodness, and truth), which are present in creatures in a limited way. While angels and souls are finite, temporal, and changeable, God's nature and communicable attributes are infinite, eternal, and unchangeable.

God is infinite in his being, presence (omnipresence), and time. He is eternal, having no beginning or end, unlike created things with a starting point but no endpoint—such as spirits, souls, the gospel, the covenant of grace, and Christ's redemption. God's unchangeableness means he remains the same in his perfections, intentions, and decrees, despite his dealings changing across different dispensations.

God's being is his nature, essence, and existence, which are infinite, eternal, and unchangeable. Unlike creatures whose being is limited and changeable, God's being is incomprehensible, omnipresent, immense, independent, and self-sufficient, with no progression in time. God affirms his eternal and unchanging existence by identifying himself as "I AM" (Exod 3:14).

God's wisdom signifies that he knows himself, all possible things, and how to dispose of them to the best ends. His knowledge is omniscient (Heb 4:13) and infallible (Rom 11:33–34). God's personal wisdom is Christ (1 Cor 1:24), to whom we can entrust our concerns, knowing he will manage them wisely for his glory.

God's power is his ability to do anything consistent with his nature—he is omnipotent (Jer 32:17). God's power manifests in creation (Rom 1:20), preservation (Heb 1:3), governance, and redemption. Boston refers to God as "the supreme Rector of the universe," highlighting his power in raising Jesus from the dead, forming the foundation of Christianity and our faith.

God's holiness is "the absolute purity of his nature." Boston emphasizes that God's holiness is perfect, universal, and unchangeable. It is most vividly demonstrated at the cross, where the eternally holy Son of God suffered for sins he did not commit. Only by fleeing to Christ, whose righteousness makes sinners acceptable, can we have hope before a holy God.

God's justice is "the perfect rectitude of his nature, whereby he is infinitely righteous and equal in himself and all his dealings with his creatures" (Deut 32:4). As sovereign Lord and supreme Judge, God has the absolute right to govern and judge creation according to his will, exercising both reward and punishment.

God's goodness means he is inherently good and the author of all good (Ps 119:68). Boston differentiates between absolute goodness, pertaining to God's inherent goodness, and relative goodness, shown through his benevolent disposition toward creation, especially his people.

Finally, God's truth means he is truthful, faithful, and error-free (Deut 32:4; Titus 1:2). His word is truth (John 17:17), forming a solid foundation for our faith in the authenticity of his revealed word. God's truth is built upon his knowledge, immutability, power, holiness, justice, and righteousness.

TEA WITH THOMAS BOSTON

1. How does understanding God as a spirit impact worshiping him "in spirit and truth," and how can this deepen your faith and worship? (John 4:24; 2 Cor 3:17; Ps 139:7–8)
2. Why does the catechism address "what is God?" (Q4) before "who is God?" (Q6) (Exod 3:14; 1 Tim 1:17; Isa 44:6–8)
3. Why is it important to understand God's incommunicable and communicable attributes in comprehending his nature? (Exod 34:6–7; Isa 40:28; 1 Pet 1:16)
4. How do God's holiness and justice balance his mercy and grace, and how do we reflect this in discipleship and parenting? (Ps 89:14; Rom 3:25–26; 9:13–16)
5. How can parents and church leaders teach God's omnipotence, omnipresence, and omniscience, and how do these traits shape worship, prayer, and evangelism? (Ps 139:1–4; Jer 23:23–24; Rev 19:6)

Silver needle is a premium white tea made from young tea buds, delicate and pure, with a light, sweet flavor that reflects divine majesty.

Heavenly Father, I praise your infinite wisdom, power, and holiness, and help me to grow in your knowledge and worship you in spirit and truth. Amen.

"That being which we can comprehend, cannot be God, because he is infinite."[1]

---

1. Boston, *Works*, 1:130 (1:77–130, 7:12–14).

Day 6

The Unity of God

> Q5. *Are there more Gods than one?*
> A. There is but one only, the living and true God.

Hear, O Israel: The LORD our God, the LORD is one.
DEUTERONOMY 6:4

We know that "there is no God but one."
1 CORINTHIANS 8:4

But the LORD is the true God; he is the living God.
JEREMIAH 10:10

THE FIRST TEXT TEACHES that God, the LORD (YHWH), is one—a being infinitely and eternally perfect, self-existent, and self-sufficient. The second text also affirms the singularity of God—"there is no God but one." The third text asserts that the LORD is the true and living God who is life itself and the source of life for all creatures. Thomas Boston combines these texts to establish the doctrine: "There is but one only, the living and true God."

Scripture calls God the *living* God to distinguish him from dead idols (Ps 115:4–6; 1 Thess 1:9). God, having life in himself (John 5:26), is the fountain of life. He gives life to all creatures. All life—natural (Acts 17:28), spiritual (Eph 2:5), and eternal (Col 3:4)—is *in* him and *from* him.

The Bible also refers to God as the *true* God, distinguishing him from all false gods. In addition to worshiping lifeless idols, unbelievers worship living creatures—even the devil (Deut 32:17). How can one discern the existence of the true God? Boston argues that the works of creation, providence, human conscience, universal consensus, and miracles in the world serve as evidence for the presence of a true God.

Beyond Scripture (1 Sam 2:2; Ps 18:31; Isa 44:6, 46:9; Mark 12:32; 1 Cor 8:4, 6), Boston establishes the truth of one God through reason. Firstly, "there can be but one First Cause," as only one being can create, preserve, and govern the world. Secondly, "there can be but one Infinite Being," as the existence of two infinite beings would entail contradiction. Thirdly, "there can be but one Independent Being," for multiple gods would either cause each other or none would be God. Fourthly, "there can be but one Omnipotent Being," as two all-powerful beings would render one redundant. If they disagreed and one could not oppose the other, that one would not be truly omnipotent. Fifthly, "a plurality of gods is destructive to all true religions," as devotion to multiple gods would divide the worshiper's loyalty (Matt 6:24). Finally, Boston emphasizes that accepting multiple gods would lead to irrational speculation about numerous deities.

Given the undeniable existence of the one, living, and true God, Boston condemns atheism as profoundly irrational and foolish (Ps 14:1). He considers it "most impious" and "of pernicious consequence both to others and to the atheist himself." In Boston's view, atheists are worse than heathens who worship multiple gods, as atheists worship none. To counter atheism, one should avoid indulging in sins, as doing so might lead one to wish there were no God to punish sinners. One should also "study God in the creatures as well as in the scriptures," as both reveal God's power.

TEA WITH THOMAS BOSTON

1. In what ways have you seen God as the living and true God in your life? (Jer 10:10; Acts 17:28; Ps 115:3)

2. Have you ever doubted God's existence, and how do creation, providence, and conscience testify to it? (Rom 1:19–20; 2:14–15; Ps 19:1–2)

3. How does Christianity differ from Judaism and Islam, and do Muslims and Christians worship the same God? How is monotheism more consistent than polytheism or atheism? (John 14:6; John 17:3; Acts 4:12)

4. Why does Boston see atheism as irrational, and how can understanding God's oneness address secularism? How can Scripture and nature strengthen our faith? (Ps 14:1; Rom 1:21–22; Job 12:7–10)

5. How can we teach the significance of God as the living God and help us remove idols from our lives? (Jer 10:10; 1 Thess 1:9; Ps 115:4–7)

Tieguanyin is a famous Chinese oolong tea with floral, vegetal notes, symbolizing the unity of divine compassion and harmony.

Heavenly Father, I acknowledge you as the one true God and ask for strength to worship and serve you with my whole being. Amen.

"There may be atheists in the church, but there are none in hell."[1]

---

1. Boston, *Works*, 1:139 (1:131–42, 7:14–15).

Day 7

The Holy Trinity

> Q6. *How many persons are there in the Godhead?*
> A. There are three persons in the Godhead: the Father, the Son, and the Holy Ghost, and these three are one God, the same in substance, equal in power and glory.

For there are three that bear record in heaven, the Father, the Word, and the Holy Ghost: and these three are one.

1 JOHN 5:7 (KJV)

IN 1 JOHN 5:5, the apostle John affirms that Jesus Christ is the Son of God and introduces supporting witnesses in verses 6 and 7. Thomas Boston expounds to reveal several truths about the Godhead: their number is three; their names and order are the Father, the Son (Word), and the Holy Spirit; they reside in heaven, revealing their glory and majesty; they bear witness that Jesus is God's Son; and they are united as one God in substance and essence.

Boston defines the Godhead as "the nature or essence of God," comprising three distinct persons. The Father is "the fountain or principle of the Deity," whose personal property is to beget the Son (Heb 1:5–6, 8). The Son is "begotten of the Father" (John 1:14, 18). The Spirit "proceeds from the Father *and* the Son" (John 15:26).

Both the Old and New Testaments attest to the plurality of persons in the Godhead. In the creation narrative, God says, "Let *us* make man in *our* image, after *our* likeness" (Gen 1:26). After the Fall, the LORD says, "Behold, the man is become as *one of us*" (Gen 3:22). The New Testament clarifies this plurality in passages like Jesus' baptism (Matt 3:16–17), the Great Commission (Matt 28:19), and the benediction (2 Cor 13:14). Boston notes that the baptismal formula shows both the singularity and plurality of the Godhead: believers are baptized in the *name* (singular) of the Father, Son, and Holy Spirit, signifying simultaneously the singularity and the plurality of the Godhead.

Scripture teaches that these three persons are one God, sharing the same substance, power, and glory. The Son is called God (Isa 9:6; John 1:1; Rom 9:5), as is the Spirit (Acts 5:3–4; 1 Cor 3:16). God's attributes are ascribed to both the Son (Mic 5:2; John 21:17; Heb 1:11–12; Rev 1:8) and the Spirit (Ps 139:7; 1 Cor 2:10, 12:6, 9–11). The works of creation, preservation, and salvation are attributed to the Son (John 1:3; Heb 1:3; John 5:21) and the Spirit (Ps 33:6; Ps 104:30; Matt 12:28). Worship is directed to the Son (Ps 2:12; John 5:23; 10:30; Phil 2:6) and the Spirit (Matt 28:19; Acts 4:23, 25; 2 Cor 13:14). Since all three persons share the same divine attributes, Boston asserts that the Godhead is undivided, with each person possessing the "one whole Godhead."

The doctrine of the Trinity is central to Christianity; without it, salvation would be impossible. Without the Trinity, faith loses its foundation. Jesus defines eternal life as knowing the Father as the only true God and recognizing the Son (John 17:3). Second, rejecting the Son severs true worship and fellowship with God, as we have access "in one Spirit to the Father" (Eph 2:18). Lastly, obedience is unattainable without living by the Spirit and being obedient to the Father, Son, and Spirit through baptism.

TEA WITH THOMAS BOSTON

1. How can we explain that the Trinity is a mystery, not a contradiction? (Deut 6:4; 1 Cor 8:6; Col 2:9)

2. How does each person of the Trinity contribute to our salvation, and how does believing in the Trinity impact worship, prayer, evangelism, and daily life? (Eph 1:3-14; 1 Pet 1:2; Titus 3:4-6)

3. What misunderstandings or heresies about the Trinity should we guard against? (John 10:33; Phil 2:6; 1 John 4:1-3)

4. What are the consequences of denying the Trinity, and how can we explain it to those from other faiths like Judaism or Islam? (John 14:6-7; 1 John 2:23; Acts 4:12)

5. How can we teach children and new believers about the Trinity and illustrate its unity and diversity? (Matt 28:19-20; Eph 4:4-6; 1 Tim 2:5)

Three-flower tea is a blend of jasmine, chrysanthemum, and lily, symbolizing the beauty and harmony of the Holy Trinity.

God, thank you for revealing yourself as the Trinity; help me understand and embrace this mystery, glorifying you in all your majesty. Amen.

"This mystery of the Trinity is so interwoven with the whole of religion that there can neither be any true faith, right worship, or obedience without it."[1]

---

1. Boston, *Works*, 1:147 (1:142-48, 7:15-16).

Day 8

The Decrees of God

Q7. *What are the decrees of God?*

A. The decrees of God are his eternal purpose, according to the counsel of his will, whereby, for his own glory, he has foreordained whatsoever comes to pass.

Q8. *How does God execute his decrees?*

A. God executes his decrees in the works of creation and providence.

In him we have obtained an inheritance, having been predestined according to the purpose of him who works all things according to the counsel of his will.

EPHESIANS 1:11

IN CHRIST, BELIEVERS OBTAIN a heavenly inheritance because God predestined them for salvation, as Paul teaches in Eph 1:11. This predestination is certain, aligning with God's purpose and decree. It is efficacious because God works "all things"—encompassing both blessings and all things within his decree—through creation and providence, following "the counsel of his will." Thomas Boston explains that God's will represents his decree and intention, with "the counsel of his will" emphasizing the wisdom and freedom in his decrees.

Boston defines God's decree as "to purpose and fore-ordain, to will and appoint that a thing shall be or not be." Nothing occurs outside God's decree, as everything depends on God as the first cause. While human decrees are distinct from their being, God's decrees are intrinsic to his being and are one singular act. Like the sun's heat can melt wax and harden clay while remaining a single action, God can decree many things as one unified act.

God's decrees cover several areas. First, God decreed the creation of all things—angels, humans, animals, and all beings. Second, God decreed to govern all his creations and their actions, including good and bad things. He even decreed the evils of sin, such as the crucifixion of Jesus (Acts 2:23) and Joseph being sold into Egypt (Gen 45:8). Boston notes, "Though sin in itself is evil, yet God's permitting it is good, seeing he can bring good out of it." However, this permission does not infringe upon human free will. Even the most casual actions of creatures fall under God's decree (Prov 16:33; Matt 10:29–30). God has decreed the rise and fall of kings and the fate of individuals, including their birth, place, and lifespan (Acts 17:26). Third, God decreed "the eternal state of all rational creatures"—angels and humans. Some angels were elected, while others were condemned (2 Pet 2:4). Similarly, some humans are elected to everlasting life (Rom 8:29–30), while others are passed over for damnation (Rom 9:22).

The ultimate purpose of God's decrees is his glory (Rom 11:36; Eph 1:12). In creation, inanimate objects glorify him through their nature (Ps 19:1; Rom 1:20), while rational beings like angels and humans praise him using their faculties (Rev 4:8–11). However, God's glory in redemption through Christ surpasses that in creation, where "his perfections and excellencies shine forth in their greatest glory." God's glory is also evident in the election for salvation and the passing over of others, showing mercy to some (Isa 43:21; 1 Pet 2:9) and righteous judgment to others (Prov 16:4).

Boston asserts that God's decrees are eternal, wise, free, unchangeable, holy, pure, and effective. Since God decrees all things, there is no room for chance or luck in a Christian's worldview (Prov 16:33). Believers should never use God's decrees as excuses for sin but find comfort, resting in God's wisdom and sovereignty.

TEA WITH THOMAS BOSTON

1. How do God's eternal, wise, free, unchanging, holy, pure, and effective decrees offer comfort in difficult times? (Ps 33:11; Rom 11:33; Jas 1:17)

2. How do God's decrees relate to creation and providence, and how does recognizing God's governance shape our view of chance and luck? (Prov 16:33; Col 1:16–17; Heb 1:3)

3. How can we reconcile evil and suffering with God's goodness, given Boston's argument that God ordains both for his glory? (Isa 45:7; Rom 8:18; Gen 50:20)

4. What is the relationship between human free will and God's decrees? Are our choices truly free or predetermined? (Prov 16:9; Phil 2:12–13; Acts 2:23)

5. How can we teach children and new believers about God's decrees, emphasizing his sovereignty, love, and justice? (Rom 11:33; Ps 139:13–16; Deut 32:4)

 Aged pu-erh is a fermented tea that matures over time, offering a deep, earthy flavor and symbolizing the eternal nature of God's decrees.

 Heavenly Father, help me trust in your sovereign plan over all things, submitting to your will and finding rest in your providence. Amen.

 "In our redemption by Christ, we have the fullest, clearest, and most delightful manifestation of the glory of God that ever was or shall be in this life."[1]

---

1. Boston, *Works*, 1:157 (1:149–67, 7:16–18).

Day 9

The Work of Creation

Q9. *What is the work of creation?*
A. The work of creation is God's making all things of nothing, by the word of his power, in the space of six days, and all very good.

By faith we understand that the universe was created by the word of God, so that what is seen was not made out of things that are visible.

HEBREWS 11:3

GOD EXECUTES HIS DECREES through creation and providence. Thomas Boston compares God's decrees to a house's blueprint, while creation and providence are the actual house built according to that plan.

Hebrews 11:3 teaches that God created the universe by his word, implying a beginning for the world. The "word of God" refers to the powerful utterance that brought everything into existence (Ps 33:6) or to Christ, who is the Word of God (John 1:1). What is visible was formed from the invisible, specifically from nothing, as seen in the doctrine of *creatio ex nihilo*, or creation out of nothing, which can only be understood through faith.

Boston calls creation out of nothing "immediate creation," contrasting it with "mediate creation," where things are shaped from preexisting matter, such as animals formed from the dust of the ground or the first woman from

Adam's rib. Mediate creation still relies on God's power, as material would not have assumed its form without divine intervention.

Unlike modern cosmologists, Boston rejects the idea of self-creation or chance. He rhetorically asks, "Can any man rationally conceive . . . a confused rout of atoms . . . should ever meet in such a fortunate manner . . . to form an entire world?" Such a view is nonsensical and only found in disordered thinking.

Scripture attributes creation to all members of the Godhead. The Father, as the "fountain of the Deity," willed creation by his authority. Psalm 33:9 states, "He spoke, and it was done; he commanded, and it stood fast." The Son, through whom all things were made (John 1:3; Eph 3:9), is attributed with the act of immediate operation. The Holy Spirit is responsible for the world's disposition and decoration, as seen in Gen 1:2, where "the Spirit of God was hovering over the face of the waters," beautifying the world after its substance was formed. Elihu in Job 33:4 says, "The Spirit of God has made me, and the breath of the Almighty gives me life."

Genesis 1 describes the world's creation in six days, though Boston notes that it could have been done in an instant. Boston believes angels were created within this timeframe, as Gen 2:1 mentions "all things" being created during those six days and angels are part of the heavenly host (1 Kgs 22:19).

All things were created by and for God (Col 1:16). Ultimately, creation glorifies God (Rom 11:36). His wisdom, power, and goodness are especially evident in creation. Since everything we have—our bodies, abilities, and life—originates from God, we should consecrate all we do for his glory.

TEA WITH THOMAS BOSTON

1. How does knowing God created all things for his glory impact our worship, daily lives, choices, and evangelism? (Col 1:16; Rev 4:11; Rom 8:19–22)
2. What is the significance of creation "out of nothing" in six days, and how does it differ from other worldviews? (Gen 1:1–2; Heb 11:3; Ps 33:6, 9)
3. How does Heb 11:3 explain the nature of faith in creation? Why is it essential to believe God created the universe through his word? (Gen 1:1; John 1:3; Rom 4:17)
4. How should Christians approach theories like evolution and the Big Bang, and can they be reconciled with the biblical creation account? (Heb 1:2; Rom 1:20; Isa 45:18)
5. How can we teach children and new believers that God created everything by his word and for his glory? (Ps 104:24; 139:13–14; Isa 43:7)

 Matcha is a powdered green tea that is whisked into a frothy beverage, vibrant and full of energy, symbolizing the work of creation.

 Heavenly Father, thank you for your creation, and may I honor you with all that I am and have for your glory. Amen.

 "The world could not make itself, for this would imply a horrid contradiction, namely, that the world was before it was, for the cause must always be before its effect."[1]

---

1. Boston, *Works*, 1:169 (1:167–77, 7:18–19).

Day 10

The Creation of Man

Q10. *How did God create man?*

A. God created man male and female, after his own image, in knowledge, righteousness, and holiness, with dominion over the creatures.

So God created man in his own image, in the image of God he created him; male and female he created them.

GENESIS 1:27

GOD DEMONSTRATES HUMANITY'S EXCELLENCE over other creatures through the way he created man. While God spoke other creatures into existence, Thomas Boston notes that God convened a council of the Trinity when creating man. Genesis 1:27 repeats the act of creation three times to emphasize that God, not angels or anyone else, created man. "Man" here includes both male and female, and both were made "very like God" to represent and imitate him in his perfections (Gen 1:26–31).

The first man's body was formed from the dust of the ground (Gen 2:7), hence the name Adam, meaning "red earth." Man's humble origin should deter pride, as human composition is no different from the earth beneath our feet. Just as man originated from the earth, he will return to it, awaiting the day of resurrection for judgment or eternal life (John 5:28–29).

The first woman's body was fashioned from Adam's rib (Gen 2:21–22). Boston emphasizes that the word *made* in verse 22 is the Hebrew word *built*, showing that woman was built like a mansion from nobler material. This foreshadows the "mystery of the church drawing her life out of Christ's sleeping the sleep of death on the cross" (Eph 5).

Unlike the creation of man's and woman's bodies, God created the soul of man from nothing (Gen 2:7). Adam was a lifeless body until God breathed the life-giving breath into him. The soul is a spiritual substance called a spirit (Zech 12:1), immortal, and does not die with the body (Eccl 12:7). God is the "Father of spirits" (Heb 12:9), creating the souls of all humans from nothing.

The image of God is most prominently reflected in the soul. It includes knowledge (Col 1:10), as Adam was created wise and "ignorant of nothing that he was obliged to know," displaying his knowledge by naming animals (Gen 2:19). It also consists of righteousness (Eph 4:24), as Adam's will perfectly aligned with God's, with a disposition toward good actions (Eccl 7:29). The image involves holiness (Eph 4:24), as his affections were pure, loving what God loves (Matt 22:37). Lastly, the image includes dominion over creatures (Gen 1:26–27), allowing Adam to manage creation. Boston summarizes, "The parts of the image of God impressed on his soul were knowledge on his mind, righteousness on his will, and holiness on his affections," with "dominion over the creatures" as part of the whole man.

Adam's original righteousness—knowledge, righteousness, and holiness—was mutable. Using the language of the *Fourfold State*, Boston stresses that Adam, in his state of innocence, possessed spiritual strength similar to that of Christians in their state of grace. Adam could obey all of God's commands, meaning God cannot be blamed as the author of sin for Adam's fall.

TEA WITH THOMAS BOSTON

1. How does being created in God's image impact your self-worth? (Gen 2:18; 1 Tim 2:13–14; 1 Cor 11:3, 8–9)

2. How does the creation of man and woman as male and female reflect God's image, and what are the implications for gender roles and the concept of gender as a continuum or social construct? (Gen 2:18–24; Matt 19:4–6; Gal 3:28)

3. What does having dominion over creation mean, and how can we balance civilization's advancement with environmental preservation? (Gen 1:26; Ps 8:5–8; Rom 8:19–21)

4. How does the Bible challenge the evolutionary view of humans, and how should Christians respond to those who see creation as a myth? (John 1:3; Heb 11:3; Rom 1:18–20)

5. How can we teach children and new believers about being made in God's image and the dignity and purpose of human life? (Gen 1:27; Ps 139:13–14; Jas 3:9)

Darjeeling is a fragrant black tea from the foothills of the Himalayas, known for its unique muscatel flavor, symbolizing the creation of humankind's unique nature.

Heavenly Father, thank you for creating me in your image and restoring me through Christ, shaping me into His likeness by the Holy Spirit. Amen.

"The only way to recover the image of God is to unite with Jesus Christ by faith."[1]

---

1. Boston, *Works*, 7:21 (1:177–85, 7:19–22).

Day 11

The Providence of God

Q11. *What are God's works of providence?*

A. God's works of providence are his most holy, wise, and powerful preserving and governing all his creatures and all their actions.

Are not two sparrows sold for a penny? And not one of them will fall to the ground apart from your Father. But even the hairs of your head are all numbered.

MATTHEW 10:29–30

JESUS ENCOURAGES HIS DISCIPLES to overcome fear by highlighting God's providence, which extends even to sparrows and the hairs on their heads. Despite their minimal value, sparrows are preserved and governed by God, who ensures no one falls without his permission.

Thomas Boston supports providence with Scripture and nature, quoting Psalm 103:19 and Acts 17:28 to emphasize God's dominion and sustaining presence. He also references Ezekiel's wheels, interpreting "the wheel inside a wheel" as symbolizing God's guiding providence. Boston stresses that biblical prophecies depend on providence, and despite apparent chaos, providence ensures hidden order and harmony. Ultimately, God governs all things to fulfill his decrees for his glory.

Providence includes all creatures and their actions, as God upholds *"all things* by the word of his power" (Heb 1:3, KJV). His providence extends to angels (Neh 9:6), demons (Matt 8:31), and every element in the universe (Ps 104; 147). Even "the most free acts of the creature's will," not only good deeds (John 15:5) but also evil ones (Acts 4:27–28), "are governed by superintending providence."

Providence involves two key acts: preservation and governance. Preservation refers to God continuously upholding all creatures in being. Boston stresses that nothing could endure even for a single moment without God's providence, as there is no inherent link between a creature's existence at one moment and the next. Since creatures cannot bring themselves into existence or sustain it independently, God's providence is vital in providing everything required to maintain creation (Ps 145:15–16).

God's providence arranges everything according to his will. Just as creatures cannot persist without his preservation, they cannot act without his permission. They do good only by his grace and commit evil only as he permits. God allows sin without causing it, as Acts 14:16 states: "In past generations, he allowed all the nations to walk in their own ways." Yet, he uses even evil for good, as seen in Joseph's words: "You meant evil against me, but God meant it for good" (Gen 50:20). Indeed, God brings "the greatest good out of the worst of evils" in the crucifixion of Christ. However, God neither implants wickedness in hearts nor tempts anyone to sin (Jas 1:13). Therefore, God is not the originator of sin.

Though involved in a world of sin, God's providence remains holy (Ps 145:17). Boston argues that just as a rider of a lame horse is not the cause of its lameness, God is not the author of sin. His providence is also profoundly wise (Isa 28:29) and supremely powerful (Prov 21:1)—nothing can obstruct God's plans or hinder their providential execution.[1]

---

1. For Boston's detailed treatment of the subject of providence, consult his famous work, *The Crook in the Lot: The Sovereignty and Wisdom of God Displayed in the Afflictions of Men*, found in Boston, *Works*, 3:497–590.

TEA WITH THOMAS BOSTON

1. How does knowing that God governs even the smallest details, like sparrows and our hairs, shape our view of daily struggles? (Luke 12:6–7; Ps 139:1–4; Prov 16:9)
2. How can God govern good and evil actions without being the author of sin? How does this help us reconcile suffering with God's goodness? (Jas 1:13–14; Rom 8:28; Isa 45:7)
3. How do God's holiness, wisdom, and power in providence bring peace amid chaos? Can you share a time when this truth reassured you? (Prov 3:5–6; Isa 55:8–9; Rom 8:28)
4. How does providence shape our understanding of prayer? Does prayer change God's plan or align us with his will? (Matt 6:9–13; Phil 4:6–7; 1 John 5:14–15)
5. What examples can help children and new believers grasp that God preserves and governs everything? (Matt 6:26; Col 1:17; Ps 104:27–30)

Rooibos is a caffeine-free herbal tea from South Africa, known for its soothing, nutty flavor and for being a symbol of God's sustaining providence.

Heavenly Father, thank you for your sovereign care over all creation and for reminding me to trust your providence in every trial. Amen.

"Even though providence reaches to and be conversant in sinful actions, yet it is pure; as the sun contracts no defilement, though it shines on a dunghill."[2]

---

2. Boston, *Works*, 1:191 (1:186–93, 7:22–24).

Day 12

The Covenant of Works

> Q12. *What special act of providence did God exercise toward man in the estate wherein he was created?*
>
> A. When God had created man, he entered into a covenant of life with him, upon condition of perfect obedience; forbidding him to eat of the tree of the knowledge of good and evil, upon pain of death.

And the LORD God commanded the man, saying, "You may surely eat of every tree of the garden, but of the tree of the knowledge of good and evil you shall not eat, for in the day that you eat of it you shall surely die."

GENESIS 2:16–17

IN HIS PROVIDENCE, GOD established a covenant of life with Adam, often called the covenant of works, as obedience to God's command is its condition. Hosea 6:7 affirms its covenantal nature: "But like Adam, they transgressed the covenant." Thomas Boston notes that the command not to eat the forbidden fruit is a supernatural revelation, not part of the natural or moral law inscribed in Adam's heart in his state of innocence (Rom 2:15). The penalty for breaking this command is threefold: natural death (separation of body and soul), spiritual death (separation of the soul from God, Eph 2:1), and eternal death (separation of both body and soul from God in hell forever, Matt 25:41). By implication, life—natural, spiritual, and eternal—was promised as a reward for obedience within the probationary period, following the principle "do this and live."

The covenant of works involves two parties: on the divine side, the triune God; on the human side, Adam, the federal and covenantal representative of humankind (Rom 5:12). No mediator was needed, as Adam, in his state of holiness, was fully capable of fulfilling the covenant (Eccl 7:29). God's command required not only external obedience but also an internal disposition of the heart—abstaining from the fruit for God's glory. Adam was expected to obey perfectly in thoughts, words, and actions, loving God with all his heart, soul, and strength. Given the unequivocal threat of "you shall surely die," this covenant allowed no room for repentance.

Boston identifies "two sacramental seals" of this covenant. The first is the tree of the knowledge of good and evil (Gen 2:17), which did not inherently make one wise, contrary to the serpent's insinuation. The fruit was not evil in itself but became so because it was forbidden. The tree's name warns Adam and Eve against gaining experiential knowledge of evil through disobedience. The second seal is the tree of life (Gen 2:9), which did not inherently grant immortality but served as a sacramental sign of eternal life. By eating it, Adam would have affirmed his faith in God's promise (Gen 3:22). However, his sin forfeited his right to this symbol of eternal life, leading God to expel him to prevent him from defiling a sacrament he no longer had access to.

God's grace and condescension are evident in this covenant. As Creator and sovereign Lord, God could have simply required obedience, which Adam inherently owed him. Yet, God went further, promising eternal life—a reward far exceeding the required obedience—if Adam remained faithful during probation. This covenant underscores the link between duty and happiness, revealing that man's chief end is to obey God, the only path to true happiness.[1]

---

1. For a detailed exposition of Boston's concept of the covenant of works, see his *A View of the Covenant of Works* in Boston, *Works*, 11:171–339. For a concise overview, see Tse, *Marrow of Certainty*, 130–35.

TEA WITH THOMAS BOSTON

1. How does Adam's required perfect obedience challenge us today, and how does Christ fulfill this standard for us? (Rom 5:19; Matt 5:48; Heb 4:15)

2. The covenant of works teaches that true happiness comes from obeying God. How does this shape our view of a meaningful life? How can we explain this to people from secular or other religious backgrounds? (John 15:10–11; Ps 1:1–3; 119:1–2)

3. In the covenant of works, obedience brought life, and disobedience brought death. How does this highlight the seriousness of sin? (Rom 6:23; Ezek 18:4; Jas 1:15)

4. How does Adam's role as humanity's representative help us understand the impact of his obedience or disobedience? Are there similar examples in politics, sports, business, or family? (1 Cor 15:22; Heb 7:9–10; 1 Sam 17:8–9)

5. How can we teach the covenant of works to children and new believers, showing both the seriousness of sin and our hope in Christ? (Gen 3:15; 2 Cor 5:21; Rom 3:23–24)

 Yerba mate is a South American herbal tea, rich in caffeine and antioxidants, symbolizing the strength of the covenant of works.

 Heavenly Father, thank you for your grace in the covenant of works, and help me live in obedience, trusting in Christ for eternal life. Amen.

 "That chariot which the first Adam drove, went not far till it was all shattered, and made unfit to carry any to heaven. . . . But come into the chariot of the covenant of grace, and ye will be safely carried in it to the land of eternal rest and glory."[2]

---

2. Boston, *Works*, 1:242 (1:229–42, 7:24–26).

PART 3

Man and Sin

(Q13—Q19)

Day 13

The Fall of Our First Parents

> Q13. *Did our first parents continue in the estate wherein they were created?*
>
> A. Our first parents, being left to the freedom of their own will, fell from the estate wherein they were created by sinning against God.

So when the woman saw that the tree was good for food, and that it was a delight to the eyes, and that the tree was to be desired to make one wise, she took of its fruit and ate, and she also gave some to her husband who was with her, and he ate. Then the eyes of both were opened, and they knew that they were naked. And they sewed fig leaves together and made themselves loincloths.

GENESIS 3:6–7

IN *THE FOURFOLD STATE*, Thomas Boston chronicles the fall of our first parents from the state of innocence—where their will extended "both to good and evil"—to the state of corrupt nature, where it extends "only to evil" (Gen 4:5). In contrast, the will of Christians in the state of grace extends "partly to good and partly to evil" (Rom 7:23), while in the state of glory, it extends "only to good" (Heb 12:23).

By eating the forbidden fruit, Boston argues, Adam "broke the whole law of God at one touch" because he "violently struck against God and man's neighbor," his posterity. Through this single act of disobedience, Adam fell from his blessed state, losing his spiritual knowledge, the holiness of his affections, and the righteousness of his will—corresponding to his threefold office of prophet, priest, and king.

Boston asserts that no one should object to God for making Adam capable of change in his goodness. It would have been either by nature or grace if Adam had been unchangeably holy. If by nature, he would have been divine; if by grace, God did him no injustice by withholding what was not owed. Had Adam remained faithful through his testing, he would have received the grace of confirmation. Moreover, God neither removed any strength he had given Adam nor instilled any sinful inclinations. Instead, God permitted the fall. God could have prevented Satan from tempting or Adam from yielding, but in God's holy and wise providence, he chose not to intervene. Adam had the power to obey or fall, and God was not obligated to prevent it. Our first parents "had a possibility of standing, yet they had not an impossibility of falling." They were, in other words, "holy but mutable."

Since serpents cannot speak, much less reason, Boston concludes that the devil—driven by "an implacable hatred against God" and "solicited by envy"—"hid himself in the body of a serpent." In his craftiness, Satan first approached Eve, "the weaker vessel." Seeing the forbidden fruit was agreeable to the taste, pleasant to the eye, and desirable to "the rational appetite" to make one wise, Eve ate and gave it to Adam.

By succumbing to Satan's insinuations, our first parents entered a state of misery, seized by the horror of conscience. God expelled them from paradise and excommunicated them from communion with him. God condemned the woman to "sorrow and pain in breeding, bearing, and bringing forth children" and subjected her to her husband, while God cursed the ground for man's sake and condemned him to "singular anxiety, weary, toilsome, and fruitless labor." Finally, since Adam broke the covenant of works, neither he nor his descendants could obtain life through it—life could now be attained only through the covenant of grace.

TEA WITH THOMAS BOSTON

1. What steps can you take to safeguard your minds and hearts from temptation, especially considering how our first parents fell? (Matt 26:41; 2 Tim 2:22; 1 Pet 5:8)
2. How does the fall challenge the common idea that humans are inherently good? (Rom 3:23; 1 John 1:8; Gen 6:5)
3. How does the doctrine of original sin, illustrated by the fall, explain the need for salvation? (Gen 3:15; Rom 5:18–21; Gal 3:21–22)
4. How does the shift from the covenant of works to the covenant of grace give hope and shape our view of suffering? (Rom 8:18–25; 2 Cor 4:17–18; Heb 12:2)
5. How can we help children and new believers cultivate a healthy understanding of the consequences of sin? (Rom 5:12; 1 John 1:9; 2 Cor 7:10)

Smoked lapsang souchong is a bold black tea with a smoky flavor, representing the deep loss and sorrow of the fall of man.

Heavenly Father, thank you for your grace that restores us through Christ, despite the fall of our first parents and our own weakness. Amen.

"If Adam in a few hours sinned himself out of paradise, O how quickly would even those who are regenerated sin themselves into hell, if they were not preserved by a greater power than their own?"[1]

---

1. Boston, *Works*, 1:254 (1:242–55, 7:26–27).

Day 14

Sin in General

> Q14. *What is sin?*
>
> A. Sin is any want of conformity unto, or transgression of, the law of God.

Everyone who makes a practice of sinning also practices lawlessness; sin is lawlessness.

1 JOHN 3:4

SIN, IN THE ORIGINAL language, is not hitting the mark or deviating from the right path. Sin cannot be defined apart from God's law because it is anything that fails to align with or transgresses God's law. Romans 4:15 states, "Where there is no law, there is no transgression." Boston distinguishes two senses of God's law. First, natural law, or conscience—what Boston calls the "light of reason"—is engraved upon every human being long before the promulgation of the law at Mount Sinai. Second, for the nation of Israel, God gave the Law of Moses, which consists of the ceremonial law governing the external worship of YHWH, the judicial law prescribing civil governance for the Jews, and the moral law summarized in the Ten Commandments.

The moral law, Boston insists, "continues in its full force and power." While Christ has come to fulfill the law and his death has abolished the ceremonial law, some aspects of the judicial law rooted in universal moral principles—such as enforcing justice, punishing criminals, and protecting widows, orphans, foreigners, and the vulnerable—remain in effect.

Therefore, the law that defines sin includes the moral law written on human hearts, the commandments revealed in Scripture and summarized in the Ten Commandments, and the ethical teachings of the gospel of Christ.

Boston differentiates between two kinds of sin. Original sin, inherited from Adam, is a lack of conformity of our *nature* to God's law. Actual sin, originating from us, is the lack of conformity in our lives—whether in heart, words, or deeds—to God's law, either by omission or commission. Since sin is a lack of perfection, Boston argues that sin is not from God but from the creature. Sin is not something to take pride in; instead, it should humble us, as we desperately need its removal. Sin should be hated, for it is utterly detestable to God.

Even the earliest stirrings of sin—before the will consents to them—are indeed sin. Any inner agreement with or delight in thoughts that go against God's law is sinful, even if they never lead to outward actions. Failing to fulfill our internal duties toward God and others is a sin, including wrongful silence and wrongful speech when truth and righteousness demand otherwise. Likewise, neglecting external duties for which we are responsible is sinful. According to Boston, any failure—no matter how small—that falls short of God's law is also a sin.

Although sin harms others and ourselves, its greatest evil lies in its offense against God. Sin is "the greatest of evils" because it directly contradicts God, who is the supreme good. Sin is an act of high rebellion against God's sovereign authority. Worse still, sin not only rejects God's rule but also submits to the devil, whose very work is sin. Sin assaults "the unspotted holiness of God," mocks his wisdom, abuses his goodness, and implicitly denies his omniscience. Ultimately, sin defies God's power and authority. Therefore, "flee to Jesus Christ," Boston urges, "for the pardon of sin."

TEA WITH THOMAS BOSTON

1. How can you guard your thoughts and desires to prevent sin? (Matt 5:28; Prov 4:23; Phil 4:8)

2. How does the distinction between original and actual sin show our need for Christ? (Rom 5:12; Eph 2:1–3; 1 John 1:8)

3. How can you explain that God's law—not human standards—defines sin? (Rom 7:7; 1 John 3:4; Ps 119:11)

4. How can you raise awareness of the seriousness of sin, especially in omissions like wrongful silence? (Luke 12:47–48; Matt 25:40–45; Jas 4:17)

5. What steps can children or young believers take to flee sin and seek Christ's pardon? (1 Cor 10:13; 2 Tim 2:22; Acts 3:19)

Dark-roast oolong is a heavily oxidized tea with a strong, rich flavor, symbolizing the sobering reality of sin.

Heavenly Father, I confess my sin against you and seek your forgiveness through Jesus Christ, my only hope for restoration. Amen.

"Sin is the mother of all evils that ever were or shall be. It is the big-bellied monster that is delivered daily of all other evils as its births."[1]

---

1. Boston, *Works*, 1:266 (1:256–66, 7:27–28).

Day 15

The First Sin in Particular

> Q15. *What was the sin whereby our first parents fell from the estate wherein they were created?*
>
> A. The sin whereby our first parents fell from the estate wherein they were created was their eating the forbidden fruit.

So when the woman saw that the tree was good for food, and that it was a delight to the eyes, and that the tree was to be desired to make one wise, she took of its fruit and ate, and she also gave some to her husband who was with her, and he ate. Then the eyes of both were opened, and they knew that they were naked. And they sewed fig leaves together and made themselves loincloths.

GENESIS 3:6–7

REGARDING ADAM AND EVE's first sin of eating the forbidden fruit, the fruit itself was not inherently evil; rather, the sin lay in their disobedience—eating it "against the express command of God." Thomas Boston reasons that our first parents were not entirely innocent before they physically ate the forbidden fruit, for their desire for it in their hearts must have preceded the act. The physical eating, however, explicitly confirmed their lust and "completed their sin" of rebellion against their Creator.

Since Adam and Eve were created with a free will to choose good, as evidenced by the tree of life, but also with the capacity to choose evil, as evidenced by the tree of the knowledge of good and evil, Boston maintains that the divine prohibition of a morally neutral act—eating the forbidden fruit—was the most fitting test of their obedience to God. Commands such as loving God, keeping the Sabbath, honoring parents, or refraining from murder, adultery, or theft would not have genuinely tested them, as these either aligned with their upright nature or were irrelevant to their circumstances. As a newly created man and woman blessed with divine gifts, they would have naturally loved God and others, making these commandments less of a challenge.

Eating the forbidden fruit was, in essence, Adam and Eve's defiant assertion that they would follow their own will rather than submit to God's. Consequently, it was not a minor offense but, argues Boston, a blatant violation of the entire Ten Commandments simultaneously. They committed idolatry by making their belly, themselves, and the devil their gods. They engaged in false worship by rejecting God's clear command and choosing their own manner of worship. They took God's name in vain by despising his attributes, disregarding his word, and misinterpreting his providence. They broke the Sabbath, disrupting the rest and service to God they were meant to enjoy. They dishonored their heavenly Father and neglected their duty to each other and their descendants. Adam became the greatest murderer by bringing death upon himself and all his offspring. They indulged in sensual desires and engaged in spiritual adultery, leading to shame, and they had to cover their nakedness. They committed theft by taking what was not theirs, eating the forbidden fruit against God's will. Their actions bore false witness against God, implying that he was withholding happiness from them and that God's word was not to be trusted. Finally, they were discontent with their happy and blessed state and coveted what was not theirs, leading to their downfall.

The effects of our first parents' disobedience were thoroughly devastating as their first sin robbed God's glory, defaced the divine image in humans, and brought miseries, death, and hell to all their descendants. O, cherish Christ, urges Boston, for the second Adam hung on a tree to redeem the sons of the first Adam and drank the cup of wrath as the bitter fruit of sin, restoring us to fellowship with our heavenly Father.

TEA WITH THOMAS BOSTON

1. How does Adam and Eve's disobedience challenge your trust and obedience to God? (Gen 3:6; Prov 3:5–6; Heb 3:12)
2. Why was the forbidden fruit a fitting test of obedience? (Gen 2:16–17; Deut 8:2; Jas 1:14–15)
3. How would you respond to those who see Adam and Eve's sin as minor? (Rom 6:23; Jas 2:10; Heb 2:2–3)
4. How do the first sin's devastating effects motivate you to pursue holiness? (Rom 6:12–14; 1 Pet 1:14–16; Gal 5:16–17)
5. How can we teach children and new believers to trust and obey God? (Deut 6:6–7; Prov 22:6; Eph 6:4)

 Spiced chai is a traditional Indian tea blend with a mix of warming spices, representing the complexity and deception of the first sin.

 Heavenly Father, keep my heart from rebellion and teach me to trust and obey your commands that I may not choose my own way over yours. Amen.

 "This fruit was not forbidden because it was evil, but it was evil because it was forbidden."[1]

---

1. Boston, *Works*, 1:268 (1:257–73, 7:28–29).

Day 16

Our Fall in Adam

Q16. *Did all mankind fall in Adam's first transgression?*

A. The covenant being made with Adam, not only for himself, but for his posterity; all mankind, descending from him by ordinary generation, sinned in him and fell with him in his first transgression.

Q17. *Into what estate did the fall bring mankind?*

A. The fall brought mankind into an estate of sin and misery.

For as by the one man's disobedience the many were made sinners, so by the one man's obedience the many will be made righteous.
ROMANS 5:19

WHEN ADAM ATE THE forbidden fruit, all his descendants by ordinary generation—except Christ—sinned in him and fell with him. Although Christ was a son of Adam (Luke 3:23, 38), Christ was not represented by Adam because Christ was born through an extraordinary generation, conceived by the Spirit, and born of a virgin. By eating the forbidden fruit, Adam imputed his first sin to all his descendants except Christ, who "was separated from sinners" (Heb 7:26) and "was not infected with the plague whereof he was to be the cleanser."

What was the basis for that imputation? Although there was a natural connection between Adam and us, Boston argues that this biological link was not the basis for the imputation of his sin, as we share a similar union with our parents, yet their sins are not imputed to us. The imputation is based on Adam acting not merely as a "private person" but as a "public person" in the covenant of works. Adam's first sin, therefore, is our sin because he was "our covenant head and representative in the covenant of works." In other words, God not merely made the covenant of works with Adam but with "all his posterity descending from him by ordinary generation."

Adam's subsequent sins, however, are not imputed any more than the sins of other private individuals are imputed. By breaking the covenant of works, Adam ceased to be our representative, as only a sinless person can serve as a representative. Nevertheless, everyone in Adam is born condemned because Adam broke the covenant while he was our sinless representative. Although the covenant is broken, Adam's descendants are not free from the covenant of works. They remain under the curse of this "broken covenant of works" (Rom 3:19)—not as a means of obtaining eternal life, for that possibility was lost in the fall. However, the covenant of works remains in effect, demanding perfect obedience from sinners and condemning them for even the slightest failure (Gal 3:10).

After the fall, every human was born into a state of "sin and misery." Not only was Adam's first sin imputed to them but also the consequences of that sin, including the guilt of eternal wrath, the loss of God's image, the corruption of human nature, and the punishments incurred by that sin—women will suffer pain in childbirth and be subject to their husbands, while men will toil in work, both facing separation from God and eventual death.

Even though we did not elect Adam to be our representative, God elected him for us, and Adam was "the most fit choice for that end." Boston claims that those who charge God as unfair "must renounce their part in Christ: for we are made righteous by him, as sinners are made guilty by Adam."

TEA WITH THOMAS BOSTON

1. How does knowing all humanity fell in Adam's first sin help you understand human depravity? (Rom 5:12; 1 Cor 15:22; Gen 3:6)

2. How does Adam, as a "public person" in the covenant of works, help explain the doctrine of original sin and our fall? (Rom 5:12–19; Gen 2:16–17; 1 Cor 15:22)

3. How does the fall and imputation concept distinguish Christianity from other religions? (Rom 3:23; 5:12; Gen 3:17–19)

4. How does the fall deepen your appreciation for God's grace in Christ? (Eph 2:4–5; Rom 5:20–21; 1 Pet 1:3–5)

5. How would you explain to a young believer why Adam's sin affected all humanity? (Gen 2:16–17; Rom 3:10–12; Ps 51:5)

 Kuding tea is a bitter Chinese tea, known for its sharp, medicinal taste, symbolizing the inherited bitterness of sin passed down from Adam.

 Heavenly Father, I recognize that through Adam's sin, I am born into sin and suffering, but I thank you for Christ, my sinless representative, who gives me salvation. Amen.

 "Adam had all his children in one ship to carry them to Immanuel's land; by his negligence he dashed the ship on a rock, and broke it all in pieces; and so he and his lay foundering in a sea of guilt: Jesus Christ lets out the second covenant as a rope to draw them to the shore."[1]

---

1. Boston, *Works*, 1:274 (1:273–78, 7:29–31).

Day 17

The Sinfulness of Man's Natural State

> Q18. *Wherein consists the sinfulness of that estate whereinto man fell?*
>
> A. The sinfulness of that estate whereinto man fell consists in the guilt of Adam's first sin, the want of original righteousness, and the corruption of his whole nature, which is commonly called original sin, together with all actual transgressions which proceed from it.

Behold, I was brought forth in iniquity, and in sin did my mother conceive me.

PSALM 51:5

THE NATURAL STATE OF humans is a sinful state, entailing original sin imputed and inherited from Adam, as well as actual transgressions incurred by us. Adam, whom Thomas Boston calls the "original of mankind," transferred original sin to us, which consists of "the guilt of Adam's first sin, the lack of original righteousness, and the corruption of his whole nature."

The first component of original sin is the guilt of Adam's first sin, which incurs "an obligation of punishment for it." This guilt, imputed to all in Adam, can only be removed through justification (Rom 3:24). The second component is the lack of original righteousness, which involves a lack of knowledge in the understanding (1 Cor 2:14), righteousness in the will (Rom 8:7), and holiness in the affections (Rom 7:14). This lack of original righteousness is not only devoid of good qualities but is also filled with evil ones; therefore, it is sinful, as it represents a failure to conform to God's law (Matt 5:48). The third component is the corruption of the whole nature, which Boston considers the worst part, rendering the sinner "utterly disabled for, and opposed to all spiritual good, and prone to the contrary evils continually."

The guilt of Adam's first sin is by imputation, a legal reckoning where Adam's sin is counted against all his descendants by his federal and covenantal headship (Rom 5:12, 19). In comparison, the lack of original righteousness and the corruption of the whole nature—which Boston calls "original sin inherent"—is not by imputation but by impartation. Adam's children, by the process of natural generation or procreation, inherit a corrupted image and nature, and the only remedy is Jesus Christ and the Holy Spirit. While God pardons the guilt of Adam's first sin immediately in justification, he begins removing the "original sin inherent" in regeneration, continues this process through sanctification, and will perfect it in glorification.

Due to the imputation and impartation of original sin, Adam's descendants will commit actual transgressions. These actual sins are, as Boston succinctly states, "breaches of God's law by omission or commission, in thoughts, words, or deeds." Therefore, people in the natural state cannot do anything genuinely good because their nature is wholly corrupt. Boston maintains that even their natural actions, such as eating and drinking, are sinful, citing Zech 7:6: "And when you eat and when you drink, do you not eat for yourselves and drink for yourselves?" Their civil actions, such as plowing and sowing, are also sinful, as Prov 21:4 states: "The plowing of the wicked is sin" (KJV). Finally, their religious actions are sinful, as "the sacrifice of the wicked is an abomination to the LORD" (Prov 15:8). A sinner is thus a carnal person, "made up of nothing but a lump of dull flesh kneaded together without spirit," whose only hope is redemption through Christ's blood and the washing of regeneration through the Holy Spirit.

TEA WITH THOMAS BOSTON

1. How does recognizing our inherited corruption affect your fight against sin? (Rom 7:14; Jer 17:9; Eph 2:3)
2. What impact did losing our original righteousness have on your relationship with God? (Rom 8:7; Matt 5:48; 1 Cor 2:14)
3. How would you explain imputation vs. impartation to people of other religions? (Rom 5:19; Eph 2:8–9; 1 Pet 1:18–19)
4. How should awareness of sin's grip affect your pursuit of holiness? (Rom 6:12–14; Col 3:5–10; 1 Pet 1:14–16)
5. What habits should young believers develop to fight inherited corruption? (Rom 12:2; Col 3:10; 2 Tim 2:22)

Black licorice root tea has a sweet yet earthy flavor, representing the unpleasantness and depth of humankind's sinful nature.

Heavenly Father, I confess my sinful nature and seek your mercy, knowing only through Christ and the Holy Spirit can I be forgiven and made new. Amen.

"As the fish is averse to come out of the water, so is the sinner from the puddle of sin, in which he delights to lie."[1]

---

1. Boston, *Works*, 1:283 (1:279–93, 7:32–35).

Day 18

The Miseries of Man's Natural State

> Q19. *What is the misery of that estate whereinto man fell?*
>
> A. All mankind, by their fall, lost communion with God, are under his wrath and curse and so made liable to all miseries in this life, to death itself, and to the pains of hell for ever.

Therefore, just as sin came into the world through one man, and death through sin, and so death spread to all men because all sinned.

ROMANS 5:12

THE NATURAL STATE OF humans is not merely a sinful state but a miserable one. The greatest misery is losing communion with God, which Adam used to have without a mediator. By Adam's fall, man lost God, "the greatest and the fountain of all other losses." Since "God is the cause and fountain of all good," losing God is, Thomas Boston reasons, "the greatest of all losses and miseries." The lost sweet fellowship with God can only be restored by "union with Jesus Christ," the sole mediator between God and humanity (Gal 3:20).

Having lost communion with God, sinners lie under God's wrath and curse. They were by nature "children of wrath" (Eph 2:1), as God's wrath abides on those who do not obey Jesus (John 3:36). They were God's enemies (Nah 1:2) and under God's curse because "cursed be everyone who does not abide by all things written in the Book of the Law, and do them" (Gal 3:10).

Under God's curse, sinners are liable to all outward and inward miseries in this life. Boston outlines a catalog of outward miseries, including war, famine, pestilence, severe diseases, physical pain, financial hardships, oppression, disgrace, difficulties in work, troubled relationships, betrayal by friends, harsh authorities, and unfaithful servants (Deut 28:15–68). Inward miseries are spiritual plagues, such as "blindness of mind" (2 Cor 4:4), "a reprobate sense" (Rom 1:28), "strong delusions" (2 Thess 2:11), "hardness of heart" (Rom 2:5), "vile affections" (Rom 1:26), and "fear, sorrow, and horror of conscience" (Isa 33:14).

Sinners are also liable to death itself, the separation of soul and body, as "the wages of sin is death" (Rom 6:23). Boston calls this death "stinged death" (1 Cor 15:56), as it still carries the full weight of sin's curse, as opposed to a believer's death, where Christ has removed death's sting by taking away sin's guilt and punishment (1 Cor 15:55). Although believers are liable to the miseries in this life and death itself, these are but "marks of God's displeasure with the sin in them, while yet he loves their persons in Christ."

Ultimately, sinners are liable to hell forever, entailing "pain of loss" and "pain of sense." The pain of loss is "total and final separation from God" (Matt 25:41), which is not a "local separation"—as if God were not in hell—but a "relative separation," an everlasting shunning of "all comfortable communication between God and them" (Matt 22:13). Being eternally separated from the chief good—God himself, they will lose all earthly pleasures, the presence of God and Christ, the fellowship of saints and angels, all glory and blessedness, any pity or compassion, all hope of deliverance, and any possibility of escape. The pain of sense is "unspeakable torment, both in soul and body," suffering the unimaginable wrath of God forever (Mark 9:43–44). "Flee from the wrath to come," Boston urges, "for it is a fearful thing to fall into the hands of the living God" (Heb 10:31).

TEA WITH THOMAS BOSTON

1. How do you experience sin's consequences daily, and how does the gospel give you hope? (Rom 7:24–25; 2 Cor 4:16–18; Phil 3:20–21)

2. Why is losing communion with God the greatest misery, and how does Scripture describe it? (Gen 3:23–24; Isa 59:2; Eph 2:12)

3. How would you answer someone who says hell is unjust or unloving? (Matt 25:41; 2 Thess 1:8–9; Rev 14:10–11)

4. How should eternal separation from God motivate our evangelism? (Matt 28:19–20; Acts 4:12; 2 Cor 5:20–21)

5. How can we teach young believers about sin's seriousness without leading them to despair? (Ps 103:8–12; 1 John 1:9; Rom 8:15)

Dandelion root tea has an earthy, slightly bitter taste and is known for its detoxifying properties, representing sin's discomfort and eventual healing.

Heavenly Father, have mercy on me, for apart from Christ, I am lost in sin and misery. Restore me to communion with you through faith in my only mediator, Jesus. Amen.

"Let men be clothed in rags, or wear a crown, the garment common to all is misery. Every sigh, tear, or sorrowful look, is a proof of this."[1]

---

1. Boston, *Works*, 1:294 (1:293–301, 7:35–38).

PART 4

Christ and Redemption

(Q20—Q28)

Day 19

Election to Everlasting Life

> Q20. *Did God leave all mankind to perish in the estate of sin and misery?*
>
> A. God having, out of his mere good pleasure, from all eternity, elected some to everlasting life, did enter into a covenant of grace, to deliver them out of the estate of sin and misery, and to bring them into an estate of salvation by a Redeemer.

Blessed be the God and Father of our Lord Jesus Christ, who has blessed us in Christ with every spiritual blessing in the heavenly places, even as he chose us in him before the foundation of the world, that we should be holy and blameless before him. In love he predestined us for adoption to himself as sons through Jesus Christ, according to the purpose of his will.

EPHESIANS 1:3–5

THOMAS BOSTON DEFINES THE doctrine of election as follows: "God left not all mankind to perish in the state of sin and misery, but having from all eternity elected some to everlasting life, brings them into a state of salvation by a Redeemer." Like all of God's decrees, the decree of election is eternal. From eternity, before creation, God the Father chose some—the elect—to be redeemed by the Son and sanctified by the Spirit while leaving others—the reprobate—to perish in their state of sin and misery. The elect, fewer in number than the reprobate (Matt 7:13–14), are chosen by grace as the means and for glory as the end, to receive eternal life and bliss in the presence of God.

God's election is entirely free, not based on any moral or civil virtues in the elect, as God alone calls, converts, changes, and renews them—despicable sinners like others—by his grace. He does not choose them based on foreseen faith, good works, or perseverance, as these are "fruits and effects" of election, not its cause (Rom 8:29; Acts 13:48). If election depended on foreseen faith or good works, Boston argues, it would mean that we choose God rather than God choosing us. Election is not a general decree to save "all that shall believe and persevere," for in that case, it might happen that none would be saved. Rather, it is a particular and definite decree, and the number of the elect "can neither be more nor fewer" (Luke 10:20). If God had willed, he could have chosen everyone or none, as he is not obligated to save anyone. Election is a secret to us, based on the "purpose of his will" (Eph 1:5) and the "mystery of his will" (Eph 1:9). It is also unchangeable—every elect person will undoubtedly receive salvation and never be lost. Election, Boston asserts, is "the foundation of God's house."

By the decree of election, in due time, all the elect will, by the Spirit's power, be regenerated, converted, and granted faith to unite with Christ the Redeemer (Titus 3:4–6). However, God's justice required complete satisfaction for sin before the elect could be delivered. His holiness abhors sin, his justice demands its penalty, his wisdom upholds the law's authority, and his truth ensures his word stands firm. Therefore, sin had to be justly satisfied for redemption to occur.

Since neither the elect nor others could satisfy God's justice (Isa 63:5), God, in his infinite grace and wisdom, "pitched upon Christ as the fittest person for managing this grand design." From eternity, Christ accepted the "office of the Redeemer" and "engaged to make his soul an offering for sin." At the cross, taking the place of the elect, Christ "satisfied offended justice" and "purchased eternal redemption for them."

TEA WITH THOMAS BOSTON

1. How does God's election deepen your trust in his love and faithfulness? (Eph 1:4–5; Rom 8:29–30; 2 Tim 1:9)
2. How does election reveal the Trinity's role in salvation? (Eph 1:3–14; John 6:37–39; Titus 3:4–6)
3. How would you answer someone who says election is unfair? (Rom 9:14–21; Matt 20:1–16; Deut 7:6–8)
4. How should election inspire us to evangelize and pray for the lost? (2 Tim 2:10; Matt 28:18–20; Rom 10:14–17)
5. How can we teach children about God's grace in election to build their trust in him? (Deut 6:6–7; 2 Tim 3:15; Matt 19:14)

Golden monkey black tea is a rare and luxurious tea from China, with sweet, malty notes, symbolizing the chosen nature of the elect.

Heavenly Father, in your sovereign grace, you have chosen me in Christ before creation—may I live holy and blameless before you in gratitude and love. Amen.

"Those that were rejected were as eligible as those that were chosen. They were all his creatures, and all alike obnoxious to his wrath by sin. It was grace alone that made the difference."[1]

---

1. Boston, *Works*, 1:304 (1:301–13, 7:38–44).

Day 20

The Covenant of Grace

> Q20. *Did God leave all mankind to perish in the estate of sin and misery?*
>
> A. God having, out of his mere good pleasure, from all eternity, elected some to everlasting life, did enter into a covenant of grace, to deliver them out of the estate of sin and misery and to bring them into an estate of salvation by a Redeemer.

You have said, "I have made a covenant with my chosen one; I have sworn to David my servant.

PSALM 89:3

Thus it is written, "The first man Adam became a living being"; the last Adam became a life-giving spirit.

1 CORINTHIANS 15:45

FROM ETERNITY, FORESEEING THAT Adam would break the covenant of works by God's decree, the Father made the covenant of grace with Christ, the second Adam, "to deliver the elect out of the estate of sin and misery" and to bring them salvation (Ps 89:3; Titus 1:2). Just as Adam federally represents all his biological descendants in the covenant of works, Christ federally represents all his spiritual descendants, the elect, in the covenant of grace. Thomas Boston is adamant that faith is the means, not the condition, of entering the covenant of grace. Just as the condition of "the first covenant" is Adam's complete obedience, the sole condition of "the second covenant," insists Boston, is Christ fulfilling all righteousness (Matt 3:15)—the righteousness that Adam failed to deliver under the first covenant.

God has chosen Christ as the Redeemer and Administrator of the covenant of grace: the former for fulfilling the covenant's condition and the latter for distributing the covenant's promise. Christ is the Mediator (Heb 9:15), Kinsman-Redeemer (Job 19:25), Surety (Heb 7:22), and Priest (Heb 7:20–22, 28) regarding the covenant's condition, while he is the Trustee (John 3:35), Testator (Heb 9:16–17), Prophet (Acts 3:22), King (Ps 2:6), and Intercessor (Heb 7:25) regarding its promise.

Regarding the condition of the covenant of grace, the righteousness that the broken covenant of works justly demands—and which Christ must fulfill—is "perfect holiness of nature, righteousness of life, and satisfaction for sin." Since God gave Adam a "holiness of nature" at creation (Eccl 7:29), the broken covenant of works justly requires it. The broken covenant of works also justly demands a "righteousness of life," as that is its explicit condition (Gal 3:12). Finally, "satisfaction for sin" must be provided as the penalty for breaking the covenant of works (Gen 2:17). Christ fulfills the righteousness required of the elect through his obedience, which, in Boston's thought, is personal, perfect (entire and exact), and perpetual (enduring throughout his trial).

The demands of the broken covenant of works become the condition of the covenant of grace. Since neither Adam nor his descendants could satisfy that condition, Christ, as the Redeemer of the covenant of grace, undertook from eternity to redeem the elect by the price of his blood (Heb 9:22) and deliver them from bondage to sin and Satan by the power of his Spirit (1 Cor 15:45). As "a public person," Christ perfectly fulfilled that condition on behalf of the elect by being "born perfectly holy, living perfectly holy, and making complete satisfaction by his death," thereby accomplishing redemption for them.

Regarding the promise of the covenant of grace, once Christ has accomplished redemption, as the Administrator of the covenant (Matt 28:18), he dispenses eternal life to all who unite with him, the head of the covenant (Isa 42:1), by faith. "Christ is the covenant," asserts Boston, such that the free offer of Christ in the gospel is the free offer of the covenant of grace to anyone who will receive it by faith.[1]

---

1. For a detailed exposition of Boston's concept of the covenant of grace, see his *A View of the Covenant of Grace* in Boston, *Works*, 8:379–604. For a concise overview, see Tse, *Marrow of Certainty*, 135–44.

PART 4: CHRIST AND REDEMPTION

TEA WITH THOMAS BOSTON

1. How does knowing that Christ fulfill what Adam could not assure you in your faith? (1 Cor 15:45; Rom 5:19; 2 Cor 5:21)

2. How does Boston's view of faith as the means to enter the covenant deepen your understanding of justification by faith? (Eph 2:8–9; Gal 3:24–26; Rom 5:1)

3. How does the covenant of grace's promise of salvation differ from other religions' views of salvation? (Acts 4:12; John 14:6; 1 Tim 2:5)

4. How does the assurance of salvation in the covenant bring you peace during trials or doubts? (Rom 8:38–39; Phil 4:7; 2 Cor 1:20)

5. What habits can young believers develop to grow in understanding the covenant and their identity in Christ? (2 Pet 3:18; 1 Tim 4:7–8; Col 2:6–7)

 Honeybush is a caffeine-free herbal tea from South Africa with a naturally sweet and smooth flavor, representing the sweetness and security of God's grace.

 Heavenly Father, thank you for Christ, who fulfilled the covenant's condition, redeemed us by his blood, and offered eternal life to me. Amen.

 "The covenant of grace held forth in the gospel, is the cord of love let down from heaven to perishing sinners shipwrecked in Adam, to save them from sinking into the bottom of the gulf, and to hale them to land. It is their duty to lay hold of the covenant by faith."[2]

---

2. Boston, *Works*, 1:335 (1:314–75, 7:38–44).

Day 21

Christ the Only Redeemer of God's Elect

Q21. *Who is the Redeemer of God's elect?*

A. The only Redeemer of God's elect is the Lord Jesus Christ, who, being the eternal Son of God, became man and so was, and continues to be, God and man in two distinct natures and one person, for ever.

But when the fullness of time had come, God sent forth his Son, born of woman, born under the law, to redeem those who were under the law, so that we might receive adoption as sons.

GALATIANS 4:4–5

THIS PASSAGE PRESENTS CHRIST as the Redeemer, who frees the church from old dispensational bondage. Paul contrasts the church's former subjection to the law with its new dispensational freedom through Christ's incarnation, obedience, and sacrificial death. By fulfilling the law and bearing its curse (Gal 3:13), Christ redeems the elect, granting believers a fuller experience of adoption and the Spirit.

To redeem is to buy back. It implies that the elect initially belonged to God but, due to Adam's fall, were sold into a corrupt state, enslaved to sin and Satan. The Redeemer of God's elect, the Lord Jesus Christ, redeemed them by his blood from this fallen condition. "Lord," asserts Thomas Boston, denotes YHWH, the true God, signifying his universal dominion (Ps 103:19). "Jesus" means Savior, for "he will save his people from their sins"

(Matt 1:21). "Christ" means the Anointed One, as God anointed him with the Holy Spirit (Acts 10:38).

The Redeemer is the Mediator between God and humans because of his "common relation to both." His relation to God is that he is the eternal Son—begotten, not made—by eternal generation, equal with God in divine essence (Heb 1:5). He must be God to endure and emerge from God's infinite wrath (Acts 2:24) and to ensure that his temporary sufferings would be of infinite value in fully satisfying God's justice (Heb 9:14). His relation to us is that he is our "near kinsman" (Heb 2:11) and our "kinsman-redeemer, who redeems by right of kin" (Job 19:25). He must be man to suffer death (Heb 2:14) in our nature, which has sinned (Ezek 18:4), and to serve as a merciful High Priest (Heb 2:16–17), enabling us to approach the throne of grace with confidence.

In a Chalcedonian-like definition, Boston expounds on the hypostatic union of our Redeemer's divine and human natures. They exist *without confusion*, as "the two natures in Christ remain distinct," meaning "the Godhead was not changed into the manhood, nor the manhood into the Godhead." This distinction affirms that the divine and human natures do not mix or merge into a third nature. They exist *without change*, as they "remain still with their distinct properties," emphasizing that neither nature loses its essential attributes—the divine nature is not made finite, nor does the human nature take on divine attributes like omnipotence or omniscience. They exist *without division*, for Christ is "not two persons, but one," akin to the soul and body making up one person, affirming that Christ is a unified whole, not a split being. Finally, the two natures exist *without separation*—Boston insists that "this union never was dissolved" and that Christ "was, and so will continue, God and man forever." Even in his death, resurrection, and ascension, the union of the two natures remains intact.

TEA WITH THOMAS BOSTON

1. How does knowing Christ as your Redeemer strengthen your security and identity in him? (Gal 4:4–5; Rom 8:15; Eph 1:7)
2. Why must Christ be both divine and human to be the Mediator between God and us? (Heb 2:14–17; 1 Tim 2:5; Rom 5:19)
3. How does Christianity's teaching of Christ as the Redeemer differ from religions that deny his deity or humanity? (John 14:6; Acts 4:12; 1 John 2:22–23)
4. How does Christ's role as Redeemer give us confidence in our struggles with sin and suffering? (Rom 8:34; Heb 7:25; 1 John 1:9)
5. Why is establishing a habit of worship and gratitude for Christ and his redemption important? (Ps 107:2; Col 3:16–17; Heb 13:15)

 Assam is a bold black tea from India with a strong, malty flavor, symbolizing Christ as the singular and strong Redeemer.

 Heavenly Father, I praise you for sending Christ, our Redeemer, to free us from bondage—grant me a deeper appreciation of adoption and the Spirit in him. Amen.

 "It was necessary he should be God and man in one person, that what of the work was done by either of the natures, might be reckoned the deed of the person of our Redeemer."[1]

---

1. Boston, *Works*, 7:46 (1:375–89, 7:44–46).

Day 22

Christ's Incarnation

> Q22. *How did Christ, being the Son of God, become man?*
>
> A. Christ, the Son of God, became man, by taking to himself a true body and a reasonable soul, being conceived by the power of the Holy Ghost, in the womb of the Virgin Mary, and born of her, yet without sin.

And the angel answered her, "The Holy Spirit will come upon you, and the power of the Most High will overshadow you; therefore the child to be born will be called holy—the Son of God.

LUKE 1:35

CHRIST'S HUMAN NATURE WAS derived from the flesh and blood of the Virgin Mary, ensuring his true kinship with humanity as a descendant of Adam, Abraham, and David. Christ did not assume a human person, as that would make him two persons; rather, he assumed a complete human nature with a body and a soul.

God could have created Christ's body from nothing or from dust, as he did with Adam, but this would not have established the necessary legal and relational connection to humanity. Instead, the Holy Spirit prepared and sanctified a portion of Mary's substance—purging it of sin—to form Christ's body (Heb 10:5; Gal 4:4). Christ's conception was by the Spirit's power, not essence. Therefore, the Holy Spirit cannot be called the "Father of Christ," as he did not contribute divine substance but enabled Christ's human nature to be without sin.

Christ's soul was not a part of Mary's soul, as spiritual substances cannot be divided, but was created directly by God from nothing, just like all human souls (Heb 12:9; Zech 12:1). This human, reasonable soul—capable of reasoning, understanding, and willing—was infused into Christ's body. Thus, Christ has two understandings and wills: an infinite divine understanding and will and a finite human understanding and will.

Boston further clarifies Christ's hypostatic union. When Christ took on human nature, it was not united like the three persons of the Godhead, who share one essence and will. Instead, Christ possesses two distinct natures and wills within one person. Unlike the soul-body union in humans, which is dissolved by death, Christ's two natures remain indissolubly united to the second person of the Godhead, even in death. Unlike the mystical union between Christ and the church, where believers remain distinct, in Christ's hypostatic union, his two natures are united in one person.

Christ must be born of a virgin, Boston explains, in part to fulfill God's first gospel promise in Gen 3:15, which calls the Messiah the "seed of the woman, not of the man." Although God could have perfectly sanctified two earthly parents to transmit an immaculate human nature to Christ, it was fitting that Christ should have a distinct conception, reflecting the infinite dignity of his person and requiring divine involvement. Boston states, "At first, Adam was produced neither of man nor woman; Eve of a man without a woman; all others of a man and a woman. The fourth way remained, namely, of a woman without a man; and so Christ was born." Most significantly, Christ must be born of a virgin and without sin to provide us with his holiness of nature, imputed to us as part of the righteousness needed for our justification before God.

PART 4: CHRIST AND REDEMPTION

TEA WITH THOMAS BOSTON

1. How does Christ's body and soul encourage you in times of suffering? (Isa 53:3–5; Heb 2:17; Rom 8:3)

2. How does the hypostatic union highlight Christ's uniqueness? (Col 2:9; John 1:14; Phil 2:6–8)

3. Why is Christ's dual nature essential in defending Christianity against misconceptions? (Heb 2:14; Rom 1:3–4; 1 Tim 3:16)

4. How can Christ's incarnation deepen our understanding of God's love? (Rom 5:8; John 3:16; 1 John 4:9)

5. What habits can young believers develop to better grasp Christ's incarnation? (Luke 2:52; Gal 4:4; Matt 28:18)

 Chamomile is a calming herbal tea, often used to aid sleep, symbolizing the humble, comforting care of Christ's incarnation.

 Lord Jesus, thank you for your incarnation, where you took on our human nature to grant us your righteousness, through which I am justified. Amen.

 "Christ as God had no mother, and as man no father."[1]

---

1. Boston, *Works*, 1:391 (1:389–403, 7:46–48).

Day 23

Christ's Offices in General

Q23. *What offices does Christ execute as our Redeemer?*

A. Christ, as our Redeemer, executes the offices of a prophet, of a priest, and of a king, both in his estate of humiliation and exaltation.

It is he who shall build the temple of the LORD and shall bear royal honor, and shall sit and rule on his throne. And there shall be a priest on his throne, and the counsel of peace shall be between them both.

ZECHARIAH 6:13

CHRIST FULFILLS THREE ESSENTIAL offices as Redeemer—Prophet, Priest, and King—based on Zech 6:13. As a Prophet, he "builds the temple of the LORD," representing his church, through the gospel, revealing divine truth as faith's foundation. As a Priest, he expiates sin, secures "peace" for his people, and intercedes before God. As a King, he reigns "on his throne," exercising authority and ruling actively, demonstrating the glory and power of redemption. These offices will be exercised despite all opposition, as he shall "sit and rule on his throne."

Boston links the threefold office to Christ's proclamation "I am the way, and the truth, and the life" (John 14:6). Christ is "the way to life" through his death in his priestly office, "the truth in his word" in his prophetic office, and "the life in his Spirit" in his kingly office, "quickening and preserving his people by his power." Addressing our misery of ignorance, guilt, sin, and bondage, God has made Christ our "wisdom, and righteousness, and sanctification, and redemption" (1 Cor 1:30). Boston asserts, "Wisdom as a Prophet, righteousness as a Priest, and sanctification and redemption as a King." Concerning the covenant of grace, Christ fulfilled the covenant condition in his priestly office and administers it through his prophetic and kingly offices.

Salvation required revelation, purchase, and application—things sinners could never achieve. Therefore, Christ became a Prophet to reveal salvation, a Priest to purchase it through his sacrifice, and a King to apply it by his Spirit. As helpless slaves, sinners could neither raise their ransom nor recognize it, much less come out of their bondage, making Christ's threefold office essential for their redemption.

Since Christ is "the Redeemer of the church in all ages," Boston argues that Christ "executed these offices in all ages," including the Old Testament. As Prophet, he guided Israel in the wilderness (Exod 23:20) and preached through Noah to the sinners of the old world (1 Pet 3:19). As Priest, he interceded for his people based on his future sacrifice (Zech 1:12). As King, he led Israel as Captain of the Lord's host, delivering them from Egypt, guiding them through the wilderness, and establishing worship and service in Canaan.

After his incarnation, Christ exercises his offices in humiliation on earth and exaltation in heaven (Phil 2:6–11). As Prophet, he taught God's will for salvation during his ministry and continues to reveal it through his Word and Spirit. As Priest, he offered himself as a sacrifice (Eph 5:2) and continues to intercede for his people (Heb 7:25). As King, he was born a king (Matt 2:2), acknowledged before Pilate (Matt 27:11) and now reigns as King of kings until all enemies are defeated (1 Cor 15:25). Christ's three offices are distinct but never separate; wherever he acts as one, he fulfills the others.

TEA WITH THOMAS BOSTON

1. How does Christ's threefold office impact your spiritual growth? (John 14:6; 1 Cor 1:30; Phil 2:9–11)
2. Why must Christ fulfill the threefold office for our redemption? (Zech 6:13; Luke 4:18–21; Heb 7:25)
3. How do Christ's offices challenge atheism and help defend our faith? (Isa 9:6; John 14:6; Acts 4:12)
4. How can recognizing Christ's offices deepen your understanding of God's plan for your life? (Rom 8:29; 1 Pet 2:9–10; Col 2:6–7)
5. How can Christ's offices motivate young believers to depend on him for salvation and sanctification? (Rom 6:13–23; Eph 2:8–10; Phil 4:13)

English breakfast is a traditional, full-bodied black tea blend, perfect for any occasion, representing Christ's balanced offices.

Heavenly Father, thank you for sending Jesus as our Prophet, Priest, and King to reveal truth, redeem us, and reign in our lives for your glory. Amen.

"As a Prophet he gives light to the blind, as a Priest he brings merit, and as a King power."[1]

---

1. Boston, *Works*, 7:46 (1:375–89, 7:44–46).

Day 24

Christ's Prophetical Office

Q24. *How does Christ execute the office of a prophet?*

A. Christ executes the office of a prophet in revealing to us, by his Word and Spirit, the will of God for our salvation.

Moses said, "The Lord God will raise up for you a prophet like me from your brothers. You shall listen to him in whatever he tells you. And it shall be that every soul who does not listen to that prophet shall be destroyed from the people."
ACTS 3:22–23

IN THIS PASSAGE, THE apostle Peter reveals to the Jews that Moses had foretold Christ as the great Prophet of the church. Peter declares that this promised Prophet has now come and urges them to heed his teachings. Moses commands the Jews to "listen to him," signifying that complete obedience must be given to Christ alone with serious consequences for disobedience.

The office of a Prophet is to redeem the elect not by price but by power, delivering them from spiritual darkness through "the strength of his light" (Acts 26:18). Christ executes his prophetic office by revealing God's will to us concerning faith for salvation and obedience for edification. Christ teaches us, as Thomas Boston succinctly puts it, how to be justified and sanctified. Christ is most fit for this office because, as God, he was "from eternity privy to the whole counsel of God" (John 1:18), and, as man, the Spirit who searches the deep things of God rested upon him (Isa 11:2).

God's will encompasses what we must know, believe, and do, forming the foundation of faith, belief, and duty. Boston explains that Christ reveals humanity's original happiness in Eden, the sin and misery caused by the fall, and our complete inability to save ourselves. Christ also makes known God's divine plan for delivering sinners from sin and wrath, showing that he alone is a "full and sufficient Savior" (Heb 7:25). He teaches that faith in him is necessary for salvation (1 John 5:12) and that we must trust in him alone as our Redeemer. He further reveals that God's will for us is holiness, "without which no one will see the Lord" (Heb 12:14).

Christ reveals God's will to us externally by his word and internally by his Spirit. His word is the Spirit-inspired Scripture of the Old and New Testaments, written and preached. Since we were by nature spiritually ignorant (1 Cor 2:14), Christ has to rescue us from the power of spiritual darkness by "joining an internal revelation by his Spirit, with the external revelation by his word." Anytime we read the Scripture and hear it preached, Christ is executing his prophetic office.

Christ is the Prophet par excellence, "the fountain-head of prophecy, revealing by his own Spirit," whereas other prophets "are but instruments by whom he spake." Christ's teachings humble the soul, revealing God's greatness while exposing human sinfulness and unworthiness. His teachings deeply impact the heart, convicting of sin and bringing comfort that surpasses earthly troubles. They sanctify and transform, leading to holiness and renewal. Christ's teachings are practical, producing obedience rather than empty speculation. They always align with Scripture, as the Spirit never contradicts God's word. Lastly, those taught by Christ develop a deep love for him, echoing a desire for God above all else. "We are to receive Christ as our prophet," Boston enjoins us, "renouncing our own wisdom, and wholly giving up ourselves to him, to be taught in things, by his word and Spirit."

TEA WITH THOMAS BOSTON

1. How have Christ's teachings humbled you and revealed God's greatness and your sinfulness? (Isa 11:2; Acts 26:18; John 1:18)
2. What biblical foundations explain Christ's role as Prophet and its connection to salvation and edification? (Acts 3:22–23; Deut 18:18; Heb 7:25)
3. How is Christ's role as Prophet unique compared to other religious leaders? (Acts 3:22–23; Luke 4:32; Matt 7:29)
4. How do Christ's teachings on salvation and holiness shape your daily life? (Heb 7:25; 1 Thess 4:3; 1 John 5:12)
5. What habits can you encourage children and young believers to engage with God's word and the Spirit? (1 Cor 2:14; Heb 12:14; 2 Tim 3:15–16)

 White chrysanthemum is a delicate floral tea with a subtle sweetness, symbolizing the clarity and vision of Christ's prophetic office.

 Lord Jesus, help me listen to you, the great Prophet, and obey your teachings, leading to salvation, transformation, and love for you. Amen.

 "Others indeed may far excel you in the knowledge of other things: but if you know Jesus Christ, and the truth as it is in Jesus, one drop of your knowledge is more valuable and desirable than a whole sea of their natural and political knowledge."[1]

---

1. Boston, *Works*, 1:433 (1:411–36, 7:51–54).

Day 25

Christ's Priestly Office

Q25. *How does Christ execute the office of a priest?*

A. Christ executes the office of a priest in his once offering up of himself a sacrifice to satisfy divine justice and reconcile us to God, and in making continual intercession for us.

For it is witnessed of him, "You are a priest forever, after the order of Melchizedek."

HEBREWS 7:17

THE OFFICE OF THE Levitical priests was to offer sacrifices and pray for the people (Heb 5:1; Num 6:22–26). The difference between their priesthood and Christ's is that theirs was a shadow, while Christ's is the substance, fulfilling what the Aaronic priests symbolized. Theologically, Thomas Boston teaches that Christ's priestly office consists of his oblation—"his once offering up of himself a sacrifice to satisfy divine justice and reconcile us to God" (Heb 9:14)—and his intercession.

Old Testament sacrifices were either thank offerings—expressing gratitude and seeking God's favor—or expiatory sacrifices, atoning for sin and satisfying divine justice. Christ's sacrifice was an expiatory offering, securing atonement for sin. Christ's offering, states Boston, began with his incarnation (Heb 10:5), continued through his life (Isa 53:2–3), and was completed at the cross and in the grave, spanning the entire spectrum of his estate of humiliation. In other words, Christ's holiness of nature, righteousness of life, and sacrificial death were the price he paid as our Priest to redeem us from sin and misery. Furthermore, Christ offered himself as a sacrifice only once, for "by that once offering, the price of our redemption was fully paid" (Heb 10:14). Although "Christ's sufferings were not infinite in continuance, yet they were infinite in value" because of "the infinite dignity of his person and his real, untainted holiness" (Heb 4:14; 7:26).

Christ's intercession differs from that of the Holy Spirit. Christ pleads "our cause in the court of heaven," while the Spirit intercedes for us "in our own hearts" and helps us "to pray for ourselves" (Rom 8:26). The difference, explains Boston, is that the Spirit "draws a poor man's petition," but Christ "presents it to the king and gets it granted to him." Christ's intercession is not as "a supplicant on mere mercy, but as an advocate pleading law and right" (1 John 2:1). The legal basis for his intercession is his fulfillment of the condition of the covenant of grace by offering himself once for all as a sacrifice for us (John 17:4).

Christ, therefore, intercedes only for those for whom he offered up himself (John 17:9). Christ's offering and his intercession, Boston reasons, "are of the same latitude and extent," joined by "an inseparable connection," as "Christ Jesus is the one who died—more than that, who was raised—who is at the right hand of God, who indeed is interceding for us" (Rom 8:34). Furthermore, his intercession is always effectual (John 11:42) and continues forever (Heb 7:25). Christ's everlasting priesthood, accordingly, is after the order of Melchizedek (Ps 110:4)—"not a sacrificing priest forever, but an interceding priest forever." Thus, "we are to receive Christ as our priest," Boston urges, "renouncing our own righteousness and wholly trusting in him, to be saved by his sacrifice of himself and intercession."

TEA WITH THOMAS BOSTON

1. How does Christ's eternal priesthood and intercession affect you? (Heb 7:24–25; Ps 110:4; 1 Tim 2:5)

2. What does "Christ as a priest forever after the order of Melchizedek" mean? (Heb 7:17; Ps 110:4; Gen 14:18)

3. How is Christ's sacrifice unique compared to other religious sacrifices? (Heb 10:4; 1 Pet 1:19; John 14:6)

4. How can you apply the truth of Christ's continual intercession in your daily struggles? (Rom 8:26–27; Heb 4:16; John 16:24)

5. How can you explain Christ's sacrifice and intercession to children or new believers? (Rom 5:8; Heb 7:25; 1 Tim 2:5)

Mint tea is a refreshing herbal tea with a cooling, invigorating taste, symbolizing the cleansing and interceding comfort of Christ's priestly office.

Lord Jesus, thank you for your perfect sacrifice and eternal intercession. I humbly trust in your mediation to reconcile me to God and save me from sin and death. Amen.

"If Christ died for all men, then he died in vain for the most part, and his death and sacrifice had little effect; for the generality of men and women will perish eternally."[1]

---

1. Boston, *Works*, 1:447 (1:437–75, 7:54–61).

Day 26

Christ's Kingly Office

> Q26. *How does Christ execute the office of a king?*
> A. Christ executes the office of a king in subduing us to himself, in ruling and defending us, and in restraining and conquering all his and our enemies.

Yet have I set my king upon my holy hill of Zion.

PSALM 2:6 (KJV)

CHRIST POSSESSES A TWOFOLD kingdom: an essential kingdom—encompassing the whole creation, as God—and a mediatory kingdom, the church, as our Redeemer. Thomas Boston asserts that Christ executes his kingly office in this second kingdom, the "holy hill of Zion." In the Old Testament, God appointed kings to save his people by "strength of hand from their enemies, and to rule them as their head" (2 Sam 3:17–18). While theirs is a temporal kingdom for the safety of their people, Christ's is "a spiritual and eternal kingdom" for the salvation of God's people (John 18:36). Christ is qualified for such a kingdom by "his infinite wisdom and power" and the Father's "committing the kingdom of providence throughout the whole world into his hand" (Isa 9:6).

Christ executes his kingly office by rescuing those he has already redeemed by the price of his blood to deliver them from his and their enemies, namely "sin, death, the devil, and the world" (Zech 9:11). They are Christ's enemies, as they oppose his kingdom but can no longer harm him. They are also our natural enemies (Acts 26:18); even now, they seek our destruction. Christ rescues us from their dominion by subduing us with "the sword of his word in the hand of his Spirit" (Eph 6:17). The word, guided by the Spirit, acts as a sword to penetrate the soul, overcoming our natural stubbornness and making us willing to submit (Heb 4:12).

Externally, Christ, as head of the church, governs us by providing laws, ordinances, and officers. His laws are the principles in the Ten Commandments (Isa 33:22), his ordinances include those for worship, discipline, and governance (1 Cor 11:2), and his officers are "pastors, teachers, ruling elders, and deacons." Internally, Christ rules by his Spirit, writing his laws on our hearts and enabling our obedience (Ezek 36:27). In this life, Christ rewards our obedience with royal favor and corrects us for our sins (Ps 19:11). He will consummate his rule in heaven by "making us perfectly holy and happy" (2 Tim 4:8).

Most significantly, Christ secures us from being brought back into the dominion of our enemies by defending, restraining, and conquering them (Ps 89:18). He defends the church, ensuring it will remain until the end (Matt 16:18). He defends all believers by pouring out his grace and working providentially on their behalf (2 Cor 12:9). Christ restrains all of his and our enemies, limiting "the kinds, degrees, and continuance of their attacks" (Job 2:6). Ultimately, he "completes our rescue" by triumphing over all of his and our enemies (1 Cor 15:25). "We are to receive Christ as our King," Boston enjoins us, "renouncing the dominion of sin, death, the devil, and the world, and wholly giving up ourselves to him, to be ruled by him as our head."

TEA WITH THOMAS BOSTON

1. When have you experienced Christ's protection from enemies? How did he defend you? (Ps 89:18; 2 Cor 12:9; Rom 8:31)

2. What is the difference between Christ's essential and mediatory kingdoms, and how do they shape your view of his kingship? (Ps 103:19; John 18:36; Col 1:16)

3. How does Christ's kingship set Christianity apart from other religions? (Matt 16:18; John 18:36; Isa 9:6)

4. What steps can you take to align your life with Christ's commands as King? (Ezek 36:27; Ps 19:11; Rom 12:1)

5. How can you help children and new believers recognize Christ's kingship in their daily lives? (Ezek 36:27; 1 Cor 11:2; Eph 6:17)

 Keemun is a high-quality Chinese black tea with a slightly smoky, fruity flavor, representing the regal and authoritative nature of Christ's kingship.

 Lord Jesus, thank you for reigning as our Redeemer, rescuing us from our enemies, and governing me by your Word and Spirit. Amen.

 "Christ shall remain the King, Head, and Husband of his church for ever."[1]

---

1. Boston, *Works*, 1:483 (1:475–90, 7:61–68).

Day 27

Christ's Humiliation

> Q27. *Wherein did Christ's humiliation consist?*
>
> A. Christ's humiliation consisted in his being born, and that in a low condition, made under the law, undergoing the miseries of this life, the wrath of God, and the cursed death of the cross; in being buried and continuing under the power of death for a time.

And being found in human form, he humbled himself by becoming obedient to the point of death, even death on a cross.

PHILIPPIANS 2:8

CHRIST'S HUMILIATION, THOMAS BOSTON explains, "belonged to the condition of the covenant of grace," which Christ voluntarily undertook (Phil 2:7–8). To fulfill his offices, particularly his priestly role, Christ the King became a servant, emptying himself of his divine glory and submitting to the law on behalf of the elect (Gal 4:4–5). In doing so, he took upon himself the burden of human servitude under the law, rendering the perfect obedience it required and enduring its curse as punishment for sin (Matt 3:15). Both his obedience and suffering were essential aspects of his humiliation (Phil 2:8). However, this state of humiliation ended with his resurrection, marking the beginning of his exaltation (Rom 14:9).

From his conception to the grave, Christ willingly endured the effects of the curse for us (Gal 3:13). He humbled himself in his incarnation, being conceived by a lowly virgin (Luke 1:48) and born in humble circumstances—"in the small town of Bethlehem, in the stable of an inn, and laid in a manger instead of a cradle"—and underwent painful circumcision on the eighth day. Throughout his life, he suffered the hardships of human existence, living a "poor, sorrowful, despised, tempted, and toiled life," experiencing hunger, thirst, and weariness (2 Cor 8:9).

At the cross, he humbled himself to "drink the bitter dregs of his Father's wrath for us." It was a painful death, as the Romans nailed his hands and feet to the tree (Luke 23:33). It was a shameful death (Heb 12:2), as he hung exposed, stripped of his clothing (Matt 27:35), recalling our "naked first parents' sinning by eating the fruit of a tree." It was a lingering death, as he remained alive on the cross from the third to the ninth hour (Mark 15:25). Above all, it was a cursed death, for "cursed is everyone who hangs on a tree" (Gal 3:13). While the law ceremonially cursed those hanged on a tree without preventing the salvation of the repentant (Luke 23:33), the curse Christ bore was real and substantial—the cross itself serving as its "sign and badge" (Gal 3:13).

After his death, Christ further humbled himself by remaining under the power of death for three days—part of the first day, the entire second, and part of the third—while his soul and body remained separated (Acts 2:31). The Apostles' Creed expresses this state as "he descended into hell," referring to the time when his soul was in paradise (Luke 23:43). While the "hardest and sharpest" aspect of Christ's humiliation was enduring the wrath of God in his soul, the "lowest" was his continued subjection to death, lying in the grave (Ps 22:15). Still, as Boston maintains, "the deeper he debased and the lower he humbled himself, the higher did he raise, and the more clearly did he manifest his love."

TEA WITH THOMAS BOSTON

1. How does meditating on Christ's humility shape your view of suffering? (Phil 2:8; 2 Cor 8:9; Heb 12:2)

2. Why did Christ need to be born in a lowly state and suffer? (Luke 2:7; Gal 4:4–5; Heb 2:17–18)

3. How would you explain why a loving God allowed Christ to suffer? (Isa 53:10–11; Heb 9:22; Rom 3:25–26)

4. What practical steps can you take to live humbly and self-sacrificially? (Matt 16:24; Luke 14:11; Rom 12:3)

5. How can you help young believers grow by teaching them Christ's humility? (Deut 6:6–7; Matt 18:3–4; Phil 2:5–7)

Barley tea is a roasted tea with a warm, earthy flavor, symbolizing the humble and common nature of Christ's humiliation.

Lord Jesus, you bore our sin, endured the curse, and drank the cup of wrath—may I live in gratitude for your redeeming love. Amen.

"When he was born, he was born in another man's house; when he preached, he preached in another man's ship; when he prayed, he prayed in another man's garden; when he rode to Jerusalem, he rode on another man's ass; and when he was buried, he was buried in another man's grave. He had nothing peculiar to himself but his cross."[1]

---

1. Boston, *Works*, 1:497 (1:490–504, 7:68–73).

Day 28

Christ's Exaltation

> Q28. *Wherein consists Christ's exaltation?*
>
> A. Christ's exaltation consists in his rising again from the dead on the third day, in ascending up into heaven, in sitting at the right hand of God the Father, and in coming to judge the world at the last day.

Therefore God has highly exalted him and bestowed on him the name that is above every name, so that at the name of Jesus every knee should bow, in heaven and on earth and under the earth, and every tongue confess that Jesus Christ is Lord, to the glory of God the Father.

PHILIPPIANS 2:9–11

THOMAS BOSTON TEACHES THAT Christ's exaltation—which the Father performs to Christ "as the reward of his suffering even unto death" (Isa 52:13)—"belongs to the promise of the covenant of grace." The first step in his exaltation was his resurrection on the third day (1 Cor 15:4). Scripture attributes Christ's resurrection to the Father, who, as a judge, raised him and discharged him from prison, having fully paid the debt of sin (Eph 1:20; Acts 2:24). Christ also ascribes the resurrection to himself, exercising divine power by "calling back his soul into his body" and taking up his life again (John 10:18). The Bible also ascribes the resurrection to the Holy Spirit, who reunites Christ's soul and body (Rom 8:11; 1 Pet 3:18). Christ rose in the same body he was laid in the grave, without corruption, now transformed into an immortal and glorious state (Luke 24:39; Acts 13:37; 1 Cor 15:43).

The second step of Christ's exaltation was his literal ascension into heaven forty days after his resurrection, that he might be "solemnly inaugurated and installed in glory" (Acts 1:3). He ascended in his human nature, argues Boston, since Christ's divine nature is omnipresent. The ascension took place at the Mount of Olives, the very place where his deepest humiliation began (Acts 1:11–12; Luke 22:39). He ascended to the highest heaven visibly and triumphantly, like a victorious conqueror (Eph 4:8, 10; Acts 1:9). The Father's role in this step was receiving Christ into heaven, affirming his glory and authority (Mark 16:19).

The third step in Christ's exaltation is his sitting at the right hand of God the Father (1 Pet 3:22). Since God is spirit and does not have a physical right hand, this phrase signifies Christ's exaltation to the highest dignity, power, and authority over all creation (Phil 2:9–10). His reign is everlasting and will never cease (Heb 10:12). The Father's action in this step is to set Christ at his right hand, demonstrating his supreme authority (Eph 1:20).

The final step in Christ's exaltation will be his return to judge the world on the last day (Acts 1:11). Christ will come again, not as a suffering servant but as the appointed Judge of all (Acts 17:31; John 5:22). His return will take place at the end of time, marked by the full display of his own and his Father's glory, accompanied by all the holy angels (Luke 9:26; Matt 25:31). His coming will be announced with a great shout, the voice of the archangel, and the trumpet of God (1 Thess 4:16). This judgment will not interrupt his reign but will instead reveal his authority to all (Matt 26:64). In this final act of exaltation, the Father will send Christ in his full glory, clothed with divine authority, to judge the world (Acts 3:20).

PART 4: CHRIST AND REDEMPTION

TEA WITH THOMAS BOSTON

1. How does Christ's resurrection shape your view of eternal life? (1 Cor 15:4; John 10:18; Acts 13:37)
2. What is the significance of Christ sitting at God's right hand? (Phil 2:9–10; 1 Pet 3:22; Eph 1:20)
3. How does Christ's ascension differ from other religious leaders' after death? (Acts 1:9; Eph 4:8, 10; Luke 22:39)
4. How does Christ's resurrection and exaltation give you hope in difficult times? (Acts 2:24; 1 Pet 3:18; Rom 8:11)
5. How can you help young believers anticipate Christ's return? (Matt 25:31; Acts 1:11; 1 Thess 4:16)

 Jade oolong is a lightly oxidized tea, vibrant and aromatic, symbolizing the brightness and elevation of Christ's exaltation.

 Heavenly Father, thank you for Christ's resurrection, ascension, and reigning at your right hand. I look forward to his glorious return to judge the world. Amen.

 "Lazarus came out with his grave-clothes on, because he was to die again; but Christ rising to an immortal life, came out free from all these incumbrances."[1]

---

1. Boston, *Works*, 1:507 (1:504–28, 7:74–78).

PART 5

Spirit and Salvation

(Q29—Q38)

Day 29

The Application of Redemption

> Q29. *How are we made partakers of the redemption purchased by Christ?*
>
> A. We are made partakers of the redemption purchased by Christ by the effectual application of it to us by his Holy Spirit.

He saved us, not because of works done by us in righteousness, but according to his own mercy, by the washing of regeneration and renewal of the Holy Spirit.

TITUS 3:5

CHRIST'S REDEMPTION—WHICH IS DELIVERANCE by payment of a price—frees sinners from the bondage of "sin, death, the devil, and the world," bringing them into a state of "eternal holiness and joy" (Titus 2:14). Redemption, Thomas Boston explains, consists of "deliverance from evil" and "restoration to the good" lost through Adam's first sin. All the lost good is, in sum, eternal life. God, however, restores more than what we lost in Adam—while Adam forfeited conditional eternal life, believers receive unconditional eternal life, which can never be lost again.

The redemption Christ purchased through his obedience and death must be personally received to be effective (John 13:8). The application of Christ's redemption belongs to the office of the Holy Spirit (Eph 2:12; Titus 3:5-6), "to whom we owe the same faith, worship, and obedience as to the Father and the Son." Without the Spirit's work, even the most compelling offer of the gospel remains ineffective, "leaving sinners imprisoned in their bondage" (John 1:11–12). The Spirit applies redemption to all for whom Christ purchased it, ensuring their salvation (Eph 1:3, 14). Through this effectual application, believers truly partake in redemption, experiencing real deliverance, like prisoners freed from a pit (Zech 9:11). As Boston explains, "Without the Spirit, without Christ; without Christ, without God."

The application of Christ's redemption is grounded in the covenant of grace, "promised to Christ for the elect" (Isa 53:10–11). Believers receive "the whole Christ, with all his benefits" now, albeit many benefits will be fully realized on the day of redemption (Eph 1:14; 4:30). Nevertheless, as Boston attests, the Spirit is "the leading benefit of Christ's purchase, which all the rest infallibly follow." The outward means by which the Spirit applies redemption is the ministry of the word (1 Cor 3:5), for "faith comes from hearing, and hearing through the word of Christ" (Rom 10:17). Inwardly, the Spirit powerfully operates on "all the faculties of the soul" (1 Thess 1:5–6), quickening the conscience, spiritualizing the affections, and affecting the whole soul so that the sinner embraces Christ with heart and goodwill.

Boston provides two signs of whether the Spirit has effectually applied Christ's redemption to a person. The first is a full recognition of one's sin and inability to save oneself, leading to a sincere seeking of Christ for both justification and sanctification (Luke 6:48; 1 Cor 1:30). The second is a growing deliverance from sin's power—though sin may still exert influence, it no longer reigns, and the individual longs to be free from it, much like a captive shedding his chains (Rom 6:14; 7:24). Given the Spirit's indispensable role in applying redemption, Boston warns against resisting (Acts 7:51), grieving, (Eph 4:30), vexing (Isa 63:10), and, worst of all, blaspheming (Matt 12:22–32) the Holy Spirit.

TEA WITH THOMAS BOSTON

1. How has the Holy Spirit made Christ's redemption real in your life and freed you from sin's bondage? (Titus 2:14; John 8:36; Rom 6:22)
2. Why is the Spirit's application of Christ's redemption necessary for salvation? (Titus 3:5; John 3:5–6; Eph 2:12)
3. How does the Spirit's role in redemption set Christianity apart from other religions? (John 1:12–13; Rom 3:20–24; Gal 3:2–3)
4. How can you avoid resisting, grieving, or vexing the Holy Spirit? (Acts 7:51; Eph 4:30; Isa 63:10)
5. How can you help children and young believers recognize their need for the Holy Spirit? (John 16:8; Ezek 36:26–27; 2 Tim 1:5)

Golden Yunnan is a rich black tea from China, known for its smooth, malty flavor, representing the transformative nature of redemption.

Heavenly Father, thank you for applying Christ's redemption to me by your Spirit, freeing me from sin's bondage so that I may walk in the joy of eternal life. Amen.

"The Father sent our Redeemer: the Son purchased our redemption; and the Holy Ghost applies it."[1]

---

1. Boston, *Works*, 1:532 (1:529–43, 7:78–80).

Day 30

Union with Christ

> Q30. *How does the Spirit apply to us the redemption purchased by Christ?*
>
> A. The Spirit applies to us the redemption purchased by Christ by working faith in us and thereby uniting us to Christ in our effectual calling.

For in one Spirit we were all baptized into one body—Jews or Greeks, slaves or free—and all were made to drink of one Spirit.

1 CORINTHIANS 12:13

PAUL EXPLAINS IN 1 Cor 12:13 the union between Christ and believers, comparing it to the two Christian sacraments. Through baptism, believers are united with Christ, signifying their incorporation into one body by the Spirit, who works faith in them and joins them to Christ. This union extends to all believers—Jews or gentiles, bond or free. The Lord's Supper illustrates the fruit of this union, where believers partake of the Spirit, receiving ongoing spiritual nourishment and growth in grace. Thomas Boston states that these sacraments demonstrate the believer's union and continued communion with Christ through the Spirit.

Christ's redemptive work is his purchase by the price of his active and passive obedience. The Holy Spirit's application of Christ's purchase to us is not external but internal (Ezek 36:27). We are made participants of the Spirit, given to us by Christ (John 20:22). The Holy Spirit is central to

Christ's purchase, both as a key part of that purchase and the One who applies it (Luke 24:49). The Spirit enters within us, applies Christ's purchase to us, uniting us to Christ (1 Cor 12:13). Union with Christ is, Boston asserts, the "leading, comprehensive, fundamental privilege of believers." It is essential for salvation because "as Adam's sin could never have hurt you, unless ye had been in him, so Christ's redemption shall never savingly profit you, unless ye be in him."

This union is real, spiritual, mysterious, intimate, and indissoluble. It encompasses the whole person—body and soul—joined to the "whole Christ" in both his divine and human nature (1 Cor 6:15). Our union with Christ is by the Spirit, given to us when we are spiritually dead in sin. The Spirit works within us to bring us to life through his transforming power. We commune with Christ and his benefits as the Spirit applies Christ's work through this union.

The Spirit's role in this union is his "working faith in us, and thereby uniting us to Christ" (Col 2:12). Receiving Christ first happens passively, when Christ, by his Spirit, enters and quickens a dead soul, uniting himself to it without any action from the soul—such is the case for "elect infants" who cannot yet exercise faith. Receiving Christ then happens actively when the soul, having been given faith by the Spirit, responds by believing and embracing Christ, thereby joining itself to him (Phil 3:12).

In the case of those elect who are "incapable of actual believing"—like infants or those with limited understanding, the Spirit can still unite them to Christ by applying Christ's redemption to them (Luke 1:15). On Christ's side, the Spirit forms the bond of spiritual union between Christ and believers. On our side, the Spirit forms faith in us (1 John 3:24). This work of God, in which the Spirit works faith in us and unites us to Christ, is our "effectual calling."

TEA WITH THOMAS BOSTON

1. How does understanding your union with Christ deepen your relationship with him? (Gal 2:20; 2 Cor 13:14; Col 2:6)
2. How does the Holy Spirit work faith in us and unite us to Christ? (Eph 2:8–9; Titus 3:5; 1 Cor 12:13)
3. How does believers' union with Christ distinguish Christianity from other religions? (John 14:20; Col 1:27; 1 John 5:20)
4. How can believers experience ongoing spiritual nourishment through communion with Christ? (John 6:56; 1 Cor 10:16–17; Col 1:27)
5. How can we help children grow in their understanding of union with Christ and the Holy Spirit? (2 Tim 1:5; Eph 6:4; Deut 6:7)

 Blended herbal infusion is a carefully crafted mix of herbs, symbolizing the harmonious union of believers with Christ.

 Heavenly Father, thank you for uniting me with Christ through the Holy Spirit, transforming me and nourishing my faith to live in communion with Christ. Amen.

 "It is true, if the firmness of this union depended entirely on the hold the sinner has of Christ by faith, it might be broke; but it depends on the hold that Christ has of the sinner by his Spirit, as the nurse has of the babe in her arms."[1]

---

1. Boston, *Works*, 1:551 (1:544–56, 7:80–83).

Day 31

Effectual Calling

> Q31. *What is effectual calling?*
>
> A. Effectual calling is the work of God's Spirit, whereby convincing us of our sin and misery, enlightening our minds in the knowledge of Christ, and renewing our wills, he does persuade and enable us to embrace Jesus Christ, freely offered to us in the gospel.

Who saved us and called us to a holy calling, not because of our works but because of his own purpose and grace, which he gave us in Christ Jesus before the ages began.

2 TIMOTHY 1:9

THE SPIRIT APPLIES CHRIST'S redemption to the elect through effectual calling, which Thomas Boston describes as "the first entrance of a soul into the state of grace," where the mystical union between Christ and a sinner is realized. In this calling, the Spirit "works faith" in the elect to unite them to Christ. The Spirit must effectually call sinners by persuading and enabling them to come to Christ in union and communion with him because, left to themselves, they are spiritually dead in sin and, therefore, both unwilling and unable to come.

Effectual calling, Boston asserts, is the third link in the chain of salvation, following foreknowledge and predestination. As the gospel call goes out, it urges "sinners of mankind" to come out "from the world lying in wickedness." However, most people hear only the outward call and reject it, as it remains ineffectual without the Spirit's work. Only the elect receive the inward, effectual call, where the Spirit convicts them by savingly illuminating their minds and renewing their wills. Boston observes that "the law discovers the disease, and the gospel the physician." The Spirit opens both "the outer door of the understanding" and "the inner door of the will" by renewing it.

Negatively, through preaching the law, the Spirit convicts the elect of their sin and misery, producing remorse, terror, and anxiety, highlighting their need for a Savior. Positively, through preaching the gospel, the Spirit, through saving illumination, renews sinners' minds and enables them to see Christ's ability and willingness to save, leading to hope. Through this work, the Spirit reveals and confirms the gospel as God's infallible word and assures sinners that it is addressed to them personally, providing a foundation for faith.

The Spirit must also renew sinners' wills to make them responsive to the gospel call. Specifically, the Spirit instills a "flexibleness or pliableness to good" (Ezek 36:26) and a "proneness and bent of the will to good" (Jer 31:18). By doing this, the Spirit overcomes the old nature of the will, giving it a new disposition that enables the elect to embrace Christ. The Spirit's operation on the sinners' minds and will is irresistible, yet "without the least violence done to their will." The Spirit persuades and enables them to embrace Christ by saving illumination and renewing their wills. This perfected persuasion leads to actual faith in Christ, which infallibly results in true conversion.

Boston insists that the gospel call, whenever it reaches any sinner, comes with full authority and permission for that sinner—elect or not—to come to Christ and be united with him. This authority is grounded in Christ, as he is "freely offered to us in the gospel."

TEA WITH THOMAS BOSTON

1. How has the Spirit deepened your understanding of sin and increased your appreciation of Christ's grace? (Rom 3:23; Eph 2:1–5; Titus 3:3–7)
2. How does the Spirit's convicting and renewing work connect to regeneration? (John 3:5–8; Titus 3:5; Ezek 36:26–27)
3. How does effectual calling differ from religious views focused on human effort to approach God? (Eph 2:8–9; Rom 9:16; John 6:44)
4. How can reflecting on effectual calling help you trust God more in your daily struggles? (Rom 8:28–30; Phil 1:6; Heb 12:2)
5. What practical steps can parents and mentors take to help children and young believers recognize the Spirit's work in their lives? (Deut 6:6–7; Eph 6:4; 2 Tim 3:14–17)

Gunpowder green tea is a tightly rolled green tea with a smoky, bold flavor, symbolizing the bursting power of effectual calling.

Heavenly Father, thank you for the Spirit's work of effectually renewing my mind and will and enabling me to embrace Christ as offered in the gospel. Amen.

"Sinners naturally are not only asleep, but dead in sins. And no less power is requisite to bring them than to raise the dead, and therefore this call is a voice that raiseth the dead."[1]

---

1. Boston, *Works*, 1:564 (1:557–75, 7:83–90).

Day 32

The Benefits of Effectual Calling

> Q32. *What benefits do they that are effectually called partake of in this life?*
>
> A. They that are effectually called do in this life partake of justification, adoption, sanctification, and the several benefits which, in this life, do either accompany or flow from them.

For those whom he foreknew he also predestined to be conformed to the image of his Son, . . . And those whom he predestined he also called, and those whom he called he also justified, and those whom he justified he also glorified.

ROMANS 8:29–30

THE GOLDEN CHAIN OF salvation in these two verses, explains Thomas Boston, consists of five links. The first two, God's foreknowledge and predestination, are invisible to the sinner until revealed through the third link, the effectual calling. The fourth link is the justification of the effectually called, which includes both justification and adoption. The fifth link is the glorification of the justified, encompassing both their sanctification in this life and their ultimate glorification in the next.

Those the Holy Spirit effectually called into union and communion with Christ receive the full benefits of Christ's redemption (Eph 1:3). However, these benefits are not granted all at once. Believers will experience some in this life, others at death, and the fullness at the resurrection. The foundational benefit from which all others flow and depend on is their union with Christ (1 Cor 1:30). The "leading benefits" that the effectually called partake of in this life are justification, adoption, and sanctification (Rom 8:30).

When sinners respond to the gospel and come to Christ, they are immediately freed from condemnation and granted absolution (Rom 8:1). No longer under the curse, they live under blessing, forgiven, and accepted as righteous. They are judged and receive the "white stone," symbolizing victory and a new identity (Rev 2:17). The law has no more demands, guilt is broken, and they are clothed in perfect righteousness.

They are adopted as God's children (Eph 1:5) and receive a new name, becoming sons and daughters of God. Taken from the "devil's family," they are now part of the household of faith, not as servants but as sons. Through the call, they are made heirs of heaven, with Christ as their Brother and God as their Father. The Spirit of adoption dwells in them, teaching them to cry "Abba, Father," and they share the same family as the saints and angels (Eph 3:15).

They are sanctified through a holy calling (2 Tim 1:9). The Spirit works in them, breaking sin's power and gradually eradicating it. The Spirit equips them with saving graces, transforming them into Christ's image (John 1:16) and enabling them to live a new life for the Lord. Like Lazarus, they are called from death to life, spending the rest of their lives shedding sin and living by the Spirit's power.

According to the Shorter Catechism Q36, other benefits accompanying or flowing from these primary blessings are "assurance of God's love, peace of conscience, joy in the Holy Ghost, increase of grace, and perseverance therein to the end." To these, Boston also adds reconciliation with God (Rom 5:1), access to God (Eph 3:12), freedom from slavery to sin and Satan (John 8:32), a right to eternal life (Rom 8:17), and, in the life to come, glorification (2 Thess 2:14).

TEA WITH THOMAS BOSTON

1. How has God's calling freed you from guilt and condemnation? (Rom 8:1; Eph 1:3; 1 John 1:9)
2. How does knowing you are a child of God affect your daily life? (Eph 1:5; Rom 8:15; Gal 4:6)
3. How has sanctification shaped your walk, and how can you grow in holiness? (1 Thess 4:3; Heb 12:14; 1 Pet 1:15–16)
4. What is the connection between predestination and effectual calling in Rom 8:29–30? (Rom 8:29–30; Eph 1:4–5; 2 Thess 2:13)
5. How can you help young believers grasp the significance of adoption into God's family? (Eph 3:15; Gal 4:6–7; Rom 8:15)

Lemon balm tea is a calming herbal tea with a light, citrusy flavor, representing the peace-giving benefits of effectual calling.

Heavenly Father, thank you for calling us to Christ, justifying, adopting, and sanctifying us, and for the assurance of your love and the promise of eternal life. Amen.

"God deals very liberally and kindly with his people that answer his call. He does not put an empty spoon into their mouths, he sets them not down to bare commons; they get much in hand, and yet far more in hope."[1]

---

1. Boston, *Works*, 1:579 (1:576–80, 7:90–91).

Day 33

Justification

Q33. *What is justification?*

A. Justification is an act of God's free grace, wherein he pardons all our sins and accepts us as righteous in his sight, only for the righteousness of Christ imputed to us and received by faith alone.

Being justified freely by his grace through the redemption that is in Christ Jesus.
ROMANS 3:24 (KJV)

ALL WHO ARE EFFECTUALLY called are also justified (Rom 8:30). Justification does not infuse righteousness or holiness but discharges sinners from guilt and declares them righteous. Since God cannot declare sinners inherently righteous, justification means God counts them as righteous. Thomas Boston states that justification changes a person's standing, not nature, before God. In justification, God removes sinners from a state of condemnation (Rom 8:33–34), where they were under the curse of the law (Gal 3:10). Through justification, God frees them from this curse (Gal 3:13) and will never accuse them again (Rom 8:1, 33–34).

Justification is not a process but an instantaneous act of God carried out "at the court of heaven" when a sinner believes in Christ (John 5:24; Rom 5:1). God, acting as judge, justifies sinners from his throne of grace, accessible through Christ (Rom 8:33–34; Heb 4:16; 2 Cor 5:19). The Spirit brings sinners, guilty and condemned by the law, to this throne through effectual calling, where God justifies them by his free grace (Ezra 9:15). It is free to us, though not free concerning Christ, who paid "the price of blood."

Boston teaches that justification consists of God pardoning all our sins and accepting us as righteous. Our sins are against God, so only he can pardon them. Pardon frees sinners from the guilt of God's revenging wrath (John 3:36), and, once justified, they can never fall under this wrath again (Rom 8:1). Justification covers all past and present sins (Mic 7:19). For future sins, God does not impute guilt leading to wrath because of Christ's righteousness (Rom 3:22; 4:6–8). However, future sins—if not repented—incur fatherly displeasure and discipline, yet God promises, "I will not remove from him my steadfast love or be false to my faithfulness" (Ps 89:30–33). Still, "pardoned sin is still sin," argues Boston, as God justifies the sinner but never his sin.

In justification, God accepts our persons, not our works (Rom 3:28). No work can be accepted until we are justified (Heb 11:6). God's acceptance of us in justification means that he grants us eternal life, viewing us as righteous in his sight (Rom 5:17–18). This righteousness meets all the demands of the law, making us truly righteous in God's eyes.

Justification is by faith alone (Phil 3:9). This righteousness by faith is not from anything we have done (Titus 3:5). Christ's righteousness is not the essential righteousness that he had from eternity but his "mediatory righteousness"—his holy nature, righteous life, and satisfaction for sin, all of which God imputes to us in justification. As the judge, God reckons this righteousness as ours in Christ by faith alone (Rom 4:6). Still, faith is not the basis of justification but the instrumental means by which God justifies sinners and reconciles them with him (2 Cor 5:19).

TEA WITH THOMAS BOSTON

1. How does knowing justification covers all your sins affect your view of God's forgiveness? (Mic 7:19; Rom 3:22; Ps 89:30–33)
2. Why is it significant that justification changes our standing before God, not our nature? (Rom 5:1; 8:33–34; Gal 3:13)
3. How does justification by faith alone set Christianity apart from other religions? (Gal 2:16; Phil 3:9; 2 Cor 5:19)
4. How does understanding justification help overcome feelings of guilt or shame? (Rom 8:1; 1 John 1:9; Isa 43:25)
5. How can you explain justification using simple language or examples to a child? (Rom 3:24; Eph 2:8–9; Gal 3:22)

Ceylon black tea is a classic, robust tea from Sri Lanka, symbolizing the bold, declarative nature of justification.

Heavenly Father, thank you for justifying me with your grace in Christ, pardoning my sin, and counting me righteous forever. Amen.

"Great and small sins, sins against the gospel and the law, the most and least heinous, in the happy hour of pardon, sink down all together into the sea of the Redeemer's blood."[1]

---

1. Boston, *Works*, 1:587 (1:581–612, 7:91–100).

Day 34

Adoption

Q34. *What is adoption?*

A. Adoption is an act of God's free grace, whereby we are received into the number, and have a right to all the privileges, of the sons of God.

And I will be a father to you, and you shall be sons and daughters to me, says the Lord Almighty.

2 CORINTHIANS 6:18

THOMAS BOSTON DISTINGUISHES BETWEEN "external and federal" adoption—pertaining to members of the visible church, such as Israel in the Old Testament (Exod 4:22–23; Rom 9:4)—and "internal and saving" adoption, which belongs uniquely to true believers, the invisible church. The latter is a legal act by which those once children of wrath become children of God.

The Father's work is justification and adoption, just as the Son's is redemption and the Spirit's is sanctification. Justification delivers us from condemnation, while adoption removes alienation. Like justification, adoption involves an instantaneous change in status—not a gradual process or a transformation of nature. It occurs when a person believes in Christ, is justified, and is reconciled to God, who becomes a Father rather than a Judge (Gal 4:4–5). However, the full enjoyment of adoption's benefits will not be realized until the last day (Rom 8:23).

By nature, we belong to the family of the devil, a "cruel and deceitful father" (John 8:44; 1 John 5:19). However, through effectual calling, God, for the sake of his Son, adopts us into his family (Eph 1:5). Adoption takes us "out of the black number of the devil's family, consisting of devils, damned spirits, and an unconverted world, bearing the devil's image." It dignifies us by making us sons of God and granting us a place among Jesus Christ, the holy angels, and the saints in heaven and on earth (Heb 2:11; 12:22–23). Christ is the Son of God by eternal generation, the angels are sons by creation in God's image (Job 38:7), and the saints are God's sons by "spiritual marriage with Christ, by adoption, and by regeneration."

Christ holds the "peculiar dignity" of being the first-born and the Elder Brother in God's family (Rom 8:29; Col 1:18). His preeminence as the first-born grants him dominion, headship, the priesthood, the blessing, and the double portion. Though all believers share in the blessing, Christ is the "prime receptacle" of the blessing, from whom it flows to his brethren (Gen 12:2–3). Through his obedience and satisfaction, Christ purchased their adoption. As sons of God, they receive all the privileges of sonship (Rom 8:17), including a new name (Rev 2:17), special immunities and freedom (Matt 17:26), and, most significantly, "special access to God and communion with him." They will also enjoy "fatherly pity, protection, provision, and correction, and the eternal inheritance" (Eph 3:12).

While justification grants us a "fundamental right" to these privileges, adoption—which follows justification—adds an "honorary right of inheritance." Until we fully receive this inheritance, God gives us the Spirit of adoption as the earnest of our eternal inheritance, sealing us with the Son's image and producing in us a "son-like disposition" toward God (Rom 8:15; Eph 1:13–14; Gal 4:6). Boston maintains that adoption is permanent: "Once a child of God, ever so."

TEA WITH THOMAS BOSTON

1. How does knowing that God has adopted you change your view of your identity and purpose? (Rom 8:15; John 1:12; 1 John 3:1)
2. How do justification and adoption relate in the broader scope of salvation? (Gal 4:4–5; Rom 8:17; Eph 1:5)
3. How does adoption in Christianity distinguish God as both Judge and Father? (John 1:12; Rom 8:15; John 8:44)
4. How can you live out the benefits of adoption in your work, family, and friendships? (Eph 3:12; Gal 4:7; Rom 8:17)
5. How can you help young believers cultivate a "son-like disposition" toward God? (Rom 8:15; Gal 4:6; Eph 1:13–14)

Milk oolong is a smooth, creamy oolong tea, symbolizing the rich and nurturing nature of adoption into God's family.

Heavenly Father, thank you for adopting me into your family through Christ, granting me eternal privileges, and sealing me with your Spirit. Amen.

"Though a new nature accompanies it, yet adoption itself is a new name, not a new nature."[1]

---

1. Boston, *Works*, 1:615–16 (1:612–53, 7:100–105).

Day 35

Sanctification

Q35. *What is sanctification?*

A. Sanctification is the work of God's free grace, whereby we are renewed in the whole man after the image of God and are enabled more and more to die unto sin and live unto righteousness.

And such were some of you. But you were washed, you were sanctified, you were justified in the name of the Lord Jesus Christ and by the Spirit of our God.

1 CORINTHIANS 6:11

THE APOSTLE PAUL REMINDS the Corinthians of both their past and present states. They were once deeply sinful—described as fornicators, idolaters, thieves, and more—with no merit to deserve God's sanctifying work. However, they are now "washed" in two ways: through sanctification, where the Holy Spirit gradually removes sin and implants grace in their hearts, and through justification, where the guilt of their sin is removed and they are clothed with Christ's righteousness, all made possible through faith in Jesus.

Thomas Boston describes sanctification as separation, purification, and preparation. It involves setting apart for holy use, as seen in the sacrament and in figures like Aaron and his sons. It is also a process of purification, where the Spirit cleanses the soul from sin. Finally, sanctification prepares people for God's service, transforming them to be holy and usable.

Boston views sanctification as twofold: initial and progressive. Initial sanctification, also called regeneration, involves the implantation of grace in the soul, where the Spirit of Christ takes possession and transforms the soul, reflecting the image of God (1 John 3:9). Progressive sanctification is the ongoing process of strengthening grace and weakening corruption, continuing throughout a believer's life and reaching perfection only at death (Acts 20:32). While both are part of the same work, Boston clarifies that initial sanctification precedes justification in order and progressive sanctification follows justification.

Sanctification is not the work of the sinner, as we cannot cleanse ourselves from sin (Eph 2:1). It is solely the work of God, requiring divine power similar to that of creation or resurrection. The entire Trinity is involved: "The Father elects, the Son redeems, and the Holy Spirit sanctifies." The Spirit's role is especially crucial: in initial sanctification, the sinner is passive and unable to act. In progressive sanctification, the sinner participates, albeit by the Spirit's power, enabling the believer to act according to God's will (Phil 2:13).

The Spirit renews the sinner's nature through two acts. First, the Spirit destroys the "body of sin"—the "old man" mentioned in Rom 6:6—breaking sin's dominion over the soul, weakening its power, and mortifying sinful desires (Rom 8:13). Second, the Spirit endows the sinner with various graces, making the person a new creation in Christ (2 Cor 5:17). This new nature, sown as a heavenly seed, grows toward perfection through the ongoing work of the Spirit.

The two parts of sanctification are mortification and vivification. Mortification involves dying to sin as the Spirit weakens sinful desires (Rom 6:4, 6), while vivification enables the sinner to live to righteousness, leading a transformed life focused on serving God and preparing for eternity (Rom 12:2). Sanctification renews the soul in knowledge, will, and affection (Col 3:10) and transforms the body into an instrument of righteousness (Rom 6:13), resulting in holiness expressed through a life of good works.

TEA WITH THOMAS BOSTON

1. How does knowing you are "washed" and sanctified by grace shape your identity and purpose? (1 Cor 6:11; Rom 8:15; Gal 4:7)
2. How do initial and progressive sanctification relate, and why is this distinction important? (1 John 3:9; Acts 20:32; Rom 6:6)
3. How does Boston's view of sanctification as separation, purification, and preparation deepen our understanding of the Spirit's work? (Lev 20:26; 1 Thess 4:3–4; 2 Tim 2:21)
4. How does the biblical view of sanctification set Christianity apart by emphasizing God's active role in transforming believers? (Phil 2:13; Titus 3:5; John 17:17)
5. How does recognizing both mortification and vivification in sanctification shape your pursuit of holiness? (Rom 6:4; 2 Cor 5:17; Rom 12:2)

Green tea is a light and refreshing tea, symbolizing the ongoing purity and refinement of sanctification.

Heavenly Father, thank you for sanctifying me by your Spirit, breaking the power of sin, renewing my heart, and enabling me to live a holy life that reflects your glory. Amen.

"Sanctification is not a new head full of knowledge, with the old heart and life; nor is it a new life, with the old heart and nature. But it is a change that goes through the whole soul and body, which must needs be followed with a new life."[1]

---

1. Boston, *Works*, 1:661 (1:653–61, 7:105–18).

Day 36

Union with Christ the Only Way to Sanctification

Q35. *What is sanctification?*

A. Sanctification is the work of God's free grace, whereby we are renewed in the whole man after the image of God and are enabled more and more to die unto sin and live unto righteousness.

And because of him you are in Christ Jesus, who became to us wisdom from God, righteousness and sanctification and redemption.

1 CORINTHIANS 1:30

THE APOSTLE PAUL HIGHLIGHTS in 1 Cor 1:30 that God's plan for salvation centers entirely on Christ. As our wisdom, Christ leads us to the true knowledge of God. He provides righteousness through his perfect obedience and sacrifice, making us acceptable to God. Christ is also our sanctification, as the Spirit applies his grace to transform us to produce true holiness. Finally, Christ is our redemption, securing victory over death and guaranteeing our future bodily resurrection. Most significantly, we are illuminated, accepted, sanctified, and redeemed only through union with Christ.

Thomas Boston argues that "union with Christ is the only way to sanctification" because sinners "derive holiness from him, whom the Father has constituted the head of sanctifying influences." True holiness, as sanctification's goal, is a heart disposition and way of life that pleases God and conforms to his law. It is universal, encompassing outward obedience and inward devotion to God's commands, where the heart, once prone to sin, is now inclined toward God. True holiness—imperfect in this life and perfected in the next—stems from love for God, shaping all religious duties, and is motivated by his command rather than self-interest. It centers on God's glory as its ultimate purpose, permeating the entire being and way of life (1 Cor 10:31).

Sanctifying grace transforms the whole person, affecting both mortification and vivification. Mortification is universal, as the genuinely sanctified person seeks to put to death all sin, including the most cherished sins, because sin opposes God (Gal 5:24). Just as death affects the whole body, not just one part, true mortification does not spare any lust. Vivification is also universal, restoring God's image in all aspects of the soul and moving the believer to embrace all known duties (2 Cor 5:17). The sanctified person is consistently holy—in private and public, before God and others.

Boston explains that holiness can only come from Christ. Originally, God made Adam holy, and had he not sinned, his descendants would have received his holiness. However, Adam's fall corrupted human nature, leaving humanity dead in sin and incapable of restoring holiness. To remedy this, God appointed Christ as the Mediator and source of sanctifying grace. Christ, being both God and man, was filled with the Spirit of holiness, and through his death and resurrection, he removed the guilt and curse of sin, making sanctification possible. However, believers must be spiritually united to Christ to receive his holiness. This union occurs when the Spirit quickens the soul, leading to faith that unites the believer with Christ. As "the head of all the saints," Christ continually supplies the Holy Spirit for their growth in sanctification, with faith being the means for believers to receive these sanctifying influences.

TEA WITH THOMAS BOSTON

1. How does knowing Christ is our sanctification impact your daily struggles with sin? (1 Cor 1:30; Rom 6:11; Col 3:3)
2. What is the Holy Spirit's role in sanctification? (Rom 8:13; Gal 5:16–25; 2 Thess 2:13)
3. How does Christ being our wisdom and sanctification show the fullness of salvation? (Eph 1:7–8; Col 2:3; 1 Cor 2:16)
4. What steps can you take to die to sin and live righteously? (Gal 5:24; Rom 6:11; Col 3:5)
5. What disciplines help children and young believers grow in sanctification? (Phil 4:6–7; Col 3:16; 1 Tim 4:7–8)

 Butterfly pea flower tea is a vibrant blue herbal tea, representing the transformation and beauty of sanctification.

 Heavenly Father, help me rely on Christ for sanctification, transforming me to live in true holiness by the power of your Spirit. Amen.

 "We cannot actually partake of Christ's holiness till we have a spiritual being in him, even as we partake not of Adam's corruption till we have a natural being from him."[1]

---

1. Boston, *Works*, 2:13 (2:5–14, 7:105–18).

Day 37

The Benefits Flowing from Justification, Adoption, and Sanctification

> Q36. *What are the benefits which in this life do accompany or flow from justification, adoption, and sanctification?*
>
> A. The benefits which in this life do accompany or flow from justification, adoption, and sanctification, are assurance of God's love, peace of conscience, joy in the Holy Ghost, increase of grace, and perseverance therein to the end.

Therefore, since we have been justified by faith, we have peace with God through our Lord Jesus Christ. Through him we have also obtained access by faith into this grace in which we stand, and we rejoice in hope of the glory of God.

ROMANS 5:1–2

THOMAS BOSTON DISTINGUISHES TWO types of benefits accompanying "justification, adoption, and sanctification." Some benefits—assurance of God's love, peace of conscience, and joy in the Holy Spirit—require evidence of grace, while others—an increase of grace and perseverance—proceed from the mere presence of grace.

"Assurance of God's love" gives believers confidence in divine love, their state of grace, and perseverance (Rom 5:1–2). Boston speaks of two kinds of assurance: "objective assurance," where God's special love and eternal salvation for a believer are always sure (2 Tim 2:19), and "subjective assurance," where the believer personally perceives this love and is confident of eternal glory. It comes through ordinary means like walking with God, self-examination, and using the sacraments (2 Pet 1:10), grounded in the "word of grace" and the "evidence of grace" revealed by "the Spirit's shining in his heart." Genuine assurance humbles the soul, tenderizes the conscience, and makes the heart heavenly. While seeking assurance is a duty, "there may be true faith, justification, adoption, and sanctification, without this assurance." Assurance, in other words, is not necessary for the "being of a Christian" but for the "well-being of a Christian."

"Peace of conscience" comes from being cleansed of guilt by Christ's blood, leading to peace with God through justification (Rom 5:1). This peace consists of an "inward calm," where the soul is free from fear of God's wrath, and "consolation and comfort of heart," giving the believer cheerful confidence before God (2 Cor 1:12). Peace is genuine when guided by God's word and maintained through an ongoing battle against sin (Gal 5:17).

"Joy in the Holy Ghost" is a spiritual joy produced by the Spirit, arising from a sense of grace received and hope of future glory (Rom 14:17). This joy, unlike the false joy of hypocrites, leads to victory over sin, strengthens obedience, and fills the believer with joy "unspeakable and full of glory" (1 Pet 1:8–9).

Grace, like a seed or morning light, naturally grows toward perfection, but its actual growth depends on receiving grace from Christ through the Spirit (1 John 3:9; Eph 4:13). True growth occurs through diligent use of means, especially exercising faith and love, and is marked by balanced growth in all areas of the new life, never resting until it reaches perfection.

Perseverance means continuing in grace until death (Col 1:23). All who have true grace will "infallibly persevere" despite Satan's temptations, worldly snares, and inner corruptions (John 10:28–29). While believers may lose the evidence and exercise of grace, they will never fall away "totally or finally" because their perseverance rests on "their inseparable union with Christ, the perpetual indwelling of his Spirit, the continual intercession of Christ, and the nature of the covenant of grace and decree of election."

TEA WITH THOMAS BOSTON

1. How do justification, adoption, and sanctification produce assurance, peace, and joy? (Rom 5:1–2; Gal 4:4–7; 1 Cor 1:30)
2. How does God's love strengthen your confidence in his promises during doubt? (Rom 8:38–39; 2 Tim 2:19; 1 John 5:13)
3. When have you experienced "peace of conscience," and how did it impact your relationship with God? (Rom 5:1; Isa 26:3; Phil 4:7)
4. How has "joy in the Holy Ghost" helped you persevere and overcome sin? (Rom 14:17; 1 Pet 1:8–9; Neh 8:10)
5. What practices can help new believers grow in grace and perseverance? (Acts 2:42; Heb 10:24–25; 2 Tim 3:16–17)

Masala chai is a spiced tea blend with a robust, full-bodied flavor, symbolizing the multifaceted blessings of justification, adoption, and sanctification.

Heavenly Father, grant me assurance, peace, and joy that I may grow in grace, persevere to the end, and walk faithfully with Christ until I reach eternal glory. Amen.

"A doubting Christian will be a staggering and weak Christian; as the soldier who has little hope of the victory will readily be fainthearted, while he that is assured is strengthened and established."[1]

---

1. Boston, *Works*, 2:18 (2:15–27, 7:118–27).

Day 38

Increase of Grace and Perseverance

> Q36. *What are the benefits which in this life do accompany or flow from justification, adoption, and sanctification?*
>
> A. The benefits which in this life do accompany or flow from justification, adoption, and sanctification, are assurance of God's love, peace of conscience, joy in the Holy Ghost, increase of grace, and perseverance therein to the end.

But the path of the righteous is like the light of dawn, which shines brighter and brighter until full day.

PROVERBS 4:18

PROVERBS 4:18 COMPARES "THE path of the righteous" to the "light of dawn" that grows brighter until the perfect day, illustrating how the justified life, marked by holiness and grace, progresses like the rising sun. This growth in grace is steady and continuous, and it perseveres until perfected in glory.

Real grace grows. Scripture testifies that grace is a living seed that grows over time (Mark 4:27), promised by God (Ps 92:12). God has appointed a certain stature for his children to reach, progressing from spiritual infancy to maturity (Eph 4:13). Divine influences and ordinances cultivate this growth (Eph 4:11–12). Thomas Boston states that a Christian grows in four ways: *inwardly* by strengthening faith, hope, and love through deeper union with Christ (Eph 4:15); *outwardly* in good works and holy living for God's glory and the benefit of others (Phil 2:12); *upwardly* in a heavenly mindset and longing for eternity (Phil 3:20); and *downwardly* in humility, self-denial, and greater awareness of sin (2 Cor 12:11).

Boston identifies true and false growth. Genuine growth is universal and balanced in all areas of spiritual life (Eph 4:15), whereas spurious growth is partial, focusing on specific aspects like knowledge while neglecting holiness and tenderness. True growth is also continuous, pressing toward spiritual maturity (Phil 3:13–14), while false growth eventually stagnates (Luke 8:14). Still, true grace does not always grow continuously but has seasons of growth and decline, though it never fully dies (1 John 3:9). Growth may be imperceptible at times, yet over time, the difference becomes evident (Mark 4:27). Growth should not be measured only by visible fruit but also by deeper roots—marked by increased tenderness, humility, and self-denial.

Perseverance is the believer's "firm and constant continuance in the state of grace" until the end of life (Matt 10:22). This perseverance applies only to true saints who possess saving grace, not to hypocrites whose superficial faith may wither and be lost entirely (John 6:66). Though believers may experience seasons of weakness where they lose "the evidence of grace" (Isa 50:10), neglect "the exercise of grace," and diminish in "the measure of grace" they once had (Rev 3:2), they can never lose grace "finally" (1 Pet 1:5) or "totally" (1 John 3:9). Even when saints stray, the Lord will ultimately restore them to ensure they do not utterly fall (Ps 37:24). Perseverance, Boston insists, is the "discriminating mark of the elect."

Boston grounds perseverance on four foundations: God's unchangeable decree of election (2 Tim 2:19), Christ's merit and intercession (Heb 7:25), the abiding presence of the Holy Spirit (John 14:16), and the covenant of grace, with its promises of divine preservation (Jer 32:40). Perseverance requires using God's ordained means, including his ordinances, providences, religious duties, and the exercise of grace, as neglecting these is inconsistent with true saving faith.

TEA WITH THOMAS BOSTON

1. How has God's grace sustained you through spiritual struggles, and how did it impact your faith? (Isa 50:10; Ps 37:24; 1 Pet 1:5)
2. What biblical foundation assures that true believers can never completely fall from grace? (Rom 8:38–39; John 6:39; Phil 1:6)
3. How does the doctrine of perseverance set Christianity apart from other religions? (John 10:28; Rom 8:38–39; Phil 1:6)
4. What practices can you adopt to foster growth in faith, hope, and love? (Eph 4:15; 2 Thess 1:3; Col 2:7)
5. How can you guide young believers to use God's means of grace to persevere in faith? (Acts 2:42; Heb 10:24–25; 2 Tim 3:16–17)

Ginseng tea is a stimulating herbal tea known for its energy-boosting properties, representing the renewal and perseverance of grace.

Heavenly Father, let my path shine brighter each day as I grow in grace, faith, and holiness until perfected in glory. Amen.

"Those who, by virtue of regeneration, may call God their Father, as well as the church their mother, shall abide in his family, and never fall out of it."[1]

---

1. Boston, *Works*, 2:32–33 (2:28–36, 7:118–27).

Day 39

The Benefits Which Believers Receive at Death

> Q37. *What benefits do believers receive from Christ at death?*
>
> A. The souls of believers are, at their death, made perfect in holiness, and do immediately pass into glory; and their bodies, being still united to Christ, do rest in their graves until the resurrection.

For to me to live is Christ, and to die is gain.

PHILIPPIANS 1:21

DEATH ENTERED THE WORLD by sin (Rom 5:12), and those outside of Christ die in their sins "under the curse of the broken law or covenant of works." However, those called into union with Christ do not die under this curse (Rom 7:4) but die "in conformity to Christ their head, that as death came in by sin, sin may go out by death." Death does not halt their participation in the benefits of Christ's purchase but instead opens it further, as believers' souls and bodies receive "more benefits of Christ's purchase at their death." Death is, asserts Thomas Boston, their "greatest gain."

The sanctification that began in the souls of believers is perfected at death, making their souls perfect in holiness (Heb 12:23). This sanctifying act, by God's free grace, completely renews believers after God's image, abolishing the remains of sin and enabling them to live in "holiness at the highest pitch" (Rev 7:14–15). This ongoing communication of grace in heaven ensures believers remain eternally united with Christ, acting through his continued influence.

At death, the souls of believers enter a glorious "state, place, and society." Their state is one of shining purity, reflecting God's image (2 Cor 3:18). The place is full of the glory of God and Christ (Rev 21:23). Believers are made perfect in holiness before entering this glory (Rev 21:27). The glorious society they join consists of God, Christ, holy angels, and glorified saints, with no intermediate state, Boston insists, between death and entering glory (2 Cor 5:8; Phil 1:23). Believers will be completely free from sin, with no struggles with temptation.

At death, the bodies of believers, still united to Christ, rest in their graves until the resurrection, unlike the wicked, for whom the grave is a place of imprisonment and despair. Believers' graves are a place of rest, like a bed perfumed by Christ's death (Isa 57:2), with the union between Christ and their bodies unbroken, even as their bodies dissolve (1 Thess 4:14; Rom 8:11). They remain in this restful state until the resurrection (Job 19:26–27).

The dead will rise again on the last day, when Christ returns for judgment (Acts 24:15; John 5:28–29). The resurrection will involve all people, both the just and unjust, with the dead rising in their original bodies, reformed by God's omniscient and almighty power. The resurrection involves reuniting the souls with the same physical bodies in the grave. However, these resurrected bodies will be changed to be imperishable, glorified, and fit for eternal life. Those still alive at Christ's return will be changed rather than dying and rising (1 Cor 15:51). The resurrection will occur in an instant at the last trumpet (1 Cor 15:52). While God will transform their bodies in qualities, the bodies will retain their original substance (1 Cor 15:52–53).

TEA WITH THOMAS BOSTON

1. How does seeing death as "gain" change your view on mortality? (Phil 1:21; 2 Cor 5:8; Rev 7:14–15)
2. How does 1 Cor 15:51–53 explain the transformation of believers' bodies at death? (1 Cor 15:51–53; Phil 3:20–21; 1 Thess 4:16–17)
3. What hope does Christianity offer about the resurrection compared to secular views? (John 5:28–29; Acts 24:15; Rom 8:11)
4. How does the resurrection affirm the dignity and value of the body? (Rom 8:11; Phil 3:20–21; 1 Thess 4:14)
5. How can we help young believers understand and live out the hope of resurrection? (Titus 2:13–14; 1 Cor 15:51–53; 2 Cor 4:14)

Lavender tea is a calming herbal tea with floral, soothing notes, symbolizing the peace and rest available at death.

Heavenly Father, thank you for the hope that through death, I am freed from sin, perfected in holiness, and brought into your glorious and eternal presence. Amen.

"A dying day is the best day for a believer that is in all his life. It is their marriage, home-coming, and redemption day."[1]

---

1. Boston, *Works*, 2:41 (2:37–41, 7:127–33).

Day 40

The Benefits at the Resurrection

> Q38. *What benefits do believers receive from Christ at the resurrection?*
>
> A. At the resurrection, believers, being raised up to glory, shall be openly acknowledged and acquitted in the day of judgment and made perfectly blessed in the full enjoying of God to all eternity.

Women received back their dead by resurrection. Some were tortured, refusing to accept release, so that they might rise again to a better life.
HEBREWS 11:35

THOMAS BOSTON TEACHES THAT at the resurrection, believers—those effectually called, justified, adopted, and sanctified—will fully partake of Christ's purchased benefits in three stages: at the resurrection itself, during judgment, and after judgment. At the resurrection, they will be raised in glory (1 Cor 15:43) by Christ's Spirit (Rom 8:11) and conformed to the likeness of Christ's glorious body (1 Cor 15:49), with incorruptible, glorious, strong, and spiritual bodies (1 Cor 15:42–44). The wicked, in contrast, will be raised in dishonor by Christ as their offended Judge (John 5:29).

Immediately after the resurrection, the general judgment will occur (Rev 20:13), where both humans and devils will be judged (2 Cor 5:10). The last trumpet will summon the living and the dead (1 Thess 4:16–17), raising the dead and transforming the living (1 Cor 15:52). Angels will gather all to the place of judgment (Mark 13:27), where Christ will sit on a glorious throne (Matt 25:31) with the righteous on his right "in the air" and the wicked on his left "on the earth" (Matt 25:33). People will give an account of their thoughts, words, and deeds (1 Cor 4:5). The good works of the righteous will serve only as evidence of their right to heaven, not the basis for it.

At the judgment, believers will be openly acknowledged and acquitted by Christ (Matt 10:32), who will declare them his faithful servants, whose names are in the book of life (Matt 25:23). Though they are already justified, this public acquittal, Boston explains, will occur before the Father, angels, and all people, with Christ pronouncing, "Come, ye blessed of my Father, inherit the kingdom prepared for you from the foundation of the world" (Matt 25:34; Rev 3:5). Their acquittal will be based on Christ's righteousness, vindicating them from worldly accusations (Isa 66:5), and they will be honored afterward by joining Christ in judging devils and the wicked (1 Cor 6:2-3).

At the judgment, the wicked will be "openly disowned and condemned" by Christ (Matt 7:23) based on their sins and ungodliness (Rom 2:16), with clear evidence convicting their consciences (Rom 2:15). After judgment, the sentence will be executed immediately, with the damned departing first. Simultaneously, the saints will witness their enemies' departure (Matt 25:46). They will be "cast out from the favourable presence of God" into hell (Rev 20), where their torments "will never have an end" (Mark 9:43-44). They, "the society of the devil and his angels," will suffer in hell forever.

After the judgment, believers will be "made perfectly blessed, in full enjoying of God to all eternity" (1 Thess 4:17), entering heaven in a state of complete happiness, free from all sin and misery (Matt 13:43). Their perfect blessedness comes from seeing God's glory "face to face" (Matt 5:8) and experiencing his goodness fully. They will enjoy God "immediately, fully, and eternally," fulfilling their ultimate purpose—forever glorifying God through perfect love, praise, and service.

TEA WITH THOMAS BOSTON

1. How should knowing that you will stand before Christ affect your daily life? (2 Cor 5:10; 1 Cor 4:5; Matt 25:31–33)

2. What does being raised with glorious, strong, and spiritual bodies mean for believers? (1 Cor 15:42–44; 15:49; Phil 3:21)

3. How can the certainty of judgment challenge moral relativism and denial of accountability? (Rom 2:16; Matt 25:31–33; Heb 9:27)

4. How does reflecting on final judgment cultivate humility and godly living? (Rom 14:10–12; 1 Cor 4:5; Heb 9:27)

5. How can parents teach children about judgment and hope in Christ? (Matt 25:31–34; Rev 20:13; John 5:24)

 Blooming tea is a visually striking flower tea which takes the form of a ball (or bulb) that "blooms" in hot water, symbolizing the burst of new life and glory at the resurrection.

 Heavenly Father, we rejoice in the hope of the resurrection; we will be raised in glory, fully acquitted, and perfectly blessed in the eternal enjoyment of you. Amen.

 "That will be the happiest day that ever their eyes saw. The day of their death was better than that of their birth; but they of their resurrection will be the best of all."[1]

---

1. Boston, *Works*, 2:45 (2:42–51, 7:133–42).

PART 6

The Ten Commandments

(Q39—Q84)

Day 41

The Duty Which God Requires of Man

Q39. *What is the duty which God requires of man?*

A. The duty which God requires of man is obedience to his revealed will.

And Samuel said, "Has the LORD as great delight in burnt offerings and sacrifices, as in obeying the voice of the LORD? Behold, to obey is better than sacrifice, and to listen than the fat of rams.

1 SAMUEL 15:22

IN THIS TEXT, SAMUEL rebuked Saul, reminding him that though he was Israel's king, he was still subject to God's command, which he disobeyed by sparing Agag and the best livestock after defeating the Amalekites. Samuel's response emphasizes that God requires all people, rulers and ruled, to obey his revealed will, which he values above all sacrifices.

Our duty to God is total obedience, asserts Thomas Boston, recognizing God as the supreme authority. As King, God commands his subjects to obey his laws; as Father, he expects respect and reverence from his children; as Lord, he demands his servants' wholehearted service; and as Lawgiver, his revealed will is the law we must follow. The duty of obedience to God applies to everyone, without exception, regardless of status, wealth, or belief, as God's law binds all. This obedience is grounded in God's revealed will as expressed in Scripture—not in his secret will (Deut 29:29), as was the case with the Jews who crucified Jesus—and must be followed diligently, for failure to do so leads to peril.

Boston outlines seven properties of obedience to God. It must be *sincere*, coming from a genuine heart rather than being hypocritical or superficial (Ps 18:23). It should also be *constant*, not sporadic or temporary but steady and unwavering in all circumstances (Ps 119:44). True obedience is *tender*, marked by careful avoidance of even the most minor sin and a deep reverence for God's holiness (1 Thess 5:22). It must be *ready*, with an immediate and willing response to God's commands, without hesitation or delay (Ps 119:60). Moreover, obedience must be *universal*, where all of God's commands are followed, as ignoring even one undermines the integrity of our obedience (Ps 119:6). It is also *absolute*, meaning it must be followed without reservation, even if it conflicts with the commands of others (Heb 11:8). Lastly, though imperfect due to human limitations, obedience to God should strive for *perfection*, recognizing that any failure is sin and ultimately relying on Christ's perfect obedience for salvation (Matt 5:48).

We owe obedience to God for several key reasons. As our Creator, he gave us life and being, making it just to obey him as our Lord and Master. He is our "chief end," the ultimate purpose of all creation, and our actions should reflect his glory. As the "conserving cause of all," God sustains us by his power, making it right to use our lives for his will and glory. Due to the "eminency of his nature," God, the most glorious being, demands our obedience. As our gracious Benefactor, he has blessed us abundantly, obligating us to serve and obey him in gratitude. Lastly, as our Governor and Lawgiver, God has established laws for all creation, and we are bound to obey his divine laws, inscribed on our hearts and revealed in his word.

TEA WITH THOMAS BOSTON

1. When have you struggled to obey God's will, and how did you overcome it? (Ps 119:11; Rom 7:19; Heb 12:11)
2. How does God's revealed will differ from his secret will, and why should believers focus on the former? (Deut 29:29; Rom 11:33–36; Matt 7:21)
3. How do the seven properties of obedience align with biblical sanctification? (1 Thess 4:3; Eph 4:22–24; 1 Pet 1:15–16)
4. How would you explain to an unbeliever why obedience to God's will is more important than rituals or sacrifices? (Matt 7:21–23; Isa 1:11–17; Mark 12:33)
5. What steps can children and young believers take to develop habits of obedience to God's will? (Prov 4:23–27; Eph 6:1–3; Col 3:20)

 Sencha is a Japanese green tea with a fresh, grassy flavor, symbolizing clarity and the duty required of man to follow God's law.

 Heavenly Father, help me obey your will with sincerity, constancy, and reverence so that I may honor you in all things. Amen.

 "The whole of the commands of God have the same divine stamp upon them. They are one golden chain: whoso takes away one link, breaks the chain; if the connection be destroyed, the whole machine falls asunder."[1]

---

1. Boston, *Works*, 2:54 (2:51–58).

Day 42

The Moral Law, the Rule of Man's Obedience

Q40. *What did God at first reveal to man for the rule of his obedience?*

A. The rule which God at first revealed to man for his obedience was the moral law.

For when Gentiles, who do not have the law, by nature do what the law requires, they are a law to themselves, even though they do not have the law. They show that the work of the law is written on their hearts, while their conscience also bears witness, and their conflicting thoughts accuse or even excuse them.

ROMANS 2:14–15

IN THIS PASSAGE, THE apostle Paul highlights that gentiles lack the written Law of Moses or Scripture. They, however, possess a natural law within, similar to the moral law but weakened by human corruption. This natural law is inherent in human nature, originating from Adam, and serves as a moral guide, with consciences excusing good actions or accusing evil ones. It reflects the moral law initially given to Adam in innocence, which is still evident in his descendants.

Thomas Boston states that before God gave the law to Moses, all humans had a law written in their hearts containing moral principles and duties to God, self, and others. This law, described in Romans 7:12 as "holy, just, and good," was in harmony with God's attributes, suitable and beneficial to humans. In Adam's state of innocence, this law was part of his moral nature, created in God's image, which consisted of righteousness and true holiness, allowing Adam to communicate with God in happiness and live in perfect moral alignment.

The Bible presents three types of laws: the ceremonial law, binding only to the Jews and abolished by Christ; the judicial law, regulating Jewish civil matters but only binding other nations to the extent of its moral equity; and the moral law, universally binding all people to obedience in holiness and righteousness. This moral law is in the hearts of all people through natural conscience (Rom 2:15), expressed in common moral principles, the Ten Commandments, and the Bible. It is, however, opposed by the carnal mind but written anew in the heart through regeneration (Heb 8:10) and fulfilled by Christ for the elect. Boston states that God reveals the moral law in three stages: to Adam in innocence, written on his heart; to the Israelites at Sinai in the Ten Commandments; and finally through Jesus Christ and his apostles, now recorded in the Scriptures.

The moral law is universal, binding all people at all times (Rom 2:14–15); perfect, comprehending all duties to God and neighbor (Ps 19:7); and perpetual, remaining unchanged and indestructible (Matt 5:18). For all people, the moral law reveals God's will and duties, exposes human inability to keep it, and shows the need for Christ. To the unregenerate, it serves as a mirror to convict sin, a restraint through commands, and a scourge that torments consciences. To believers, although they are not under the law as a covenant of works for justification or condemnation—as Christ fulfilled its demands and bore its penalty (Gal 3:13)—they remain under it as "a rule of life," guiding their conduct and stirring their gratitude for Christ's perfect obedience on their behalf.

TEA WITH THOMAS BOSTON

1. How does knowing that the moral law is in your heart shape your daily walk with God? (Rom 2:15; Ps 19:7; Heb 8:10)

2. How do ceremonial, judicial, and moral laws differ in purpose and application today? (Col 2:16–17; Matt 5:17–18; Rom 2:14–15)

3. How would you explain to an unbeliever that the moral law points to a moral Lawgiver? (Eccl 3:11; Ps 19:1–4; Acts 17:24–28)

4. How would you respond to someone claiming conscience alone is enough for a moral living? (Rom 2:15; Jer 17:9; Eph 4:18–19)

5. How can we teach children and young believers that God's moral law is written in their hearts? (Deut 6:6–7; Prov 22:6; 2 Tim 3:15)

 Shou pu-erh is a dark, aged Chinese tea known for its earthy and weighty flavor, representing the moral law in all its gravity.

 Heavenly Father, write your holy law afresh on my heart, that I may joyfully obey you and walk in gratitude for Christ's perfect fulfillment. Amen.

 "But believers are still under the law as a rule of life, according to which they are to regulate their hearts and lives. It is the pole star that must direct their course to heaven, and is of singular use to provoke and excite them to gratitude to Christ."[1]

---

1. Boston, *Works*, 2:64 (2:59–65).

Day 43

The Moral Law Summarily Comprehended in the Ten Commandments

Q41. *Where is the moral law summarily comprehended?*

A. The moral law is summarily comprehended in the Ten Commandments.

Why do you ask me about what is good? There is only one who is good. If you would enter life, keep the commandments.

MATTHEW 19:17

IN MATTHEW 19:17, JESUS tells a young man seeking life through the law to keep the commandments, referring to the Ten Commandments, encompassing the entire moral law. The man mistakenly understood the law only externally, but Christ revealed the law's deeper demands, exposing his error. God gave the Ten Commandments to the Israelites, who emerged from their Egyptian bondage, because, states Thomas Boston, "they that cast off Satan's yoke, must take on the Lord's." They were given audibly with great majesty at Mount Sinai to instill reverence. God also wrote them on stone tablets, symbolizing their permanence and pointing to the need for a Mediator, ultimately fulfilled in Christ.

Boston argues that God gave the Ten Commandments to renew and confirm the remnants of the natural law, which had been corrupted by the fall, leaving humanity ignorant of its actual state. The natural law was defective in several ways. It could not reveal Adam's first sin or the hidden evils of the heart. As human lifespans shortened and divine revelations became less frequent, ignorance of God and his law increased, necessitating the law's renewal at Sinai to preserve its knowledge. Ultimately, the law exposed human inability to meet its demands, pointing to the need for a Mediator who could fulfill both the law's commands and penalties.

The Ten Commandments summarize the law, condensing its broad scope into key principles. They serve as the foundation for all duties in Scripture, expounded by Christ, the prophets, and the apostles. Boston summarizes the Ten Commandments as follows. The first concerns the object of worship; the second, the means of worship; the third, reverence for God's name; the fourth, sanctifying the Sabbath; the fifth, duties to others as "superiors, inferiors, and equals"; the sixth, preserving life; the seventh, preserving chastity in "heart, speech, and behaviour"; the eighth, lawful gain and growth of wealth; the ninth, maintaining and promoting truth, especially in testimony; and the tenth, contentment "with our condition" and charity toward others. Each commandment also forbids what is contrary to its requirements.

To properly understand the Ten Commandments, Boston outlines several key principles. First, the commandments address not only outward actions but also inward motivations. They demand perfection, meaning partial obedience is unacceptable. For every forbidden sin, God requires the opposite duty; for every duty commanded, God prohibits the opposite vice. Each sin or duty encompasses all similar actions, such as when God forbids murder, he also forbids hurting others, along with envy, malice, and revenge. Moreover, prohibiting an effect also prohibits its cause, as when God forbids the desecration of the Sabbath, he also forbids the actions that lead to it. The commandments of the second table of the law must yield to those of the first when they conflict—our love for others must yield to our love for God. Furthermore, what God forbids is never lawful; what he commands is always our duty. Lastly, we are responsible for ensuring others are mindful of its commands and prohibitions.

TEA WITH THOMAS BOSTON

1. How do the Ten Commandments shape your worship and walk with God? (Exod 20:3–6; Matt 22:37–38; John 14:15)
2. How do the Ten Commandments reveal the law's deeper meaning beyond external obedience? (Matt 19:17; Mark 7:6–8; 1 Sam 16:7)
3. How does God's moral law differ from atheism or other religions? (Rom 2:14–16; Col 2:8; 1 Cor 1:18)
4. Which areas of your life are you most challenged to obey the commandments? (Jas 1:22–25; Rom 6:12–14; Ps 119:9–11)
5. How does teaching children the Ten Commandments help them understand God's holiness and their need for a Savior? (Ps 119:11; Prov 22:6; Rom 7:7)

 Lemon-ginger tea has a sharp, zesty taste, representing the healing and sharp admonishment found in the Ten Commandments.

 Heavenly Father, help me to live according to your commandments, in heart and action, recognizing my dependence on the Spirit. Amen.

 "These two tables were afterwards laid up in the ark of the covenant, in order to be fulfilled by Christ, who is the end of the law for righteousness to every one that believeth."[1]

---

1. Boston, *Works*, 2:67 (2:66–73).

Day 44

Love to God and Our Neighbor, the Sum of the Ten Commandments

> Q42. *What is the sum of the Ten Commandments?*
>
> A. The sum of the Ten Commandments is to love the Lord our God, with all our heart, with all our soul, with all our strength, and with all our mind; and our neighbor as ourselves.

And he said to him, "You shall love the Lord your God with all your heart and with all your soul and with all your mind. This is the great and first commandment. And a second is like it: You shall love your neighbor as yourself.

MATTHEW 22:37–39

CHRIST TEACHES THAT LOVE for God is the foundational command, guiding and regulating how we love ourselves and others. While distinct, the love for our neighbor is equally authoritative and must be paired with love for God, as it serves as the basis for fulfilling the duties of the second table. The Ten Commandments are, Thomas Boston asserts, "a law of love," primarily focused on the heart—"the seat of love." Their purpose is to unite people with God and each other, as holiness is the "cement of hearts."

Love for God requires "knowledge," understanding who God is—a Trinity—and his infinite, eternal, and unchangeable attributes. True love also involves choosing God as our "chief good and portion," our ultimate satisfaction (Ps 73:25). Cleaving to God is another aspect, as love unites the soul to him. High thoughts of God follow as we esteem him with the utmost regard, recognizing him as "the best and greatest" (Song 5:10). Love for God also involves deeply desiring him in this life and the next. Finally, resting in God brings joy and pleasure in him (Song 1:13).

The love required for God is sincere, with our hearts "with him, to him, and for him" (Prov 23:26). It is "strong and vigorous," demanding all our strength (Matt 22:37). It is pure, loving God for his intrinsic excellencies, not just for his gifts (Song 1:3). It is superlative, loving God above all else (Luke 14:26). It is intelligent, grounded in understanding (Mark 12:33). Lastly, it is efficacious, working through actions that serve God's glory and fulfill the law (1 John 3:18). This love is due to God, Boston teaches, because of God's "transcendent excellency and absolute loveliness."

Regarding loving our neighbor, Boston asserts that everyone is our neighbor—"known or unknown, friend or foe, good or bad" (Luke 10:29). While we should hate our neighbors' sins, we are to love them as persons. This principle supports loving our enemies despite their wrongdoing, as they share the common human nature and the potential for happiness with us through God's grace (Matt 5:44).

We must "esteem" our neighbors, recognizing that God creates them (1 Pet 2:17). We are called to "benevolence," desiring the welfare of others and wishing them the best for now and eternity while sharing in their joys and sorrows (Luke 6:31). This love expresses itself through "beneficence," where we seek to do good to others as we would want for ourselves (Matt 7:12). It also includes "complacency," or delight in the good qualities of others, especially in the saints, who reflect the beauty of God's work (1 Pet 2:17). Finally, we are to love our neighbor *as ourselves* by wishing and doing good for them with genuine respect, sincerity, and consistency, regardless of their actions toward us.

TEA WITH THOMAS BOSTON

1. How does loving God supremely affect your daily walk with him? (Deut 6:5; Ps 73:25; Song 1:13)

2. How does your love for God influence your love for others? (Matt 22:39; Luke 14:26; 1 John 3:18)

3. How is loving God wholeheartedly unique to Christianity compared to other beliefs? (Matt 22:37; Deut 10:12; Luke 14:26)

4. How can we practically love our enemies, and how can we grow in this? (Matt 5:44; Luke 10:29; 1 Pet 2:17)

5. How can we help children and young believers understand the importance of loving God and others daily? (Matt 22:37–39; 1 John 3:18; Mark 12:33)

 Rose tea is a fragrant herbal infusion with sweet floral notes, symbolizing the love and devotion due to God and neighbor.

 Heavenly Father, help me love you with all my heart, soul, mind, and strength, and love my neighbors as myself, seeking their good and honoring you in all I do. Amen.

 "Little love to our neighbour is a sad sign of little love to God."[1]

---

1. Boston, *Works*, 2:82–83 (2:74–84).

Day 45

The Preface to the Ten Commandments

Q43. *What is the preface to the Ten Commandments?*

A. The preface to the Ten Commandments is in these words: I am the Lord thy God, which have brought thee out of the land of Egypt, out of the house of bondage.

Q44. *What does the preface to the Ten Commandments teach us?*

A. The preface to the Ten Commandments teaches us that because God is the Lord, and our God, and Redeemer, therefore we are bound to keep all his commandments.

I am the LORD your God, who brought you out of the land of Egypt, out of the house of slavery.

Exodus 20:2

Some view these opening words as part of the first commandment, but the Shorter Catechism considers them a preface to all the commandments. The preface highlights the speaker, the Lord—whom Thomas Boston identifies as "particularly Jesus Christ, who gave this law in the name of the Trinity" (Acts 7:38; Heb 12:24–26)—who brought Israel out of Egypt and commissioned Moses from the burning bush (Exod 3:2–8).

The preface provides three reasons to obey. The first reason is "I am the Lord" (YHWH), signifying God's unity—he is the one true God without "partner, equal, or rival"; the reality of his being—unlike idols existing only in human imagination, God is a "real and true being"; his "necessity, eternity, and unchangeableness"—everything derives existence from him and depends on his will, while he is self-existent and eternal; and, lastly, the "constancy and perpetuity" of his nature and will—"I am that I am" means he remains the same, unchanging in "nature, will, and purposes." The name YHWH entails four reasons for obeying his commandments: his infinite excellence and perfection make him the natural Lord of all, deserving our submission (Jer 10:7); as Creator, he gave us life and governs us as a potter controls his clay (Ps 100:2–3); as supreme Governor and Lawgiver, his will is our law, and disobedience is the highest injustice (Jas 4:12); and, as Preserver, he sustains our existence, and without him, we would vanish like sunbeams without the sun (Rev 4:11).

The second reason for obedience is God's covenant relationship with his people—expressed in the phrase "thy God"—established with Abraham (Gen 17:7) as a covenant of grace, not works, which predates the law and led to Israel's deliverance (Gen 15:13–14). This covenant applies externally to the visible church and savingly to the elect (Rom 4:11–13), binding believers to obedience, not as a condition for salvation (Matt 22:32)—since God declares himself their God before giving commandments. Consent to the covenant obligates obedience (Heb 8:10), brings the honor of serving God, grants privileges such as regeneration and justification (Luke 1:74–75), and aims to restore fallen humanity to holiness and conformity to God (Song 3:9–10).

The third reason for obedience is rooted in God's deliverance of his people from Egypt, demonstrating his faithfulness to his covenant with Abraham and serving as a powerful reminder of his mercy and power. This miraculous deliverance freed Israel from cruel bondage, idolatry, and oppression (Deut 4:20) and was a type of spiritual deliverance through Christ from sin, Satan, and hell (Heb 2:15; 1 Thess 1:10). It highlights God's greatest benefit to his people, binding them to obedience by gratitude (Rom 2:4), and enables them to serve the Lord freely in holiness (Luke 1:74–75), reflecting their spiritual liberation.

TEA WITH THOMAS BOSTON

1. How does knowing God as Creator, Sustainer, and Redeemer shape your devotion and obedience? (Ps 100:2–3; Rev 4:11; Heb 12:24)
2. What does YHWH reveal about God's nature, and how does it compel obedience? (Exod 3:14; Jer 10:7; Jas 4:12)
3. How does God's covenant highlight the uniqueness of biblical salvation over other religions? (Gen 17:7; Rom 4:11–13; Jer 31:33)
4. How does reflecting on God's deliverance strengthen your trust during struggles? (Exod 20:2; 1 Thess 1:10; Heb 2:15)
5. How can you teach young believers that obedience flows from love, not fear? (Heb 8:10; Rom 2:4; Luke 1:74)

 Saffron tea is a rare and luxurious tea known for its vibrant color and rich flavor, symbolizing the royal and foundational nature of the commandments.

 Heavenly Father, you delivered your people and established a covenant of grace—help me to respond with joyful obedience, serving you in holiness all my days. Amen.

 "The true way to attain to the obedience of these commandments, is first to believe that God is our God in Christ, and then to set about the performance of them; first to believe, then to do."[1]

---

1. Boston, *Works*, 2:89 (2:84–91).

Day 46

The First Commandment (1)

Q45. *Which is the first commandment?*

A. The first commandment is, Thou shalt have no other gods before me.

Q46. *What is required in the first commandment?*

A. The first commandment requires us to know and acknowledge God to be the only true God, and our God, and to worship and glorify him accordingly.

You shall have no other gods before me.

Exodus 20:3

Every commandment has an affirmative and a negative aspect. The affirmative implies the negative and vice versa. In the first commandment, the negative is "you shall have no other gods before me," which implies the affirmative, "you shall have me as your God." Thomas Boston teaches that the chief duties of this command are knowing, acknowledging, worshiping, and glorifying the one true God.

We must first know God (1 Chr 28:9), as knowledge is the foundation of religion. We must understand God's existence as the true God (Heb 11:6) and his nature. While we cannot fully comprehend him, we must, Boston maintains, know God as revealed in his "word and works," including his unity (Deut 6:4), Trinity (1 John 5:7), and "infinite, eternal, and unchangeable nature" in the works of "creation, providence, and redemption." We can gain this knowledge through studying God's word, prayer, sermons, and other means of spiritual growth.

Secondly, we must acknowledge God as the only true God and our God (Deut 26:17), which involves firmly believing in his existence and nature as revealed in his word and works. It also includes choosing God as "our God and portion," rejecting other idols, and entering into a "personal covenant" with him (Ps 16:2). We must choose God with "serious deliberation," sever from idols, and embrace faith in Christ as part of the covenant. Acknowledging God also involves recognizing his perfections—his spirit, unchangeableness, omnipresence, omniscience, and omnipotence—and living in a way that reflects them. Moreover, we must acknowledge him through our actions and words, professing our faith openly, even in times of persecution. Such a profession brings glory to God and is fitting for the redeemed (Rom 10:9; 1 Pet 3:15).

Finally, we must worship God and glorify him as our personal God. The first commandment focuses on internal worship, while the second addresses external worship. Internal worship involves our whole being—understanding, will, affections, conscience, memory, and soul. Our mind must be focused on God, thinking about him, meditating on his greatness, esteeming him highly, and believing his truth. Our will must also engage in internal worship, where we choose God as our portion, make him our chief end, deny ourselves, and humbly submit to his will in all circumstances. We must renounce our will and accept God's sovereignty in his commands and providence. Our affections must be devoted to God, with love, desire, delight, joy, sorrow for sin, zeal for his honor, and fear of offending him. Moreover, our conscience must be submitted to God, ensuring that it aligns with his law and rightly accuses or excuses our actions according to his truth. Our memory must also remember God and his works, particularly his word and the great work of redemption. In essence, the whole soul must be engaged in worship, with all faculties directed toward God, from prayer to every other act of devotion, ensuring that we do everything with God as our ultimate end.

TEA WITH THOMAS BOSTON

1. When have you needed courage to acknowledge God, and how did it shape your faith? (Rom 10:9; Matt 10:32–33; 1 Pet 3:15)
2. How do God's infinite, eternal, and unchangeable attributes shape our worship? (Mal 3:6; Ps 90:2; Isa 40:28)
3. How does the first commandment distinguish biblical monotheism from polytheism? (Exod 20:3; Isa 45:5; 1 Cor 8:4–6)
4. How can we cultivate a heart that remembers and meditates on God's works? (Ps 77:11–12; Deut 8:11–14; Heb 2:1)
5. How can we teach children and young believers to reject idols and embrace the covenant of grace with God? (Josh 24:15; 1 Thess 1:9; 2 Cor 6:16–17)

 Sacred tulsi tea is an herbal infusion made from holy basil, known for its calming and devotional qualities, representing the first commandment's call for exclusive devotion.

 Heavenly Father, help me to know you truly, acknowledge you faithfully, and worship you wholeheartedly, that I may glorify you as the only true God. Amen.

 "The altar of our heart should never be without thank-offerings, because we are ever in God's debt; and our good things received while here are more than our evil things, though the latter are deserved, the former not."[1]

---

1. Boston, *Works*, 2:102 (2:92–103).

Day 47

The First Commandment (2)

Q47. *What is forbidden in the first commandment?*

A. The first commandment forbids the denying, or not worshiping and glorifying, the true God as God, and our God; and the giving of that worship and glory to any other, which is due to him alone.

Q48. *What are we specially taught by these words, "before me," in the first commandment?*

A. These words "before me" in the first commandment teach us that God, who sees all things, takes notice of, and is much displeased with, the sin of having any other God.

You shall have no other gods before me.

EXODUS 20:3

THOMAS BOSTON CLAIMS THAT God forbids three sins in the first commandment: atheism, profaneness, and idolatry. Atheism can be speculative or practical. "Speculative atheism" arises from a corrupt mind and is either absolute—denying God's existence—or comparative, denying the true God revealed in Scripture (Ps 14:1; Eph 2:12). "Practical atheism"—whether "heart-atheism" or "life-atheism"—denies God through actions (Titus 1:16). "Heart-atheism" shows a life devoid of reverence for God's presence, word, and works (Ps 36:1). It ignores God's omnipresence and omniscience, treating worship, providence, and redemption with indifference. "Life-atheism" manifests in living as if God does not exist, mocking religion, making no profession of faith, or living contrary to belief, sometimes abandoning faith under persecution (Mark 8:38). All types of atheism undermine faith, and believers must repent and seek Christ's grace to overcome their influence.

Profaneness is "not worshiping and glorifying the true God, as God," dishonoring him by neglecting or opposing the internal duties of worship. Profaneness of the mind includes ignorance of God, false beliefs about his nature, neglecting to think of him, and harboring doubts, errors, or carnal security (Hos 4:6). The will's profaneness involves refusing or falsely covenanting with God, making pacts with the devil, and prioritizing self-interest or human approval over God (Gal 1:10). Profaneness of the affections includes lacking love for God, indulging in carnal desires, resisting communion with him, and taking pleasure in sin (Rom 1:30). Profaneness of the conscience involves allowing it to be misled, failing to restrain sin, or neglecting duty (Isa 5:20). Memory's profaneness includes forgetting God's works and remembering what should be forgotten (Jer 2:32). The whole soul's profaneness neglects heartfelt prayer, fails to give thanks, attributes good to other sources, and resists the Holy Spirit, all of which dishonor God by failing to engage the soul fully in worship (Eph 4:30).

The first commandment also forbids "gross external idolatry" and "subtle heart idolatry." Gross idolatry includes pagan practices—such as worshiping multiple gods, celestial bodies, and deified humans (Job 31:26–27)—and Roman Catholic practices, like venerating saints, angels, the sacramental bread, the cross, and relics, which Boston deemed "heathenism in a new dress" (Matt 4:10). Heart-idolatry occurs when people prioritize anything above God, manifesting in loving something more than God, desiring created things over God, rejoicing more in worldly things than in God, grieving more over worldly losses than sin against God, being more passionate about personal interests than God's honor, fearing people or circumstances more than God, and placing more confidence in human resources than in God. God hates both forms of idolatry and will bring judgment, as in the cases of Israel's golden calf and Demas's love for the world (2 Tim 4:10). Boston calls for repentance for idolatry, relying on Christ's blood for forgiveness and the Spirit's work to cleanse hearts.

TEA WITH THOMAS BOSTON

1. How might you be tempted to deny or neglect God in daily life? (Jer 2:32; Matt 7:21–23; Eph 2:12)

2. What is the difference between speculative and practical atheism, and how does it affect faith? (Ps 14:1; Rom 1:21; Titus 1:16)

3. How do "gross-idolatry" and "heart-idolatry" differ, and why are both dangerous? (Exod 20:3; Rom 1:30; Matt 4:10)

4. What steps can you take to avoid neglect or indifference in your worship of God? (Rom 1:30; Isa 29:13; Ps 14:1)

5. What habits can you encourage in young believers to help them avoid "heart-atheism"? (Ps 36:1; Eph 2:12; Titus 1:16)

 Linden flower tea is a soothing floral tea, representing heart-centered allegiance and devotion in the first commandment.

 Heavenly Father, I confess the many ways I fail to honor you fully. Renew my heart to worship you in spirit and truth. Amen.

 "Love ourselves we may, our souls, our bodies; but the love of God must regulate our love to ourselves, and we must love ourselves in God and for our God, not more than God, nor as much."[1]

---

1. Boston, *Works*, 2:113 (2:103–27).

Day 48

The Second Commandment (1)

Q49. *Which is the second commandment?*

A. The second commandment is, Thou shalt not make unto thee any graven image, or any likeness of anything that is in heaven above, or that is in the earth beneath, or that is in the water under the earth; thou shalt not bow down thyself to them, nor serve them; for I the Lord thy God am a jealous God, visiting the iniquity of the fathers upon the children unto the third and fourth generation of them that hate me: and showing mercy unto thousands of them that love me, and keep my commandments.

Q50. *What is required in the second commandment?*

A. The second commandment requires the receiving, observing, and keeping pure and entire all such religious worship and ordinances as God has appointed in his word.

Exodus 20:4–6

THE FIRST COMMANDMENT DEALS with the object of worship, while the second "the means and ways" of worship. Thomas Boston points out that Roman Catholic catechism absorbs the second commandment into the first—and splits the tenth commandment into two—to prevent exposing their practices that heavily rely on idols and images.

The second commandment requires "receiving, observing, and keeping pure and entire all religious worship and ordinances appointed by God in his word." Boston lists these ordinances to include: Prayer—public, private, and secret, involving petition, confession, and thanksgiving, without a mandated form (Acts 2:42; Matt 6:6); Praises—through singing psalms, publicly and privately, with simplicity and grace in the heart (Ps 149:1; Col 3:16); Reading and hearing God's word—publicly and privately (Acts 15:21; John 5:39); Preaching and hearing the word—including the ministry and its maintenance as a divine ordinance (2 Tim 4:2; 1 Cor 9:14); Administering and receiving the sacraments—baptism and the Lord's Supper (Matt 28:19; 1 Cor 11:23); Fasting—public, private, and secret (Joel 2:12; Matt 6:17); Church government and discipline—with Christ-appointed officers, pastors, doctors, ruling elders, deacons, with a Presbyterian structure of parity and subordination (Heb 3:5; Acts 15); Instructing in the Lord's ways—by ministers and family heads (Gen 18:19); and Spiritual conference and swearing (Deut 6:7).

Our duty toward these ordinances, Boston asserts, is fourfold: Receive them in "our principles and profession" as a sign of subjection to God (Mic 4:5); Observe them in practice, such as praying, singing, and submitting to church discipline (Matt 18:20); Keep them pure by avoiding human inventions and adhering to their divine form (1 Cor 11:2); Keep them intact, neither adding nor subtracting from them (Deut 12:32). Consequently, we must "disapprove, detest, and oppose" all unauthorized worship—superstitious or idolatrous—and work to remove it according to our roles (Deut 7:5).

God requires both internal and external worship. While internal worship focuses on the heart, external worship involves outward actions that glorify God. Some claim that their hearts are devoted to God without engaging in outward worship, but this neglect leaves them vulnerable to idolatry. Since God is the Lord of both body and soul, Boston reasons that believers should worship him with both. Outward worship glorifies God before others, serves as a sign of inward devotion, and strengthens faith through practices like prayer and the Lord's Supper. The commandment further obliges believers to follow God's ordinances, rejecting idolatry and ensuring we neglect nothing in worship.

TEA WITH THOMAS BOSTON

1. What dangers arise when human traditions shape worship, and how can they distort true worship? (Matt 15:9; Col 2:8; Mark 7:7)

2. How does the second commandment emphasize worshiping God in his prescribed way, not human inventions? (Deut 12:32; Col 2:20–23; Lev 10:1–3)

3. How does the second commandment set Christianity apart from religions that create images for worship? (Isa 40:18–20; Acts 17:29; 1 Cor 8:4)

4. How do worship elements—prayer, singing, and hearing the word, sacraments—strengthen your faith and relationship with God? (Ps 149:1; Col 3:16; 2 Tim 4:2)

5. What practical ways can young believers cultivate worship habits? (Matt 6:9–13; Acts 2:42; Heb 10:25)

 Plain green tea is a simple yet refreshing tea, symbolizing pure worship and reverence in the second commandment.

 Heavenly Father, help us worship you with heart and action, keeping your ordinances pure while rejecting all false worship. Amen.

 "Is not God the God of the whole man, the body as well as the soul? Is it not highly reasonable, then, that we worship God with outward bodily worship, as well as with the inward worship of the heart?"[1]

---

1. Boston, *Works*, 2:140 (2:127–43).

Day 49

The Second Commandment (2)

Q51. *What is forbidden in the second commandment?*

A. The second commandment forbids the worshiping of God by images, or any other way not appointed in his word.

Q52. *What are the reasons annexed to the second commandment?*

A. The reasons annexed to the second commandment are God's sovereignty over us, his propriety in us, and the zeal he has to his own worship.

Exodus 20:4–6

THE FIRST COMMANDMENT DEALS with internal worship, while the second addresses external worship, prohibiting creating images for religious purposes (Lev 26:1). These images include graven images (statues carved from wood or stone) and any likeness of things in heaven (birds, sun, moon, stars, God, angels, saints), or on earth (men, beasts, trees, dead bodies), or in the sea (fish). This broad prohibition aims to prevent idolatry by banning all representations for worship, such as depicting the Holy Spirit as a dove or crafting images of invisible beings like God or saints, which is impious and idolatrous. The command is comparatively long because, as Thomas Boston argues, it addresses explicitly humanity's natural inclination to corrupt worship (Jer 2:11), the inherent bias toward idolatry (Rom 1:23), the zeal accompanying such practices (Jer 50:38), and God's "particular zeal for his own worship," leaving no place for image-making (Deut 4:16–19).

This commandment, moreover, forbids worshiping these images, including bowing to them (even slightly, such as bowing the head or knee) or serving them through acts like setting them up, carrying them in processions, building temples or altars, making vows, praying, offering incense, or dedicating days to them (Exod 20:5). Boston rejects the Roman Catholic distinction between absolute and relative worship—the former for worshiping God alone and the latter giving honor to images or saints as a means of honoring God—asserting that no degree of religious reverence toward images is permissible, as they are incapable of receiving even civil honor (Gen 23:7).

The prohibition extends beyond images to all corruptions of God's worship, following the principle that naming one sin—images—includes all similar sins. Thus, the command broadly forbids inventing or adding anything to God's worship and ordinances without a scriptural warrant, such as practices honoring images and relics, church ceremonies (e.g., crossing in baptism, kneeling, festival days), or any human-devised worship elements (Deut 12:30–32). It also prohibits complying with, approving, or using such unauthorized practices, regardless of who institutes them—pope, king, or council—emphasizing adherence solely to God's word (Matt 15:9). In general, the second commandment forbids worshiping God in ways not appointed by his word, including neglecting worship, altering ordinances, showing contempt, mocking worshipers, and hindering or opposing worship in public, family, or private settings.

The reasons for the second commandment are rooted in God's sovereignty, which gives him the sole authority to establish laws for his worship (Jer 7:31). His ownership or propriety of us requires our loyalty, rejecting idolatry and superstition, just as a faithful wife remains devoted to her husband (Hos 9:1). Moreover, God's zeal for pure worship, like that of a jealous husband, leads him to punish false worship to the third and fourth generation (Lev 10:1–2) while showing mercy to those who love and obey him for thousands of generations.

TEA WITH THOMAS BOSTON

1. How does the second commandment challenge your worship practices, and are there subtle forms of idolatry you need to address? (Deut 4:15–19; Jer 2:11; Matt 6:24)

2. What is the biblical basis for prohibiting worship through images, and how does Scripture define proper worship? (Lev 26:1; Deut 12:30–32; John 4:23–24)

3. How can Christians defend worshiping God as God has prescribed rather than creating their own rituals? (Isa 29:13; Deut 12:32; 1 Cor 10:20–21)

4. How can you apply the second commandment's teaching on worship purity to your church's liturgy and personal devotion? (2 Kgs 17:33–34; 1 Pet 2:9; Heb 12:28–29)

5. How can you teach children or new believers to worship God according to his word and avoid creating their own forms of worship? (Deut 6:6–7; Col 3:17; Ps 78:5–7)

White peony is a delicate white tea, symbolizing the simplicity and reverence needed in true worship of God.

Heavenly Father, help us worship you in spirit and truth, rejecting idolatry and honoring you alone, according to your word. Amen.

"Though Christ be a man, yet he is God too, and therefore no image can nor may represent him. . .He is now glorified, and so cannot be pictured as he is even in his human nature."[1]

---

1. Boston, *Works*, 2:151 (2:143–57).

Day 50

The Third Commandment (1)

Q53. *Which is the third commandment?*

A. The third commandment is, Thou shalt not take the name of the Lord thy God in vain: for the Lord will not hold him guiltless that takes his name in vain.

Q54. *What is required in the third commandment?*

A. The third commandment requires the holy and reverent use of God's names, titles, attributes, ordinances, word, and works.

You shall not take the name of the LORD your God in vain, for the LORD will not hold him guiltless who takes his name in vain.

Exodus 20:7

Thomas Boston states that the first commandment concerns *who* we worship, the second *how*, and the third *in what manner*. To take God's name in vain means using it falsely—by invoking his name to lie or swear falsely; lightly—by using his name without reverence, purpose, or just cause; and wickedly—by using it in cursing or blasphemy.

Boston outlines what God's name entails. First, it includes the names God takes for himself in Scripture, such as YHWH, Lord, God, and I AM, along with the names of the Father, Son (Jesus Christ, Immanuel), and Holy Spirit. Second, it includes the respective titles assumed by the persons of the Trinity, such as the God of Abraham, the King of kings, and the Comforter. Third, it refers to God's attributes—his eternal, unchangeable, infinite, and omniscient nature, as well as his mercy, grace, and justice. Fourth, God's name entails his ordinances, such as prayer, praise, sacraments, oaths, and lots. Fifth, his word, especially in Scripture, is how God reveals his name. Lastly, God's works—including creation, providence, and judgment—display his name.

Our duty regarding God's glorious name involves using it appropriately in all its parts, as he has provided it for us. We must actively use God's name as we are called, in thought—meditating on his names and attributes (Prov 30:4), in words—speaking or writing about it to glorify him, a duty for all and especially for those gifted to write, and in deeds—practicing religious duties like prayer, reading, hearing, communicating, and swearing by his name in lawful oaths (1 Pet 3:15). This use is necessary for God's glory (1 Cor 10:31), our good (Prov 18:10), and the good of others by commending God's name to them (John 17:26).

Boston asserts that we must also use God's name "holily and reverently" in all these actions, with faith—believing in what his name represents (Heb 11:6), fear—approaching with reverence (Deut 28:58), and singleness of purpose. We must use God's names and titles with awe, recognizing his sovereignty (Jer 5:22). We should handle his attributes reverently, applying them appropriately (Ps 130:4). When engaging in God's ordinances—prayer, singing, preaching, or hearing—we must honor his authority (Jer 4:2). We must swear lawful oaths in truth, judgment, and righteousness, ensuring the matter is true, understood, and just, glorifying God (Josh 7:19). When using lots, we must approach them reverently, trusting in God's decision (Prov 16:33). We should treat God's word with godly fear, obeying in both hearing and action (Ps 138:2). Likewise, we should use God's works to honor him and benefit ourselves and others. Ultimately, our conduct must align with the name we profess, as inconsistency causes his name to be blasphemed (Phil 1:27; Rom 2:24).

TEA WITH THOMAS BOSTON

1. How can you deepen your reverence for God's name daily? (Prov 30:4; Ps 130:4; 1 Cor 10:31)
2. What does it mean that God's name includes his names, titles, attributes, and works? (Exod 3:14; Matt 28:19; Ps 138:2)
3. How does the biblical view of God's name differ from using divine names in other religions or secular contexts? (Exod 20:7; Isa 42:8; 1 Pet 3:15)
4. How can you ensure prayer, worship, and sacraments honor God's name? (Jer 4:2; Mal 1:11; Col 3:17)
5. How can you teach children or young believers to honor God's name? (Deut 6:6–7; Prov 22:6; Eph 6:4)

 Peppermint tea is a refreshing herbal tea, representing fresh speech and clarity in honoring God's name.

 Heavenly Father, help us to honor your holy name in thought, word, and deed with reverence, faith, and sincerity. Amen.

 "To speak of God is the great end of speech that is given to man, made to be the mouth of the creation; and therefore our tongue is called our glory, by which we ought to contribute to the displaying of the glory of God."[1]

---

1. Boston, *Works*, 2:161 (2:157–64).

Day 51

The Third Commandment (2)

Q55. *What is forbidden in the third commandment?*

A. The third commandment forbids all profaning or abusing of anything whereby God makes himself known.

Q56. *What is the reason annexed to the third commandment?*

A. The reason annexed to the third commandment is that however the breakers of this commandment may escape punishment from men, yet the Lord our God will not suffer them to escape his righteous judgment.

You shall not take the name of the LORD your God in vain, for the LORD will not hold him guiltless who takes his name in vain.

Exodus 20:7

THOMAS BOSTON STATES THAT believers violate the third commandment by neglecting to use God's name as required and by abusing or profaning it. We fail to honor God's name when we do not meditate on his titles and attributes, fail to speak of him for his glory and the good of others, neglect to profess our faith when called upon, and misuse his ordinances. Similarly, declining a lawful oath when duty requires it is also a failure to honor God's name. Profaning God's name occurs when we use it ignorantly, irreverently, superstitiously, or wickedly. Ignorance of God's nature leads to using his name in vain. Irreverence occurs when his name is spoken carelessly in casual conversation. Using God's name superstitiously—such as invoking it without faith for healing or protection—also profanes it. More gravely, profane swearing, sinful imprecations, perjury, and blasphemy directly dishonor God.

God's name is abused or profaned in ordinances like prayer, praise, reading, hearing his word, and taking oaths. We take his name in vain in prayer when we pray hypocritically, coldly, or without faith and fail to prepare our hearts beforehand or reflect on our prayers afterward. Singing psalms without understanding or affection likewise profanes God's name. Similarly, hearing God's word inattentively, without understanding or with a critical spirit, dishonors his name. Oaths, whether taken unlawfully or with mental reservations, misuse God's name. Refusing a lawful oath—when required for God's glory and the good of others—is also sinful. Misusing lots—whether by treating them irreverently, using them for trivial matters, or turning an appeal to God's providence into a game—profanes his name. Finally, we dishonor God's name when his word is misapplied, used for vain arguments, treated irreverently, or when his works and creatures are abused for sinful purposes. Hypocrisy, scandalous conduct, and reviling religion all dishonor God's name.

Boston claims we also break the third commandment by malignancy, hypocrisy, and dishonorable living. Malignancy opposes God's truth, while hypocrisy turns worship into an empty ritual (2 Tim 3:5). Believers dishonor God when they are ashamed of their faith or when their actions bring reproach. Apostasy worsens this dishonor by preferring evil over God's ways.

The reason attached to this commandment is that God will not hold guiltless those who take his name in vain. While people may excuse themselves or avoid human punishment, God will personally address the matter and punish those who profane his name. No one will escape judgment; each offender will be singled out and punished as if he or she were the only one guilty. God's honor compels him to punish those who dishonor his name, ensuring no one escapes. Ultimately, God will glorify his name, whether in mercy or judgment.

TEA WITH THOMAS BOSTON

1. How do you prepare your heart and ensure sincerity in your prayers? (Matt 6:5-6; Ps 62:8; Rom 12:12)
2. How can we avoid misusing God's name in prayer, praise, or reading his word? (Deut 28:58; Jer 4:2; Ps 138:2)
3. How should we respond to those who use God's name irreverently in public? (Isa 8:13; Ps 111:9; 1 Pet 3:15)
4. How does misusing God's name in everyday speech affect our Christian witness? (Matt 5:34-37; Eph 4:29; 2 Cor 6:17)
5. What practices can help young believers avoid hypocrisy in worship or prayer? (2 Tim 3:5; Isa 29:13; Matt 15:8)

 Hyssop tea is an herb known for its cleansing properties, symbolizing sacredness, and purity in our speech and actions.

 Heavenly Father, help me honor your name in all I think, say, and do, guarding against hypocrisy and irreverence, that I may glorify you in everything. Amen.

 "How is the name of God abused by ignorant persons, while they mention the name of one they know not whom, and speak of him they know not what?"[1]

---

1. Boston, *Works*, 2:165 (2:164-85).

Day 52

The Fourth Commandment (1)

Q57. *Which is the fourth commandment?*

A. The fourth commandment is, Remember the Sabbath day, to keep it holy. Six days shalt thou labor, and do all thy work: but the seventh day is the Sabbath of the Lord thy God: in it thou shalt not do any work, thou, nor thy son, nor thy daughter, thy man-servant, nor thy maid-servant, nor thy cattle, nor thy stranger that is within thy gates: for in six days the Lord made heaven and earth, the sea, and all that in them is, and rested the seventh day: wherefore the Lord blessed the Sabbath-day, and hallowed it.

Q58. *What is required in the fourth commandment?*

A. The fourth commandment requires the keeping holy to God such set times as he has appointed in his word; expressly one whole day in seven, to be a holy Sabbath to himself.

Q59. *Which day of the seven has God appointed to be the weekly Sabbath?*

A. From the beginning of the world to the resurrection of Christ, God appointed the seventh day of the week to be the weekly Sabbath; and the first day of the week, ever since, to continue to the end of the world, which is the Christian Sabbath.

Exodus 20:8–11

THE FOURTH COMMANDMENT CONCERNS the time of worship. Remembering the Sabbath means keeping it holy by ceasing from labor. Thomas Boston teaches that Scripture speaks of three types of Sabbath rest: temporal rest, referring to the weekly Sabbath; spiritual rest, which is the soul's rest from sin (Heb 4:3); and eternal rest, celebrated in heaven where saints rest from their labors (Heb 4:9, 11). The focus here is on the weekly Sabbath, where God has put "a note of remembrance" upon this command, emphasizing the need for careful observance and honoring of this sacred day.

In the Old Testament, the Jews had several holy days, which Christ abolished by fulfilling the law. The fourth commandment, Boston argues, is "remember the Sabbath Day to keep it holy"—not "remember the Seventh day"—emphasizing the moral duty to observe a Sabbath for worship on the seventh day in the Old Testament or the first day since Christ's resurrection. Boston condemns holidays devised by humans (1 Kgs 12:33), as God alone can "make a holy day; for who can sanctify a creature but the Creator, or time but the Lord of time?"

This command binds all people throughout all ages. God appointed this command and gave it to Adam before any ceremonial laws (Gen 2:3). The Sabbath remains a moral obligation for all, not just Jews. Christ also affirmed its enduring nature, even after "divine authority" changed the Jewish Sabbath of the seventh day to the Christian Sabbath of the first day (Matt 24:20).

Believers must observe the Sabbath as a 24-hour day, not just from sunrise to sunset or only during public worship. As opposed to the Jewish Sabbath from Friday evening to Saturday evening, the Christian Sabbath runs from Sunday morning to evening (John 20:19; Matt 28:1). After all, the Sabbath commemorates Christ's resurrection, which occurred early in the morning on the first day of the week, the Lord's Day (Rev 1:10). Psalm 118:24—"This is the day that the LORD has made; let us rejoice and be glad in it"—prophesizes the Sabbath of the first day of the week, referring to the day of Christ's resurrection, when Jesus, the rejected stone, became the cornerstone. The psalmist calls for rejoicing and thankfulness, celebrating this day as a reminder of God's work of redemption.

TEA WITH THOMAS BOSTON

1. How do you prepare your heart for the Sabbath, and what changes can you make to observe it better? (Exod 20:8–11; Ps 118:24; John 20:19)
2. How does the command to keep the Sabbath holy distinguish Christianity from atheism and other worldviews? (Isa 58:13–14; Matt 24:20; Heb 4:9–11)
3. How do temporal, spiritual, and eternal rest shape your understanding of the Sabbath? (Heb 4:3; 4:9–11; Gen 2:2–3)
4. What steps can you take to keep the Sabbath holy in your routine? (Deut 5:12–15; Matt 28:1; Rev 1:10)
5. How can you teach children or young believers the importance of observing the Sabbath for spiritual growth? (Lev 23:3; Ps 118:24; John 20:19)

 Tazo Calm Chamomile is a decaffeinated blend designed for rest and rejuvenation, symbolizing the restful, intentional observance of the Sabbath.

 Heavenly Father, help me honor the Sabbath as a sacred day of rest and worship, remembering Christ's resurrection and the call to rejoice in it. Amen.

 "All days are his; but this is his in a peculiar manner, Rev. 1:10. He has set a mark on it for himself to be reserved to himself."[1]

---

1. Boston, *Works*, 2:201 (2:186–97).

Day 53

The Fourth Commandment (2)

Q60. *How is the Sabbath to be sanctified?*

A. The Sabbath is to be sanctified by a holy resting all that day, even from such worldly employments and recreations as are lawful on other days; and spending the whole time in the public and private exercises of God's worship, except so much as is to be taken up in the works of necessity and mercy.

Q61. *What is forbidden in the fourth commandment?*

A. The fourth commandment forbids the omission, or careless performance, of the duties required, and the profaning the day by idleness, or doing that which is in itself sinful, or by unnecessary thoughts, words, or works, about our worldly employments or recreations.

Q62. *What are the reasons annexed to the fourth commandment?*

A. The reasons annexed to the fourth commandment are God's allowing us six days of the week for our own employments, his challenging a special propriety in the seventh, his own example, and his blessing the Sabbath day.

EXODUS 20:8–11

Thomas Boston urges believers to sanctify the Sabbath by "holy rest" and "holy exercise." To sanctify the Sabbath means to set it apart for God's use, dedicating it to worship and service. It is a day of rest from worldly work and recreation, including labor, studies, and civil duties. However, works of necessity and mercy to preserve life or prevent harm are exceptions, such as extinguishing a fire or saving an animal, or good works like caring for the sick or helping the poor.

Both people and animals are to rest on the Sabbath, with the command emphasizing that the head of the household, children, servants, and even strangers must not profane the day. The Sabbath rest is made holy by respecting God's command.

The Sabbath is also sanctified by holy exercise, including public worship (word, sacraments, prayer) and private worship (family devotion). These activities should focus on stirring up grace and love for God. The day should be marked by a withdrawal from earthly concerns and a delight in spiritual activities, making the Sabbath a time for physical rest and spiritual renewal. "Our delights should be heavenly this day," asserts Boston, "not to please the flesh but the spirit."

Believers violate the Sabbath by omitting duties, such as failing to prepare for it and neglecting private, family, or public worship. It is also profaned by "careless performance," where duties are done hypocritically, with a worldly mindset, or with a cold, heartless attitude. Idleness violates it, such as unnecessary sleeping or idle conversation. Sinful actions, like swearing or discouraging others from worship, further profane the day. Finally, unnecessary thoughts or actions, like focusing on worldly work or recreation, violate it. These violations require repentance and reliance on Christ's atoning blood for forgiveness.

The reasons annexed to this command are unique, as no other command has such a positive and negative aspect. God is concerned with the Sabbath "on which all religion depends" as its observance or disregard reflects the condition of the rest of our religious practice. People often diminish the service of this day, either by considering "resting from labor" as sufficient to keep the Sabbath or by assuming the keeping ends after public worship. This commandment has less inherent clarity than others. While a Sabbath is morally natural, the requirement of one day in seven is based on God's will.

TEA WITH THOMAS BOSTON

1. Do you struggle to keep the Sabbath holy? How can God's grace help? (Isa 58:13–14; Heb 10:24–25; Matt 11:28)

2. Why does God require rest and worship on the Sabbath, and how do these reflect his character? (Gen 2:3; Exod 31:13; Lev 19:30)

3. How does delighting in God on the Sabbath renew your soul and strengthen your faith? (Ps 92:1–4; Col 3:16; Rev 1:10)

4. How can you avoid profaning the Sabbath through idleness or neglect? (Isa 58:13; Mal 1:13; Heb 10:25)

5. How can you teach children or young believers to value the Sabbath and develop godly habits? (Exod 20:8–11; Deut 6:6–7; Prov 22:6)

Hojicha is a roasted green tea with a warm, nutty flavor, perfect for quiet contemplation and honoring the Sabbath.

Heavenly Father, help me to honor the Sabbath with holy rest and worship, setting aside worldly concerns to delight in you and renew my spirit. Amen.

"The Sabbath-rest resembles that of heaven, which is a rest without a rest, wherein the soul is most busy and active, serving the Lord without weariness."[1]

---

1. Boston, *Works*, 2:196 (2:197–204).

Day 54

The Fifth Commandment (1)

Q63. *Which is the fifth commandment?*

A. The fifth commandment is, Honor thy father and thy mother: that thy days may be long upon the land which the Lord thy God gives thee.

Q64. *What is required in the fifth commandment?*

A. The fifth commandment requires the preserving the honor and performing the duties belonging to every one in their several places and relations, as superiors, inferiors, or equals.

Honor your father and your mother, that your days may be long in the land that the LORD your God is giving you.

Exodus 20:12

THE FIRST FOUR COMMANDMENTS focus on "piety toward God," while the last six emphasize "righteousness toward man." Thomas Boston explains that the fifth commandment—"Honor your father and your mother"—applies not only to natural parents but also to superiors, including seniors (1 Tim 5:1–2), the gifted (Gen 4:20; 45:8), and those in authority—husbands, masters, church leaders, and rulers. It likewise applies to inferiors (such as children, wives, and servants) and equals (including siblings, friends, and neighbors), in keeping with Christ's command to "love your neighbor as yourself." Since God assigns honorable roles to all, we must show inward esteem and outward respect to others (1 Pet 2:17).

The fifth commandment, the first of the second table, emphasizes relational duties and influences the sixth to tenth commands. Disobedience often begins with rejecting parental authority (Prov 30:17). This command is directed toward inferiors, as submission is challenging due to human pride. At the same time, referring to superiors as "fathers and mothers" reminds them to treat their inferiors with kindness (Num 11:12) and encourages inferiors to honor their superiors willingly (1 Cor 4:14–15). Boston states that God ordains roles—superiors, inferiors, and equals—to reflect his sovereignty, enhance societal harmony, and maintain order in a fallen world.

The relationship between husband and wife, the first in the world and foundational for all others, is governed by God's laws that promote harmony when followed and chaos when neglected. A wife must submit to her husband in heart, words, and actions but only insofar as it aligns with her duty to God (Col 3:18–19). This submission is reasonable due to God's ordinance, the woman's weaker nature, and the harm caused by rejecting it. A husband must love his wife and fulfill all responsibilities with kindness, avoiding bitterness in heart, words, or deeds, which balances authority with compassion (Eph 5:25–31). The duties husband and wife owe to each other include conjugal love, cohabitation, peaceful living, pleasing one another, companionship and joy, mutual honor, sympathy and support, faithfulness, and spiritual care.

In the relationship between parents and children, children are to obey their parents in all lawful things, including love, reverence, respectful behavior, submission to guidance and correction, bearing with their parents' weaknesses, and supporting them in need. Parents are responsible for their children's care from the womb through adulthood, including protecting their unborn child, praying for their children, providing for their physical and spiritual needs, and ensuring raising them in the covenant. Parents are to exercise their authority gently, avoiding provocation that could discourage their children (Col 3:20–21).

The relationship between masters and servants involves mutual duties. Servants are to obey their masters in all lawful matters, with sincerity and fear of God, not just when being observed. Masters, in turn, are to treat their servants justly and fairly, providing what is owed by law and charity, keeping in mind that they, too, have a heavenly Master to whom they are accountable (Col 3:22; 4:1).

TEA WITH THOMAS BOSTON

1. How does understanding the roles of superiors, inferiors, and equals in the fifth commandment reflect God's design for order in society? (1 Pet 2:17; Num 11:12; 1 Cor 4:14–15)

2. How does the fifth commandment influence the sixth to tenth? (Exod 20:12; Matt 7:12; Prov 30:17)

3. How does Christianity's view of authority differ from secular or atheistic views on family and leadership? (Rom 13:1–2; 1 Tim 5:1–2; Col 3:22)

4. How can you show respect for those in authority at work or in church, especially when you disagree with them? (1 Pet 2:13–17; Rom 13:1–2; Eph 6:5–8)

5. How can we teach children to honor their parents and those in authority, following Christ's example? (Eph 6:1–3; Col 3:20; 1 Tim 5:1–2)

Golden osmanthus oolong is a fragrant tea with floral notes, symbolizing the honor and fragrance of the fifth commandment.

Heavenly Father, help me honor the roles you have ordained in my relationships, submitting with love and humility to promote peace and order. Amen.

"The wisdom of God is to be adored, this command having a general influence on all the rest, so that we cannot transgress the rest but we transgress this in the first place."[1]

---

1. Boston, *Works*, 2:206 (2:204–51).

Day 55

The Fifth Commandment (2)

Q65. *What is forbidden in the fifth commandment?*

A. The fifth commandment forbids the neglecting of, or doing anything against, the honor and duty which belongs to every one in their several places and relations.

Q66. *What is the reason annexed to the fifth commandment?*

A. The reason annexed to the fifth commandment is a promise of long life and prosperity (as far as it shall serve for God's glory, and their own good) to all such as keep this commandment.

Honor your father and your mother, that your days may be long in the land that the LORD your God is giving you.

Exodus 20:12

The fifth commandment forbids neglecting or acting against the honor and duty owed in various relationships. Thomas Boston states that husbands and wives sin against one another in many ways. They violate conjugal love through unkindness, neglect, selfishness, unreasonable suspicions, and public shaming. They fail to show sympathy, reproach one another, and speak contemptuously, all contrary to marital love. They break faithfulness through infidelity, desertion, and neglecting their duty to care for one another's souls, often correcting faults in anger or public shame. Wives sin by rejecting reverence, acting imperiously, and being disobedient, like Queen Vashti (Esth 1:10–12). Husbands sin by being harsh, domineering, failing to protect or provide, mistrusting, and even beating their wives (Eph 5:25, 29).

Children sin by disobeying, dishonoring, and cursing their parents (Prov 30:17), resisting instruction (Prov 5:7), rejecting correction (Prov 13:18), and refusing discipline (Deut 21:18–19). Some mock their parents' weaknesses, waste resources, and act hard-heartedly in distress (Prov 19:26), while others dishonor them by choosing careers or marrying without consent (Gen 26:34–35). Parents sin by neglecting their children's spiritual and moral upbringing, fostering idleness, or teaching vice. Some overindulge or favor one child over another (Gen 25:28), while others are harsh, breaking their children's spirits with extreme discipline and bitter words (Col 3:21).

Masters and servants sin against each other in various ways. Servants sin by disrespecting, disobedient, and performing their duties with pride or resentment. Some openly refuse or complete tasks poorly, showing irreverence and refusing correction. Many are unfaithful, offering eye service that results in loss or dishonesty, while others bring scandal to religion by resisting good or religious duties (Eph 6:5–6). Masters sin by withholding fair wages, overworking servants, denying time for rest and worship, and showing constant harshness. They neglect the spiritual well-being of their servants, failing to care for their souls (Eph 6:9).

The reason attached to this command is a promise of long life and prosperity (Eph 6:2), encouraging obedience. Long life is a mercy, as it is an honor (Prov 16:31), a time for the exercise of godliness (2 Tim 2:22), a means to experience God's goodness (1 John 2:13), and an opportunity to glorify God and serve his kingdom (Phil 1:23–24). It is "the first command with promise" because, argues Boston, it is the first and most significant of the second table, encompassing all others. Violating any command starts with dishonoring parents. This command is unique, offering a specific promise, unlike the general mercy of the second commandment. While the law requires perfect obedience, Christ, through the new covenant of grace, renews the promise for believers, offering rewards for sincere obedience through faith in him (1 Tim 4:8).

TEA WITH THOMAS BOSTON

1. How do you honor your relationships with your spouse, parents, and friends? (Eph 5:25; Prov 30:17; 1 Pet 2:17)

2. What does the fifth commandment teach us about reflecting God's holiness and authority in relationships? (Eph 5:25–33; Col 3:20–21; 1 Pet 5:1–5)

3. How can you explain the fifth commandment to someone who thinks respect for authority is outdated? (1 Tim 5:1–2; Rom 13:1–2; Titus 3:1)

4. How can you show the relevance and benefit of Christianity's view on authority in today's world? (Eph 5:25–29; Prov 29:2; 1 Pet 3:7)

5. How can we teach children and young believers to honor authority in their daily lives at work, home, and church? (Rom 13:1–2; Eph 6:5–8; Col 3:22–24)

Apple cinnamon tea has a comforting, sweet-spiced flavor, symbolizing the warmth and familial bonds of the fifth commandment.

Heavenly Father, help me honor our relationships with kindness and reverence, reflecting your love and bringing glory to your name. Amen.

"He that sins before a child, sins twice, for he may expect that his sin shall be acted over again."[1]

---

1. Boston, *Works*, 2:227 (2:251–60).

Day 56

The Sixth Commandment (1)

Q67. *Which is the sixth commandment?*

A. The sixth commandment is, Thou shalt not kill.

Q68. *What is required in the sixth commandment?*

A. The sixth commandment requires all lawful endeavours to preserve our own life and the life of others.

You shall not murder.

EXODUS 20:13

THE SIXTH COMMANDMENT EMPHASIZES preserving life, recognizing that life belongs to God, who alone has the authority to take it. It applies to both our own life and the life of our neighbor, forbidding us from killing either ourselves or others. God succinctly states this commandment, along with the next three, because, Thomas Boston argues, "there is more light of nature for them than those proposed at greater length." While the command is short, it carries great significance, as it aligns with the natural law that underscores the sanctity of life. The command reflects the principle that we are not the masters of our own or others' lives, and it is rooted in the broader moral teaching to love our neighbor as ourselves.

The fifth commandment requires us to preserve both our souls and bodies. To preserve the soul—the most precious part of a person—is to avoid sin, which is a deadly poison that wounds the soul and leads to eternal death (Prov 11:19). One must nourish the soul through means of grace, "eating Christ's body, and drinking Christ's blood" (John 6:53–58).

Boston outlines three lawful means of preserving the body. First, self-defense against unjust violence done to us (Luke 22:36), using minimal force and avoiding vengeance (Luke 6:29). Second, providing for the body's necessities—moderating food, shelter, clothing, rest, exercise, and medicine (Eph 5:29). Third, regulating affections is essential for physical and spiritual well-being as a calm disposition promotes health, even as uncontrolled passions harm both body and soul (Prov 17:22).

We must preserve our neighbor's soul by living a holy life that edifies others (Matt 5:16). We should "instruct, warn, reprove, and admonish" them when necessary (Jude 23), offering comfort in distress and praying for them. We cannot, like Cain, ask, "Am I my brother's keeper?" We are responsible for one another's spiritual well-being.

We must, teaches Boston, preserve our neighbor's life, including protecting the innocent against unjust violence as opportunity allows, whether concerning their name, goods, or life (Ps 82:3–4; Prov 24:11–12), following the people's example in saving Jonathan's life (1 Sam 14:45). We must provide necessities to those in need, for withholding them makes us guilty before God (Jas 2:15–16). Cultivating charitable thoughts, love, compassion, meekness, and kindness helps prevent harm (Eph 4:31–32). A "peaceable, mild, and courteous" demeanor (Prov 15:1) in appearance, words, and conduct preserves life. Lastly, regarding injuries, we should interpret situations favorably (1 Cor 13:5, 7) and avoid conflict whenever possible, even relinquishing our rights, as Abraham did with Lot. We should endure genuine wrongs (Col 3:12–13), practice patience, seek reconciliation, forgive offenses, and respond to evil with good (Matt 5:44).

TEA WITH THOMAS BOSTON

1. How do you reflect on the sanctity of life and preserve your soul and body? (1 Cor 6:19–20; Matt 5:16; 1 Pet 2:2)

2. How does preserving life impact your daily decisions, relationships, and self-care? (Eph 5:29; Prov 3:7–8; Rom 12:1)

3. How does the sixth commandment contrast with secular views on euthanasia and abortion? (Ps 139:13–16; Jer 1:5; Exod 20:13)

4. How does the sanctity of life counter the idea that humans are merely evolved animals? (Jas 3:9; Acts 17:26; Col 1:16)

5. How can you help young believers understand the sacredness of their soul and body? (1 Tim 4:8–10; 1 Cor 6:19–20; Eph 6:4)

Red clover tea is a light and earthy herbal tea, symbolizing life-affirming values and honoring the sanctity of life in the sixth commandment.

Heavenly Father, help us to honor the sanctity of life by preserving both our own and our neighbor's soul and body. Amen.

"Where the choice is, suffer or sin, God requires and calls us in that case to suffer."[1]

---

1. Boston, *Works*, 2:261 (2:260–65).

Day 57

The Sixth Commandment (2)

> Q69. *What is forbidden in the sixth commandment?*
>
> A. The sixth commandment forbids the taking away of our own life, or the life of our neighbor unjustly, or whatsoever tends thereunto.

You shall not murder.

EXODUS 20:13

THE SIXTH COMMANDMENT FORBIDS the unjust taking of one's own life or another's, as well as anything that leads to it. Thomas Boston argues that we destroy our own souls by neglecting salvation and the means of grace (Prov 8:34, 36), since the soul's life depends on prayer, knowledge, public ordinances, and private duties. Ignoring these leads to spiritual self-destruction. Resisting God's "quickening work in the soul" suppresses convictions and hinders spiritual recovery (Prov 29:1). Persisting in impenitence despite God's calls to repentance leaves one resolutely in ruin (Ezek 18:30–31). Ultimately, unbelief and rejecting Christ (John 5:40) is equivalent to soul-murder.

The command forbids taking one's own life—like Saul, Ahithophel, and Judas—a grave sin condemned by God's law and civil laws. It also prohibits actions that indirectly lead to self-harm, such as entertaining suicidal thoughts (Jonah 4:3), "discontent and fretfulness" (Ps 37:8), "immoderate grief" (2 Cor 7:10), and anxiety over life's cares (Matt 6:31). Neglecting one's body by denying necessary food, sleep, and care (Col 2:23) is equally forbidden, as is intemperance in eating, drinking, or indulging in sensual pleasures, which shortens life and ruins the soul (Luke 21:34). Excessive labor (Eccl 2:22–23) and exposing oneself to unnecessary dangers (Matt 4:7) also violate this command. Thus, God requires us to preserve our bodies through moderation, care, and trust in him.

Boston argues that this command forbids killing a neighbor's soul, which happens by living a sinful example (Matt 18:7), using liberty uncharitably (Rom 14:15), or directly contributing to another's sin—whether by "commanding, counseling, joining, provoking, soliciting, or teaching" falsehood (Isa 5:20). It also includes consenting to sin (Acts 9:1) or neglecting one's duty to prevent or recover others from sin (Ezek 3:18). Failure to warn, admonish, or reprove others, as in Eli's case (1 Sam 3:13), contributes to their ruin. Indifference toward a sinner's condition (Ezek 9:4) or rejoicing at their sin (Prov 14:9) further adds guilt.

The commandment also forbids unjustly taking a neighbor's life, except in cases of public justice (Gen 9:6), lawful war (Judg 5:23), and necessary self-defense (Exod 22:2–3), where God—the Lord of life and death—authorizes judgment. Any other act of taking life is murder, including direct killing, as in Cain's case, and unjust executions, wars, and duels. Beyond physical murder, indirect forms are also condemned, such as "heart-murder" through anger, envy, hatred, revenge, rejoicing in others' misfortunes, and cruelty. "Tongue-murder" includes quarrels, bitter words, railing, reviling, mocking, and cursing, which can cause profound harm. "Eye-murder" is expressed through wrathful looks and gestures of hatred. "Hand-murder" occurs both by omission—neglecting to help those in need—and by commission—through acts of oppression, persecution, or physical violence. Furthermore, one can be guilty by causing others to sin or consenting to unjust actions, as seen in David's role in Uriah's death. Boston urges self-examination, recognizing the spiritual depth of the commandment and seeking Christ's blood for cleansing from guilt.

TEA WITH THOMAS BOSTON

1. How does neglecting prayer and Scripture lead to spiritual harm, and how can you avoid this? (Prov 8:34, 36; 29:1; John 5:40)
2. How can you guard against harmful thoughts or feelings during personal struggles? (Jonah 4:3; Ps 37:8; 2 Cor 7:10)
3. How does the Christian view of life challenge the evolutionary perspective of human existence? (Acts 17:26; Col 1:16; Jas 3:9)
4. What steps can you take to prevent anger, envy, or hatred from damaging your relationships? (Matt 5:21–22; Eph 4:31–32; 1 Pet 3:9)
5. What habits can help young believers avoid actions that harm themselves or others? (Prov 4:23; Matt 7:12; 2 Cor 7:10)

Turmeric tea is an earthy, warming beverage known for its healing properties, representing the protection of life mandated by the sixth commandment.

Heavenly Father, help me honor the sanctity of life by guarding my heart, avoiding harm to myself and others, and seeking your forgiveness through Christ. Amen.

"The tongue, however little a member it is, is the Lord of life and death."[1]

---

1. Boston, *Works*, 2:273 (2:265–76).

Day 58

The Seventh Commandment (1)

Q70. *What is the seventh commandment?*

A. The seventh commandment is, Thou shalt not commit adultery.

Q71. *What is required in the seventh commandment?*

A. The seventh commandment requires the preservation of our own and our neighbor's chastity, in heart, speech, and behavior.

You shall not commit adultery.

EXODUS 20:14

THE SEVENTH COMMANDMENT FOCUSES on preserving both our own and our neighbor's chastity and purity. Since God is holy and the devil is unclean, we must strive for purity in every aspect of life. Thomas Boston asserts that God places this command after the sixth to emphasize that chastity is as important as life itself. The commandment forbids adultery, all forms of uncleanness, and anything that leads to such sins.

The seventh commandment calls us to preserve chastity in heart, speech, and behavior, with duties that apply to single and married life. In single life, purity is angelic, while impurity is devilish. In married life, conjugal chastity involves fidelity to one's spouse and moderation within the marriage, as described in 1 Thess 4:3-5, which emphasizes sanctification and abstaining from fornication. Chastity begins with the heart, where we must guard our thoughts and affections (Job 31:1). Chastity also extends to speech, where our words must be pure and gracious, reflecting the condition of our hearts (Col 4:6). Finally, chastity encompasses our behavior, ensuring we keep our bodies undefiled and present ourselves modestly (1 Pet 3:2).

To preserve chastity, we must, Boston urges, guard our senses, particularly our eyes and ears, which are entry points for temptation (Prov 7:21-22). Temperance in "meat, drink, sleep, and recreation" is also necessary, as excessive indulgence can lead to impurity (Luke 21:34). Moreover, we must avoid corrupt company, as bad associations can erode virtue (Prov 5:8-9). Honest work counters idleness, which often leads to temptation, as seen in the lapses of David and Dinah (2 Sam 11:2; Gen 34:1). For those who lack the gift of celibacy, marriage serves as a safeguard against fornication (1 Cor 7:2, 9). Within marriage, conjugal love and affection should protect the relationship, preventing it from becoming a snare (Prov 5:19-20). Lastly, we must avoid situations leading to sin, as Joseph wisely fled from temptation (Gen 39:12).

The command also requires us to preserve the chastity of others in heart, speech, and behavior. We are responsible for preventing others' sin—otherwise, if we cause it, we share in the guilt. To preserve others' chastity, we must avoid actions that may tempt them. For example, modest apparel (1 Tim 2:9) and appropriate behavior can prevent others from stumbling, as seen in the story of Judah and his daughter-in-law (Gen 38:14-16) and David's sin with Bathsheba (2 Sam 11:2). Moreover, we must help protect others' purity, offering support and correction as needed, such as encouraging married couples to live in love, rescuing those in danger, and guiding children and servants away from harmful influences. Our bodies are temples of God, and we must keep them pure, as defiling them brings God's judgment (1 Cor 3:16-17).

TEA WITH THOMAS BOSTON

1. How can you guard your heart against impure thoughts and maintain mental purity? (Job 31:1; Matt 5:28; Phil 4:8)

2. How does the command to preserve chastity impact your daily habits, and how can you live it out more intentionally? (1 Pet 3:2; Rom 12:1-2; 2 Tim 2:22)

3. How would you explain the importance of chastity in a world that values sexual freedom? (1 Cor 6:18-20; 1 Thess 4:3-7; Rom 12:2)

4. How does self-control in food, sleep, and recreation help preserve purity, and how can you apply this? (Luke 21:34; 1 Cor 9:27; Gal 5:22-23)

5. How can you help young people avoid temptation and develop habits to preserve chastity? (Prov 5:8-9; Eph 5:3; 2 Tim 2:22)

 Rose and hibiscus tea is a vibrant floral tea with tart and sweet notes, symbolizing the pure love and beauty of the seventh commandment.

 Heavenly Father, help me preserve purity in heart, speech, and behavior, guarding against sin and honoring your holiness in all I do. Amen.

 "The corruption of the heart makes people liable to be chained with Satan's fetters by the ears as well as the eyes."[1]

---

1. Boston, *Works*, 2:278 (2:276-80).

Day 59

The Seventh Commandment (2)

> Q72. *What is forbidden in the seventh commandment?*
> A. The seventh commandment forbids all unchaste thoughts, words, and actions.

You shall not commit adultery.

EXODUS 20:14

THOMAS BOSTON OUTLINES VARIOUS sins condemned under the seventh commandment, warning against all forms of sexual immorality. It includes unnatural lusts such as homosexuality (Rom 1:24–27), bestiality (Lev 18:23), and incest (Lev 18:6), emphasizing that such unnatural acts can never be legal. Adultery—including bigamy and polygamy—is also forbidden, with both parties held accountable for the sin (Heb 13:4). Fornication between single persons is similarly condemned (Col 3:5–6), as it brings God's wrath (Eph 5:5). Rape, or forcing someone into sexual immorality, is a capital crime (Deut 22:25). "Secret uncleanness," whether in waking or sleeping moments, is also forbidden (Eph 5:12). Lastly, "immoderate and unseasonable use" of the marriage bed, or engaging in prostitution, is prohibited (1 Thess 4:3–4; 1 Cor 7:5).

The commandment, contends Boston, forbids various uncleanness beyond gross acts. First, uncleanness in the heart includes "unclean imaginations, thoughts, purposes, and affections," even if not acted upon, as they are sinful before God (Matt 5:28; 15:19). A habitual, sinful mindset is especially abominable. Second, uncleanness in words refers to obscene language and corrupt communication, which reflect a filthy heart (Eph 4:29). Such speech is dangerous, leading others into sin, and even disguised filthy expressions can be harmful. Finally, uncleanness in actions includes behaviors like wanton looks (2 Pet 2:14), immodest actions (Isa 3:16), and suggestive behavior (Prov 7:13). These actions, even if not entirely explicit, can lead to further sin and defile both the actor and the observer.

Boston then elaborates on all occasions that may lead to lust or corrupt chastity. These include immodest apparel (Prov 7:10), which entices lust instead of fulfilling God's purpose for clothing. Keeping bad company is another danger, as Solomon warns to avoid the path of a strange woman (Prov 5:8), and Joseph's flight from temptation serves as a model. Idleness is "the nursery of all filthiness" (Ezek 16:49). "Intemperance, gluttony and drunkenness" increase susceptibility to uncleanness (Prov 23:30–33; Jer 5:8). Promiscuous dancing, often considered harmless, is an incentive to lust and has been condemned by both Scripture and the church (Rom 13:13; 1 Pet 4:3). Unnecessary delay of marriage (1 Cor 7:7–9), unjust divorce (Matt 5:32), and a lack of conjugal affection can also lead to sexual immorality. Lastly, the Catholic doctrines of forbidding lawful marriages (1 Tim 4:3), permitting unlawful unions (Mark 6:18), and promoting celibacy through entangling vows are further violations of this commandment.

Boston urges those who have fallen into uncleanness to repent and walk humbly, recognizing that God may leave lasting consequences as a mark of his displeasure, even if they forget the sin. Those who remain standing must be vigilant, especially young people, as this sin often entices the youthful, leaving lasting marks of God's judgment even into later years. To guard against sexual sins, believers should rely on Christ's strength, maintaining a spiritual mindset while guarding their hearts and senses. They must mortify sinful desires, avoid immodest company and careless speech, and pray earnestly for God's protection (Ps 119:37).

TEA WITH THOMAS BOSTON

1. How can you guard your heart and maintain purity? (Prov 4:23; Matt 5:28; Phil 4:8)
2. How can Christians defend biblical marriage and purity today? (Matt 19:4–6; Eph 5:3; Rom 12:2)
3. What steps help avoid temptation and protect purity? (Prov 5:8; 1 Cor 6:18; Ps 119:37)
4. How can you speak pure and edifying words? (Eph 4:29; Col 3:8; Matt 12:36)
5. How can you help youth rely on God and stay accountable? (Phil 4:13; Ps 119:9–11; Gal 5:16)

 Strawberry leaf tea has a mild, earthy flavor, symbolizing faithfulness and nurture in the seventh commandment.

 Heavenly Father, grant me strength to walk in purity, guard my heart and mind against all uncleanness, and help me rely on your grace to resist temptation. Amen.

 "Watching over our senses. These are the ports at which Satan breaks in, and ruins people's purity."[1]

---

1. Boston, *Works*, 2:277 (2:280–85).

Day 60

The Eighth Commandment (1)

Q73. *Which is the eighth commandment?*
A. The eighth commandment is, Thou shalt not steal.

Q74. *What is required in the eighth commandment?*
A. The eighth commandment requires the lawful procuring and furthering the wealth and outward estate of ourselves and others.

You shall not steal.

EXODUS 20:15

THE EIGHTH COMMANDMENT CONCERNS protecting and promoting people's "goods and outward estate" through lawful means. It highlights that Christianity extends to civil actions such as "working, buying, and selling," emphasizing that God's law governs every aspect of life. It affirms private ownership of property, rejecting the idea of a universal sharing of goods. While forbidding theft, it also requires actively seeking the well-being of oneself and others through honest means.

Thomas Boston lists seven ways to seek and promote our wealth and outward estate lawfully. First, we must look to God for provision, recognizing that success comes from him (Deut 8:18; Matt 6:11). Second, we should balance diligent effort with trust in God, avoiding both laziness and anxiety (1 Tim 5:8; Ps 127:1). Third, we must engage in a lawful calling, using it diligently and skillfully to avoid idleness (Eph 4:28; Prov 10:4). Fourth, we are to enjoy the fruits of our labor to meet our needs and condition (Eccl 5:18–19) while avoiding waste. Fifth, God calls us to frugality, wisely managing resources without extravagance or miserliness, so that we can do good to others (Prov 21:20; John 6:12). Sixth, we should avoid actions that may harm our financial stability, such as unnecessary lawsuits, rash guarantees, or engaging in ventures beyond our ability (1 Cor 6:1–8; Prov 11:15). Lastly, we must cultivate moderation toward worldly goods by valuing them rightly, avoiding covetousness, and being content with God's provision (Phil 4:5; Heb 13:5).

God commands us to promote and protect others' wealth by giving everyone their due by fulfilling obligations in all relationships (Rom 13:7) and treating others as we want to be treated, following the golden rule (Matt 7:12). Specifically, God commands us to protect our neighbors from harm and loss when we have the opportunity, making us responsible for each other's well-being (Deut 22:1). We must also act with integrity in all our dealings, ensuring honesty, faithfulness, and justice to avoid stealing or deceit (Ps 15:2; Zech 7:10). Practically, Boston teaches that if we wrong someone, whether through theft, fraud, or carelessness, we are obligated to make restitution, returning stolen goods or their value and doing all we can to repair the damage (Lev 6:2–4; Luke 19:8). In matters of loans, we should lend generously to those in need (Matt 5:42), ensuring that we only borrow what we can repay and avoid causing harm to others (Exod 22:14). Lastly, giving to the poor is an essential duty, where we are to help according to our ability, prioritizing those in greatest need, especially fellow believers, and doing so with a generous and compassionate heart (Luke 11:41; Gal 6:10). In sum, the duty of giving to the poor should be carried out with sincere motives to honor God, with respect and dignity for the poor, in a cheerful and voluntary spirit, and in an amount proportionate to what the Lord has provided—guided by wisdom and love.

TEA WITH THOMAS BOSTON

1. In what areas of your life do you need to rethink your attitudes toward wealth and possessions? (Matt 6:19–21; Luke 12:15; 1 Tim 6:9–10)
2. Why does the eighth commandment affirm private property, and how does it reflect God's design for society? (Exod 20:15; Deut 19:14; Acts 5:4)
3. How does Christianity's view of wealth differ from secular materialism and greed? (Matt 6:24; Luke 16:13; 1 Tim 6:6–10)
4. How can you cultivate contentment and avoid covetousness and waste? (Phil 4:11–13; Heb 13:5; Prov 30:8–9)
5. How can you help children and young believers develop habits of generosity and frugality? (Prov 21:20; Deut 15:10–11; 2 Cor 9:7)

Yerba mate is a bold, energizing tea, symbolizing honest labor and the stewardship required by the eighth commandment.

Heavenly Father, help me honor you by promoting the well-being of others through honest work, wise stewardship, integrity, and generous giving. Amen.

"For though our good works and honest dealings with men will not save us, yet our ill works and unrighteous dealings will damn us."[1]

---

1. Boston, *Works*, 2:289 (2:286–93).

Day 61

The Eighth Commandment (2)

> Q75. *What is forbidden in the eighth commandment?*
>
> A. The eighth commandment forbids whatsoever does, or may, unjustly hinder our own, or our neighbor's, wealth or outward estate.

You shall not steal.

EXODUS 20:15

THE SINS FORBIDDEN IN the eighth commandment are unjustly hindering our own wealth and others' wealth. Thomas Boston specifies various ways we could hinder our wealth. Idleness, or failing to engage in honest work, leads to poverty and sin, exposing one to danger and temptation (2 Thess 3:11). "Carelessness, sloth, and mismanagement" in our work result in missed opportunities and can ultimately lead to theft (Prov 18:9). Neglecting God's blessing by failing to acknowledge his role in providing wealth denies his power and provision (Deut 8:18). "Wastefulness and prodigality" squander resources and often result in poverty and disarray (Prov 21:17). Engaging in rash decisions, such as unnecessary lawsuits or unwise ventures, can ruin one's financial stability (1 Cor 6:6–8; Prov 11:15). Anxious care over wealth, driven by distrust and worry, robs one of the comfort and peace that possessions should bring (Matt 6:31). Finally, sordidness, when people hoard wealth without being enjoyed or used appropriately, renders possessions as useless as if they did not exist (Eccl 6:1–2). Since we are merely stewards of

God's resources, we must manage them faithfully, recognizing that we are accountable to God and must use them according to his will.

We could hinder our neighbor's wealth by direct or indirect stealing. People steal directly, either secretly (theft) or violently (robbery). Examples include "stealing of persons," kidnapping people for sale or use (1 Tim 1:9–10), and "stealing of substance," whether from the public (harming the nation), the church (sacrilege; Rom 2:22), or private individuals (single theft), with even small thefts excluding one from heaven (1 Cor 6:9–10).

Indirect stealing originates in the heart through discontent, envy, and covetousness (Heb 13:5), leading to sinful actions. Boston identifies these actions as including idleness—when healthy individuals live without working and become a burden to others (Eph 4:28)—and illicit gain, which involves profiting from sinful activities such as unlawful trades, bribery, or the sale of spiritual things. Family frauds occur when husbands waste family resources, wives or children embezzle, or servants steal from their masters (Titus 2:9–10). Cheating in commerce involves exploiting others by lying about wares, tampering with goods, or using false measures (Lev 25:14). "Fellowship fraud" includes defrauding partners in shared ventures (Lev 6:2). Neighborhood violations occur when people move landlines or damage properties (Prov 22:28) or betray those who rely on us. Hiring injustice occurs when people abuse hired goods, shirk work, or withhold wages (Jas 5:4). Other forms of theft include retaining goods by not restoring lost or stolen items (Deut 22:1–2), borrowing issues by failing to repay loans or refusing to lend to the needy (Luke 6:35), and uncharitable use through hoarding wealth unjustly, which harms communities (Isa 5:8). Oppression denies others their rights through power (Ezek 22:7), and partaking with thieves involves encouraging, receiving, or ignoring theft (Ps 50:18). Finally, unmercifulness is considered theft, as withholding charity from the poor robs them of their God-given right (Eph 4:28).

TEA WITH THOMAS BOSTON

1. How can you cultivate contentment and trust in God's provision? (Heb 13:5; Phil 4:11–13; 1 Tim 6:6)
2. How does Scripture condemn both direct and indirect stealing? (1 Tim 1:9–10; 1 Cor 6:9–10; Lev 6:2)
3. How does Christian stewardship differ from secular views of wealth? (Deut 8:18; Matt 6:24; 1 Tim 6:10)
4. How does biblical teaching on generosity challenge materialism and individualism? (Luke 12:15; 2 Cor 9:7; Acts 20:35)
5. How can you teach young believers the value of honest work? (Prov 22:6; Eph 4:28; 2 Thess 3:10)

Chicory root tea has a robust, slightly bitter flavor, symbolizing hard work and contentment in the eighth commandment.

Heavenly Father, help me to be a faithful steward of your gifts, avoiding idleness, dishonesty, and greed. Amen.

"Laziness will make a thief, either directly or indirectly."[1]

---

1. Boston, *Works*, 2:287 (2:293–312).

Day 62

The Ninth Commandment (1)

Q76. *Which is the ninth commandment?*

A. The ninth commandment is, Thou shalt not bear false witness against thy neighbor.

Q77. *What is required in the ninth commandment?*

A. The ninth commandment requires the maintaining and promoting of truth between man and man, and of our own and our neighbor's good name, especially in witness bearing.

You shall not bear false witness against your neighbor.
Exodus 20:16

Thomas Boston emphasizes the sacredness of truth, which reflects God's very nature as truth itself. He contrasts truth and light with lies and darkness. The ninth commandment to uphold truth involves two key aspects. First, we must speak the truth consistently (Eph 4:25), exercising discretion and avoiding excessive talk. Truth requires harmony of "the tongue with the heart" (Ps 15:2), meaning we should speak as we think, lest we become false speakers despite speaking factual words. Moreover, our words must align with reality, for mistaken beliefs cannot make falsehoods true (2 Thess 2:11). Second, we must bear witness faithfully. In judicial witness-bearing, we must truthfully testify when called by civil or ecclesiastical authority. In extrajudicial witness-bearing, even outside formal settings, we must speak the truth when asked or when we witness unjust accusations against a neighbor, vindicating their innocence if we know the truth.

Witness-bearing, whether judicial or extrajudicial, is a divine calling that upholds justice and honors God. Judicial witness-bearing requires truthfulness when called by lawful authority, while extrajudicial witness-bearing obliges individuals to speak the truth in private matters or defend an innocent neighbor. In both cases, the truth must be spoken "fully, freely, clearly, and sincerely" without concealing relevant facts or distorting reality. In addition, maintaining a good name is a duty for all believers, as a good reputation is precious (Prov 22:1). This involves speaking truthfully about oneself, prudently concealing unnecessary secrets (Prov 25:9–10), and defending our reputation when unjustly attacked. Maintaining a good name requires avoiding evil actions and appearances of evil (1 Thess 5:22), as a righteous life naturally preserves one's reputation. Following Paul's exhortation, Christians must pursue what is true, honest, just, pure, lovely, and praiseworthy, safeguarding their witness and name (Phil 4:8).

The ninth commandment also calls us to maintain and promote our neighbor's good name, consistent with truth by holding a charitable opinion and hoping the best for them (1 Cor 13:7), desiring and rejoicing in their reputation even if it surpasses our own (Rom 1:8), grieving over their faults and the dishonor sin brings (2 Cor 12:21), covering their weaknesses with love rather than exposing them (1 Pet 4:8), and acknowledging their gifts and graces, however small (1 Cor 1:4–7). We are also called to defend their innocence when unjustly accused (1 Sam 22:14), be slow to accept negative reports and quick to welcome good ones (1 Cor 13:6–7; Ps 15:3), discourage slanderers and tale-bearers (Ps 101:5), and give loving admonition and correction to prevent sin and preserve their reputation (Lev 19:17). Boston prescribes these actions as vital to fulfilling the command to love our neighbor and protect their reputation, seeing it as an essential part of living in harmony and truth with others.

TEA WITH THOMAS BOSTON

1. How do you understand truth in your daily life, and how can you apply it to your conversations? (Prov 12:17; Ps 15:2; Eph 4:25)

2. Think of a time you defended someone's reputation—how did you handle it, and what was the outcome? (1 Sam 22:14; 1 Cor 13:6–7; Lev 19:17)

3. How does the command to bear witness to the truth challenge the modern relativistic view of truth? (John 18:37; Isa 5:20; Zech 8:16)

4. What steps can we take to protect our own and others' reputations in everyday life? (Prov 25:9–10; 1 Thess 5:22; Jas 3:5–10)

5. What habits can we teach young believers to help them speak the truth and avoid gossip? (Matt 12:36–37; 1 Pet 4:8; Prov 16:28)

 Ginkgo biloba tea is known for its cognitive-enhancing properties, symbolizing the wisdom and caution required in the ninth commandment.

 Heavenly Father, help me uphold truth in all my words and actions, faithfully bearing witness to justice and protecting my reputation and others. Amen.

 "Truth is to the soul as light is to the body; and they that walk in the light, will walk in truth."[1]

---

1. Boston, *Works*, 2:312 (2:312–17).

Day 63

The Ninth Commandment (2)

Q78. *What is forbidden in the ninth commandment?*

A. The ninth commandment forbids whatsoever is prejudicial to truth, or injurious to our own or our neighbor's good name.

You shall not bear false witness against your neighbor.

Exodus 20:16

The ninth commandment forbids anything that harms truth, which is sacred to God. Thomas Boston states that people can harm truth judicially and extrajudicially. Judicially, truth suffers in courts when judges pervert justice, such as when they "pervert judgment, respecting persons, and passing unjust sentences" (Prov 17:15), when people make false accusations or forged charges (Luke 19:8), when defendants deny just charges (Prov 28:13), or when witnesses conceal or distort the truth (Lev 5:1). Extrajudicially, truth is harmed in everyday conversation through unfaithfulness in keeping promises (Rom 1:31), silence when truth should be spoken (Lev 5:1), and speaking unseasonably (Eccl 3:7), maliciously (Ps 52:2–3), or falsely (Matt 26:60–61). Moreover, equivocation or deceptive language violates the commandment (Gen 26:7–9). The commandment requires honesty and integrity in public and private life, emphasizing the need to defend and uphold truth in all situations.

Boston categorizes lies into four types: "jesting lies"—false statements made humorously or playfully to deceive for amusement (Hos 7:3);

"officious lies"—told to benefit oneself or others, such as covering faults or excusing wrongs (Job 13:7); "pernicious lies"—harmful false reports spread with the intent to harm another person, considered a severe sin (Prov 6:17); and "rash lies"—false statements made out of surprise or carelessness, such as the incorrect report about Absalom's actions (2 Sam 13:30).

This command forbids actions that harm our reputation. We can breach it in our hearts—by thinking too highly or too lowly of ourselves (Rom 12:16); in our actions—by engaging in immoral behavior that damages our reputation (1 Sam 2:24); and in our words—by unnecessarily revealing faults (Prov 25:9–10), unjustly accusing ourselves (Job 27:5–6), or denying sins when called to confess (Prov 28:13).

The ninth commandment forbids actions that harm our neighbor's reputation in several ways. We may be guilty in our hearts through unjust suspicions, assuming the worst of others without cause (1 Tim 6:4), uncharitable judging, condemning others harshly beyond what their actions justify (Matt 7:1), or misconstructing others, always interpreting their actions negatively, even when innocent (Rom 3:8). We may also be guilty of contempt—underestimating and belittling others, especially for their virtues (Luke 18:9–11), or envy—resenting the well-deserved success or reputation of others (Num 11:29) or rejoicing in their disgrace (Jer 48:27). Fond admiration, excessively idolizing people, can lead to imitating their vices (1 Cor 4:6).

Boston identifies various ways the tongue can harm others' reputations. These include remaining silent when one should defend others, unnecessarily revealing faults, exaggerating minor mistakes, reviving past sins, betraying secrets, undermining someone's deserved reputation out of envy, spreading false reports, slandering, backbiting, tale-bearing, encouraging slander, rejecting someone's defense, mocking or scorning others, and using abusive language to attack someone's character. They damage relationships and reputations, underscoring the importance of speaking with care and charity.

TEA WITH THOMAS BOSTON

1. Have you ever been convicted for speaking carelessly or harming someone with your words? How did it affect your relationship with them and God? (Prov 18:21; Eph 4:29; Col 3:8)

2. How can you actively uphold truth and integrity in your relationships? (Ps 51:6; John 8:32; 1 Tim 3:15)

3. How does understanding the seriousness of lies in the ninth commandment help us engage with people of other faiths who view truth differently? (Prov 6:16–19; Rom 3:4; 1 John 2:21)

4. How can you speak the truth in love, even when difficult? (Eph 4:15; Col 3:9; 1 Tim 2:8)

5. What habits can help young believers avoid lying or harmful speech? (Ps 34:13; Matt 5:37; Jas 3:5–10)

Clove tea has a warm, aromatic flavor, symbolizing discernment and integrity in the ninth commandment.

Heavenly Father, help me uphold truth and protect others' reputations with integrity, love, and justice. Amen.

"They who value not their reputation, will hardly be found to value either their souls or bodies."[1]

---

1. Boston, *Works*, 2:315 (2:317–31).

Day 64

The Tenth Commandment (1)

Q79. *Which is the tenth commandment?*

A. The tenth commandment is, Thou shalt not covet thy neighbor's house, thou shalt not covet thy neighbor's wife, nor his man-servant, nor his maid-servant, nor his ox, nor his ass, nor anything that is thy neighbor's.

Q80. *What is required in the tenth commandment?*

A. The tenth commandment requires full contentment with our own condition, with a right and charitable frame of spirit toward our neighbor, and all that is his.

You shall not covet your neighbor's house; you shall not covet your neighbor's wife, or his male servant, or his female servant, or his ox, or his donkey, or anything that is your neighbor's.

EXODUS 20:17

THOMAS BOSTON STATES THAT the tenth commandment strikes the root of sin by addressing the heart's sinfulness and discontentment that fuel the violations of other commandments. It requires us to be weaned from worldly desires and remain indifferent to what we have or lack. This includes holding possessions loosely (Luke 14:33), viewing created things as temporary (Ps 4:6), relying on God for security (1 Sam 2:1), and using material goods moderately (1 Cor 7:29-31). The commandment shows that even lawful things can become objects of lust.

This commandment requires complete contentment with our condition, recognizing that while sin in our state is not from God, all other circumstances are according to his will. True contentment means submitting to God's will by accepting his choice of our comforts (Ps 47:4); resigning to his providence, whether in abundance or need (Matt 16:24); and aligning our minds to our circumstances, as Paul exemplified (Phil 4:11-12). True contentment, Boston argues, lies not merely in passive submission but in willingly embracing God's decisions.

True contentment requires submitting to God's will without complaint (Mic 7:9), remaining quiet and patient under hardships (Lam 3:27-29), and being at ease without what we lack (Phil 4:6, 12). It involves bearing the absence of comforts with joy in the Lord (Hab 3:17-18), finding pleasure even in affliction (2 Cor 12:10), and recognizing our condition as best for us at the time (Job 1:21). Finally, it means resting patiently in our condition "without the least squint look for a change of it, till God's time come" (2 Sam 15:25-26).

We should be content with our condition because God, the Creator, governs all things wisely (Matt 20:15) and "Infinite Wisdom" guides our situation for a greater purpose (Matt 10:30). All the good in our lives is undeserved (Lam 3:22), and even hardships are mixed with mercy. Moreover, the struggles we face result from our sin (Lam 3:39), and therefore, we should not complain but accept our lot with humility (Mic 7:9).

This command requires us to love our neighbor as ourselves, not just in word or deed but from the heart, recognizing that they are God's creation (Rom 13:9). We should respect what belongs to our neighbor, taking care of their possessions as we would our own (Deut 22:1). We must desire their welfare and prosperity, including their honor, life, and good name, even for our enemies, when it aligns with God's honor and their spiritual good (Rom 12:20). God calls us to rejoice in our neighbor's welfare, avoiding jealousy or coveting what they have (Rom 12:15). We must sympathize with them in their afflictions, sharing in each other's sorrows. However, Boston states that no one can perfectly obey this command, as all are born with original corruption, lacking the holy nature required by the law. People can only fulfill it through regeneration, where they are renewed by partaking in the new nature of Christ.

TEA WITH THOMAS BOSTON

1. How can we cultivate contentment instead of comparing ourselves to others? (Ps 47:4; Matt 16:24; Phil 4:11–12)

2. What does the tenth commandment reveal about the root cause of sin? (Exod 20:17; Jas 4:1–3; Matt 15:19)

3. How does contentment with God's provision distinguish Christianity from secularism or atheism? (Matt 20:15; 1 Sam 2:1; Ps 47:4)

4. How can we grow in loving our neighbors and desiring their well-being, even when difficult? (Rom 13:9; Gal 6:2; Deut 22:1)

5. How can we avoid coveting and instead rejoice in our neighbor's blessings? (Rom 12:15; Matt 7:12; Heb 13:5)

 Lemongrass tea is a light, citrusy tea, representing clarity and honesty in keeping the tenth commandment.

 Heavenly Father, grant me contentment in your will, a heart that loves my neighbor, and trust in your wisdom, through Christ my Lord. Amen.

 "Contentment makes a man happy and easy in every condition. It is the stone that turns all metals into gold, and makes one to sing and rejoice in every condition."[1]

---

1. Boston, *Works*, 2:341 (2:332–50).

Day 65

The Tenth Commandment (2)

Q81. *What is forbidden in the tenth commandment?*

A. The tenth commandment forbids all discontentment with our own estate, envying or grieving at the good of our neighbor, and all inordinate motions and affections to anything that is his.

You shall not covet your neighbor's house; you shall not covet your neighbor's wife, or his male servant, or his female servant, or his ox, or his donkey, or anything that is your neighbor's.

Exodus 20:17

THE TENTH COMMANDMENT FORBIDS discontent with one's own condition and envy toward others. It also forbids lustful desires and inordinate affections toward what God has either withheld or set aside for others. It calls us to align our hearts with God's will, rejecting discontent and covetousness.

Thomas Boston states that discontent with our condition arises from "tormenting passions," which flow from a heart uneasy with our circumstances, presupposing a desire for what we lack and rebelling against God's will. Discontent shows itself in sorrow, anger, and even "heart-blasphemy" that questions God's wisdom, justice, and mercy. It comes from blinded judgment, pride, unmortified desires, and unbelief. The consequences are severe. It breaks communion with God, disrupts spiritual and daily responsibilities, and harms relationships. It also torments the soul, weakens the body, kills joy, breeds ingratitude, and leads to greater sins like murder, occult practices, and blasphemy. Discontent is a rebel against providence, a despiser of grace, and "a hell in the bosom, and a lively emblem of the pit of darkness." Remedies include embracing God in Christ, humility, faith, avoiding fixation on personal crosses, religious exercises, busyness, early curbing, living by faith, and cultivating gratitude (1 Thess 5:18).

The tenth command addresses envy and grudging against our neighbor's condition. Envy emerges when we desire or resent the prosperity of others. It can manifest in sorrow over their success, anger at their well-being, and a deep sense of injustice when others seem to have more than us (1 Cor 13:4). This sinful attitude stems from a covetous heart and prideful selfishness. Envy also damages our relationship with God, as we resent his blessing others (Matt 20:15). It harms our neighbors by fostering ill will or even wishing them harm (Gen 37:11). The consequences of envy are far-reaching: it disrupts personal peace, destroys relationships, and even fuels extravagant sins, such as murder or hatred (1 Kgs 21). The cure for envy lies in finding our satisfaction in God alone, embracing his provision, and cultivating a heart that rejoices in others' blessings rather than resenting them. Learning to love God and our neighbors with humility enables us to rejoice in the good fortune of others, as John the Baptist did, demonstrating a selfless and godly attitude (John 3:30).

Boston warns that we can lust for what we possess and what belongs to others. Lust for one's own possessions becomes sinful when we cling too tightly, pursue excessively, or seek unlawful ends, disregarding God's honor and the purpose of our possessions (1 Cor 6:12; Luke 14:33). Lust for our neighbor's possessions is inordinate when we desire the unlawful or pursue lawful items for wrong reasons, showing impatience, discontent, or obsession (Matt 14:4; Gen 25:30). Lust progresses from innocent desire to full-blown sin, warring against grace and bringing spiritual harm (Rom 7:7). It leads to ungodliness, deceit, and worldly desires (Titus 2:12), harming both the soul and body.

TEA WITH THOMAS BOSTON

1. How do you deal with discontentment, and how can the tenth commandment guide you? (Exod 20:17; 1 Thess 5:18; Phil 2:3–4)

2. Have you struggled with envying others' success? How can you learn to celebrate their blessings in light of God's will? (1 Cor 13:4; Matt 20:15; Gen 37:11)

3. How does practicing contentment reflect trust in God's sovereignty and wisdom? (Rom 8:28; Prov 14:30; Ps 131:1–2)

4. How would you respond to someone who views discontentment as a healthy drive for success rather than a sin? (Phil 4:11–12; Jas 1:14–15; Eccl 5:10)

5. What habits can we teach young believers to guard them from envy and discontentment? (Col 3:16–17; Heb 12:1–2; Prov 4:23)

Cinnamon bark tea has a warm, spicy flavor, symbolizing the inner purity and contentment required to resist covetousness.

Heavenly Father, help me reject discontent, envy, and lust, and cultivate gratitude, humility, and love for you and others. Amen.

"Discontent is in the heart like a serpent gnawing the bowels, and makes a man as a moth to himself, consuming him."[1]

---

1. Boston, *Works*, 2:352 (2:350–74).

Day 66

Man's Inability to Keep the Law Perfectly

> Q82. *Is any man able perfectly to keep the commandments of God?*
>
> A. No mere man since the fall is able in this life perfectly to keep the commandments of God, but does daily break them in thought, word, and deed.

Surely there is not a righteous man on earth who does good and never sins.
ECCLESIASTES 7:20

ECCLESIASTES 7:20 EMPHASIZES THE universal sinfulness of humanity, asserting that no one is perfectly righteous. Thomas Boston distinguishes between being "evangelically just" (justified by grace) and "legally just" (perfectly obedient to the law), with the latter impossible for humans (Ps 143:2). Since Christ had not yet appeared, this statement in Ecclesiastes applies to all people on earth, whereas only in heaven do the redeemed attain such perfection.

Boston stipulates that legal perfection is complete conformity to God's commands, requiring a "perfection of the principle of action"—loving God with all one's heart; a "perfection of the parts of obedience"—where failure in one part makes one guilty of all (Jas 2:10); a "perfection in degree"—where obedience must reach the highest standard, as sincerity alone is insufficient;

and a "perfection of duration"—where obedience must continue without lapse to the end.

Before the fall, Adam could perfectly keep God's commands, as he was created upright and given the strength to obey. After the fall, Christ perfectly kept the law, fulfilling what Adam failed to do, offering salvation for the elect through his complete obedience in every aspect—principle, parts, degree, and duration. Saints in heaven will attain perfect obedience, having been set free from sin and all the possibility of sinning (Heb 12:23). However, no human in this life—elect or not—can perfectly obey due to sin's corruption. Believers will attain perfection only in the afterlife, as spiritual growth is gradual.

While the godly may do good, they still sin daily by breaking God's commands in deeds, words, and thoughts. They do what is contrary to God's command or fail to do what is required—publicly, privately, or secretly. They speak what they should not, failing to speak what they should or speak inappropriately (Jas 3:6). Believers also sin by entertaining improper thoughts, neglecting good ones, or failing to govern their thoughts as the law requires (Matt 5:28).

Boston states that perfection is not attainable in this life for several reasons. Scripture affirms that all people sin and that anyone claiming to be without sin is self-deceived (1 John 1:8). Even the best have both corrupt and gracious principles, leading to an ongoing spiritual struggle until death (Gal 5:17). The need for constant prayer for forgiveness (Matt 6:12) shows that sin remains, as sinless people do not need pardon. Moreover, the spirituality and breadth of God's law, combined with human weakness, demonstrate that perfection is unattainable, and those who claim to have reached it misunderstand the law's true nature. Regarding John's statement that "whosoever is born of God does not commit sin" (1 John 3:9), Boston clarifies that it does not mean saints are completely sinless but rather that they do not sin with full consent, delight, or habitually, as unregenerate people do. It also refers to saints not committing "the sin unto death" (1 John 5:17–18).

TEA WITH THOMAS BOSTON

1. How do you feel the tension between wanting to obey God and struggling with sin? (Rom 7:18–19; Gal 5:17; 1 John 1:8)
2. Which is hardest to submit to God—your thoughts, words, or deeds? How can you grow? (Ps 19:14; Col 3:17; 2 Cor 10:5)
3. How does Christ's perfect obedience fulfill what Adam failed to do? (Rom 5:18–19; Phil 2:8; Heb 5:8–9)
4. How would you explain that being born of God does not mean Christians are sinless? (1 John 1:8–10; 3:9; 5:17–18)
5. How can parents and mentors help young believers develop habits of confession and prayer? (Matt 6:12; 1 John 1:9; Col 4:2)

Sage tea has an earthy flavor, reflecting the humility and discernment needed to recognize our daily sins and dependence on God's grace.

Heavenly Father, I acknowledge my inability to keep the law. Help me depend on Christ's perfect obedience and pursue holiness in the Spirit. Amen.

"Let the struggling saints long for heaven, for there the perfection they would fain be at shall be attained, and not till then, comforting them under all their failures."[1]

---

1. Boston, *Works*, 2:383 (2:374–83).

Day 67

Sin in Its Aggravations

> Q83. *Are all transgressions of the law equally heinous?*
> A. Some sins in themselves, and by reason of several aggravations, are more heinous in the sight of God than others.

Then he said to me, "Have you seen this, O son of man?
You will see still greater abominations than these."
EZEKIEL 8:15

THOMAS BOSTON HIGHLIGHTS THAT Ezek 8:15 reveals the increasing severity of Israel's sins, shown to Ezekiel in a vision. All sin is a grave offense against God, but some are greater than others. Ezekiel first saw idolatrous practices, including the image of Baal near the altar (v. 5), secret idol worship in the chambers (v. 10–11), and women weeping for Tammuz (v. 14). However, the greatest abomination was the public worship of the sun at the temple's entrance (v. 16), showing deeper contempt for God by taking place in a sacred place.

Sin's heinousness refers to its great offensiveness to God. Sin displeases God, grieves his Spirit (Jer 44:4), and provokes his loathing, as seen in metaphors like "filthiness, uncleanness, and vomit" (Rev 3:16). Sin is contrary to God's nature and will, disturbing his holiness like smoke to the eyes (Isa 65:5). While "every fault is offensive, but some faults are heinous offences" (Ps 5:4–5), implying degrees of severity. Even the smallest sin is great in God's sight (Exod 34:7). However, just as some mountains are higher than others, some sins are more grievous, such as murder (Gen 4:10) and oppression (Hab 2:11), which are described as "crying sins" that provoke God's wrath. Others, like blasphemy, idolatry (Ezek 8), unbelief, and rejecting Christ (2 Thess 1:8) are incredibly offensive. The most heinous sin, however, is "the sin against the Holy Spirit" (Matt 12:31).

Some sins, explains Boston, are more heinous than others due to various aggravating factors. The first factor is the person offending—sins committed by notable individuals, such as magistrates, ministers, or parents, are more grievous because their positions carry greater responsibility and influence (Rom 2:21; Luke 12:47–48). Second, the parties offended determine the severity of the sin. Sins against God, his Son, and the Holy Spirit are more heinous than sins against fellow humans (1 Sam 2:25; Acts 5:4). Sins against superiors, loved ones, or God's people, as well as those affecting the common good, are more grievous (Prov 30:17; Matt 18:6). Third, the quality of the offense aggravates sin—sins that violate the letter of the law, are scandalous, or cause irreparable harm are more serious. Sins "consummated by action" are more heinous than "merely in the heart" (Jas 1:15). Fourth, the manner of sinning matters. Deliberate, presumptuous, repeated sins are worse than those committed through weakness or ignorance. Fifth, the time of commission makes a difference—sins committed on the Lord's Day, immediately before or after worship, or during divine judgments, are more offensive (2 Kgs 5:26). Sixth, the place of commission heightens sin's severity—sins committed in places where the gospel is preached or done publicly are more grievous than those done in secret (Isa 26:10). All these factors contribute to the varying degrees of heinousness in sin. "Repent, and flee to the blood of Christ for pardon," urges Boston, "if so be our heinous sins may not be our ruin."

TEA WITH THOMAS BOSTON

1. How does recognizing some sins as more heinous affect your view of personal sin and its impact on your relationship with God? (Ezek 8:15; Ps 5:4–5; Isa 65:5)

2. How do varying degrees of sin help us understand God's justice in punishment? (Ezek 8:15–16 ; Exod 34:7; Matt 12:31)

3. How can the doctrine of degrees of sin help you explain sin's seriousness? (Rom 2:21; 2 Thess 1:8; Isa 26:10)

4. How can recognizing the severity of sin motivate you to resist sin more deliberately? (Ezek 8:16; Jas 1:15; Luke 12:47–48)

5. What habits can you encourage young believers to resist sin and grow in God's holiness? (Jas 1:15; 2 Kgs 5:26; 1 Pet 1:14–16)

Schisandra berry tea has a unique five-flavor profile, reflecting the layered seriousness of sin in its aggravations—some sins are more grievous and call for deeper repentance.

Heavenly Father, grant me true repentance and draw me to the cleansing blood of Christ, that my sins—great and small—may not be my ruin. Amen.

"There are no small sins before God, though some are greater than others; but the least of them is great in itself, and great in his sight."[1]

---

1. Boston, *Works*, 2:385 (2:384–89).

Day 68

The Desert of Sin

> Q84. *What does every sin deserve?*
> A. Every sin deserves God's wrath and curse, both in this life and that which is to come.

For all who rely on works of the law are under a curse; for it is written, "Cursed be everyone who does not abide by all things written in the Book of the Law, and do them."

GALATIANS 3:10

THOUGH SOME SINS ARE more heinous than others, every sin deserves damnation, as "cursed be anyone who does not confirm the words of this law by doing them" (Deut 27:26). The law condemns every sinner for omissions or commissions. Even the slightest breach of the law brings condemnation. The punishment pronounced is God's wrath and curse, extending to this life and the next. Since this verdict is the voice of God's perfect justice, it ensures that no punishment exceeds what sin deserves.

Thomas Boston states that God's wrath, though described as anger, is not an emotional disturbance in God but a holy and just response to sin. God is utterly displeased with sinners, making their souls detestable and provoking God's holy anger (Ps 5:4–5). God's wrath is more dreadful than perpetual darkness or earthly misery (Ps 90:11). He deals with sinners as enemies, reserving wrath and vengeance for them (Nah 1:2; Isa 1:24). Alongside his inescapable wrath, God's curse separates sinners to evil, devoting them to destruction. This curse subjects sinners to all the dreadful effects of God's wrath, where every misery and plague converges (Deut 29:21).

In this life, God's wrath and curse encompass "all the miseries" one experiences, such as physical suffering, relationship troubles, loss of reputation, and financial difficulties. They also affect the soul, causing blindness, hardness of the heart, vile affections, and guilt, leading to death and the separation of soul and body. In the life to come, they result in eternal death, damnation, and eternal punishment in hell, creating "a shoreless sea of miseries."

Boston shows from Scripture that every sin deserves God's wrath and curse, as the wages of sin is death, specifically eternal death (Rom 6:23, 5:12; Job 24:19). Every sin is a breach of the law, and breaking even one command makes a person guilty of all, deserving God's wrath (Jas 2:10). Christ died for all the sins of his elect, enduring God's wrath and curse on their behalf (1 Pet 3:18; 1 John 1:7), proving they truly deserve it. Even the least sin can condemn a person if not forgiven (Matt 5:19; 12:36–37), and without forgiveness, these sins will be eternally punished.

Every sin deserves infinite punishment because sin is "an infinite evil." The guilt and defilement of sin remain forever unless God, in his mercy, removes it. Since the offense is against the eternal God and the sinner cannot expiate it, the punishment must be eternal. Sin is an offense against an infinite God, whose supreme dignity makes every transgression deserving of infinite punishment. Just as human justice considers the status of the one offended, sin against God—of infinite majesty—calls for punishment of infinite duration. Sin rejects God's sovereignty (Jas 2:10–11), abuses his goodness (Exod 20:1–2), defiles his holiness (Hab 1:13), and breaks his eternal law (1 John 3:4; 1 Sam 15:23), and thus deserves eternal punishment.

TEA WITH THOMAS BOSTON

1. How does understanding that every sin deserves God's wrath shape your daily view of sin? (Ps 5:4–5; Nah 1:2; Deut 27:26)
2. How does the doctrine of God's wrath reveal the severity of sin and our need for Christ's atonement? (Rom 6:23; Isa 1:24; 1 Pet 3:18)
3. How does God's wrath challenge the modern idea of a tolerant, non-judgmental deity? (Deut 27:26; Ps 5:4–5; Rom 6:23)
4. What are practical ways to develop a habit of confessing sins and seeking forgiveness? (Matt 12:36–37; 1 John 1:7; Jas 2:10)
5. How can children and young believers learn to appreciate God's holiness and Christ's mercy? (Exod 20:1–2; 1 Sam 15:23; Ps 5:4–5)

Jasmine silver needle tea has a pure and delicate aroma, reflecting the holiness of God against which every sin is measured.

Heavenly Father, I confess that every sin deserves your wrath, and thank you for Christ's mercy that saves me from the punishment I deserve. Amen.

"There is more ill in the least sin than the greatest sufferings."[1]

---

1. Boston, *Works*, 2:393 (2:389–93).

PART 7

Faith and Repentance

(Q85—Q87)

Day 69

The Means of Salvation in General

Q85. *What does God require of us, that we may escape his wrath and curse, due to us for sin?*

A. To escape the wrath and curse of God, due to us for sin, God requires of us faith in Jesus Christ, repentance unto life, with the diligent use of all the outward means whereby Christ communicates to us the benefits of redemption.

How shall we escape if we neglect such a great salvation? It was declared at first by the Lord, and it was attested to us by those who heard.
HEBREWS 2:3

HEBREWS 2:3 UNDERSCORES THAT the way to escape God's wrath and curse is not by evading or resisting God, as he is omniscient and omnipotent, but by embracing the salvation he has provided—through faith and repentance. Sinners can avoid perishing by accepting the gospel and its means of salvation.

Thomas Boston stresses that faith in Christ is "absolutely necessary" to escape God's wrath and curse due to sin. Without faith, one cannot please God (Heb 11:6), no matter how much sorrow or effort one puts into personal holiness. Faith is a "duty of the gospel," without which God can neither accept sinners nor their actions (John 3:18). It is through faith that one enters into the covenant of grace with Christ, uniting with him and receiving the benefits of salvation, including justification (Rom 5:1) and sanctification (Acts 15:9). Salvation and damnation hinge on faith—those who believe will receive salvation, but those who do not will receive damnation (Mark 16:16).

Repentance is indispensable for escaping God's wrath and curse; no adult can be saved without it. While infants and those incapable of actual faith and repentance are saved by the Spirit's work in them, Scripture clearly teaches that those who do not repent will perish (Luke 13:5). "Heaven's door is bolted against all impenitent sinners," states Boston, and they face eternal condemnation (Rev 21:27). John the Baptist, Jesus, and the apostles preached that repentance, like faith, is a core duty of the gospel, underscoring that one cannot escape judgment without repentance (Ezek 18:30–31). True faith always produces genuine repentance, as seen in Zech 12:10, where mourning follows looking upon the pierced Savior. Since Christ grants repentance as a gift (Acts 5:31), impenitent sinners remain outside salvation and must perish.

Although required by God, faith and repentance are not within human power. They are gifts of God and the result of his special grace (Acts 5:31), and without his sovereign will to give them, sinners remain in unbelief and impenitence. Faith receives Christ and his righteousness (John 1:12), while repentance, arising from godly sorrow and flowing from faith, leads to life (2 Cor 7:11), securing the great end of salvation.

Using "outward means" is necessary, as God communicates the benefits of redemption through them. God has commanded them, as God bestows grace and salvation through these means (Rom 10:17). Neglecting the means shows contempt for grace, and their diligent—not superficial—use is required (1 Cor 3:6–7). Outward means—like reading, hearing, and praying—prepare us for experiencing legal convictions, fear, sorrow for sin, and natural (though not saving) desires for grace. Although God has not promised to save those who merely use outward means, it is "possible and probable," states Boston, that God may grant saving grace in the process (Acts 8:22).

TEA WITH THOMAS BOSTON

1. How have you experienced the need for faith and repentance in your walk with God? (Heb 11:6; John 3:18; Rom 5:1)
2. When have you neglected the means of grace, and how did it affect you? (Heb 2:3; Prov 8:34; Rom 10:17)
3. How do faith and repentance unite us with Christ and secure salvation's benefits? (John 1:12; Gal 2:16; Acts 15:9)
4. How can you be more diligent in using the means of grace, such as Scripture, sacraments, and prayer? (Acts 2:42; 1 Cor 11:26; 1 Thess 5:17)
5. How can you deepen your sense of repentance and godly sorrow for sin? (Zech 12:10; 2 Cor 7:11; Acts 5:31)

Chrysanthemum and goji berry tea combines sweetness with clarity, symbolizing repentance and faith.

Heavenly Father, grant me true faith and heartfelt repentance, for only through your grace can I escape your wrath and embrace the salvation found in Christ. Amen.

"If one should weep for his sins till no moisture were left in his body, fast his flesh to a skeleton, and watch ever so carefully against his sin, if he has not faith, he is a lost man; he cannot please God, but must lie for ever under his displeasure."[1]

---

1. Boston, *Works*, 2:395 (2:393–99).

Day 70

Faith in Jesus Christ

> Q86. *What is faith in Jesus Christ?*
>
> A. Faith in Jesus Christ is a saving grace, whereby we receive and rest upon him alone for salvation, as he is offered to us in the gospel.

But to all who did receive him, who believed in his name,

he gave the right to become children of God.

JOHN 1:12

JOHN 1:12 HIGHLIGHTS SAVING faith's nature and fruit—adoption into God's family. Thomas Boston defines faith as "a saving grace" that unites one with Christ to become "an heir of heaven." Faith involves receiving Christ as offered in the gospel and resting on him—trusting him for salvation. However, not all have faith—only the elect, regenerated by the Spirit, receive Christ and salvation. This saving faith distinguishes itself from "historical faith" with mere intellectual assent (Jas 2:19), "temporary faith" that fades under trials (Luke 8:13), and "faith of miracles" (1 Cor 13:2), as even unbelievers may possess them.

Saving faith is not a meritorious work (Rom 3:27–28) but an instrument by which one apprehends Christ and his righteousness (Rom 3:22). It does not originate from human free will (John 6:44) but is "a special gift of God" (Phil 1:29), produced by divine power (Col 2:12) and attributed to the Father, Son, and especially the Spirit (Gal 5:22). God ordinarily begets faith through the word "preached, heard, or read" (Rom 10:17). This faith is found in elect sinners who are first convinced of their sin (John 16:8–9) and then quickened by God's Spirit, as regeneration precedes faith (Gal 3:23–24).

Boston states that faith's general object is God's word, but its special focus is the gospel promise (Acts 16:31), particularly Christ as Savior. Faith trusts in God's authority, the certainty of his promises, and Christ's power to save (Heb 7:25). Though maybe mixed with doubt, true faith ventures upon Christ (Mark 9:24). The personal object of faith is God—Father, Son, and Holy Spirit (John 14:1)—with Christ as the central focus of justifying faith, symbolized by the bronze serpent (John 3:14–15). Faith's secondary objects are Christ's righteousness and the benefits of salvation (Phil 3:8–9).

The saving acts of faith involve receiving Christ as offered in the gospel, entailing accepting him as a Prophet to teach (Matt 17:5), as a Priest for righteousness (Isa 45:24), and as a King to obey (Isa 26:13). Faith also rests on Christ in all his offices, depending on him as a Prophet for wisdom, a Priest for atonement, and a King for deliverance from sin. The end of these acts of faith is "Christ's whole salvation"—from sin (Matt 1:21), from wrath (1 Thess 1:10), and "the guilt, defilement, dominion, and indwelling of sin."

Faith results in justification and sanctification, as faith receives and rests on Christ alone for these benefits (Gal 2:16). Therefore, faith involves turning away from reliance on oneself and looking to Christ for all aspects of salvation. The ground and warrant of faith is the gospel offer, which includes God's invitation to sinners to come to him freely (Isa 55:1), his declaration of pleasure in their believing (John 6:29), and his command to believe in Christ (1 John 3:23), all of which provide the assurance and basis for faith.

TEA WITH THOMAS BOSTON

1. How has faith in Christ changed your relationship with God and assured you of being his child? (John 1:12; Rom 8:15; Gal 4:6)

2. How is saving faith different from intellectual assent, temporary faith, or faith in miracles? (Jas 2:19; Luke 8:13; 1 Cor 13:2)

3. How can we show skeptics that faith in Christ is based on God's promises and historical reality? (Luke 24:25–27; Acts 17:2–3; 1 Cor 15:3–6)

4. How does accepting Christ as Prophet, Priest, and King shape our daily lives? (Matt 17:5; Isa 26:13; 45:24)

5. How can we keep our faith strong and steadfast in trials? (Matt 7:24–25; Jas 1:2–3; 1 Pet 1:6–7)

Angelica root tea's sweet, earthy flavor evokes the deep peace and renewal that come from receiving and resting in Christ by faith.

Heavenly Father, strengthen my saving faith so I may more fully trust Christ as my Prophet, Priest, and King, resting on him alone for salvation. Amen.

"The soul has a burden of weakness and ignorance, and therefore rests on him as a Prophet; a burden of guilt, but rests on him as a Priest, laying the weight on his blood; a burden of strong lusts and temptations, but rests on him as a King."[1]

---

1. Boston, *Works*, 2:404 (2:399–411).

Day 71

Repentance unto Life

Q87. *What is repentance unto life?*
A. Repentance unto life is a saving grace, whereby a sinner, out of a true sense of his sin and apprehension of the mercy of God in Christ, does, with grief and hatred of his sin, turn from it unto God, with full purpose of, and endeavor after, new obedience.

When they heard these things they fell silent. And they glorified God, saying, "Then to the Gentiles also God has granted repentance that leads to life."
ACTS 11:18

REPENTANCE ALWAYS ACCOMPANIES TRUE faith in Christ, making the two inseparable. In Acts 11:18, the believing Jews conclude from Peter's account that God "has granted repentance" to the gentiles. Repentance is a gift from God, just as faith is, as God alone "works it in the heart."

Thomas Boston distinguishes between legal and evangelical repentance. Legal repentance, as seen in Judas, arises from fear of punishment without a changed heart and is not saving (Matt 27:3). Evangelical repentance, as seen in David (Ps 51:4), is unique to the elect, marked by sorrow for sin as an offense against God. The key difference is that legal repentance focuses on escaping wrath (Gen 4:13), while evangelical repentance grieves sin itself. The former leads to death, while the latter leads to life (2 Cor 7:10).

Repentance unto life is a saving grace that disposes the soul to turn from sin to God. It is not "a transient action, a sigh for sin, a pang of sorrow for it" but an enduring grace that becomes a permanent disposition of the heart, prompting continual repentance (Zech 12:10). It is not a one-time experience at the beginning of one's faith but an abiding grace throughout life, with the heart smitten by repentance at conversion and never fully healed until the glory of eternal life. Unlike legal repentance, which is temporary and a "common grace," evangelical repentance is a saving grace inseparably linked to eternal life, distinguishing the believer from a hypocrite.

The author of repentance is not human, as no human can change the heart (Jer 13:23). Repentance is a free gift from God, "wrought by the power of his Spirit in the heart" (Ezek 36:26–27; Jer 31:18–19). Even notorious sinners, like Manasseh and Paul, can experience repentance through God's work. God's word is how the Spirit brings about repentance. Boston explains that the law "breaks the hard heart" (Jer 23:29), preparing it for repentance, while the gospel "melts the hard heart" and draws the sinner to God, with the soul being "driven by the law, but drawn by the gospel."

Repentance involves a true sense of sin, where sinners recognize and feel the weight of their sin (Ps 51:3; Acts 2:37), leading to realizing their need for Christ. It also entails understanding God's mercy in Christ (Joel 2:12–13), where sinners, through faith, grasp forgiveness in Christ. Without seeing Christ's mercy, sinners may fall into despair or torment, but true repentance comes only through Christ (Zech 12:10). Repentance involves humiliation and conversion. Humiliation includes sorrow for sin (Zech 12:10), shame (Rom 6:21), self-loathing (Ezek 36:31), and confessing sins to God (Jer 3:13). Conversion consists of turning away from sin and turning to God, leading to a life of sincere dedication to God's will (Acts 24:16).

TEA WITH THOMAS BOSTON

1. How has ongoing repentance shaped your daily Christian walk? (Acts 3:19; Matt 4:17; 1 John 1:9)
2. How does distinguishing between legal and evangelical repentance help us understand true repentance? (Matt 27:3; Ps 51:4; Gen 4:13)
3. Why is repentance essential to true faith, and how do they work together in salvation? (Acts 11:18; Mark 1:15; Eph 2:8–9)
4. What areas of your life need repentance and renewed dedication to God's will? (Acts 24:16; 2 Tim 2:19; Luke 9:23)
5. What steps can you encourage new believers to take to live a life of repentance and faith? (Acts 2:38; Rom 12:1–2; 1 John 1:9)

Licorice root tea's naturally sweet, herbal flavor reflects the tender mercy of God in Christ, whose restorative grace leads sinners to true repentance.

Heavenly Father, grant me true repentance so I may turn from sin, embrace your mercy in Christ, and live in faithful obedience to your will. Amen.

"The sinner goes from God by the high-way of pride and self-conceit; but always comes back the low way of humiliation."[1]

---

1. Boston, *Works*, 2:414 (2:411–16).

PART 8

The Word, Sacraments, and Prayer

(Q88—Q107)

Day 72

Christ's Ordinances in General

> Q88. *What are the outward and ordinary means whereby Christ communicates to us the benefits of redemption?*
>
> A. The outward and ordinary means whereby Christ communicates to us the benefits of redemption are his ordinances, especially the word, sacraments, and prayer; all which are made effectual to the elect for salvation.

With joy you will draw water from the wells of salvation.
ISAIAH 12:3

ISAIAH 12:3 PORTRAYS THE joy of drawing from the "wells of salvation," symbolizing the life-giving grace of Christ's redemption (John 4:14, 7:37). Thomas Boston perceives these wells as the church's ordinances established by God to sustain believers. Whether recalling Israel's wells in the wilderness or the Feast of Tabernacles' water-drawing ritual, the imagery highlights the abundant spiritual provision found in Christ. These provisions flow to believers through the means of salvation, the instruments through which Christ, by his Spirit, conveys grace to the soul. These means, Boston teaches, can be outward, inward, ordinary, or extraordinary.

The "inward means" is faith, through which Christ's grace reaches the soul (Heb 4:2), enabling repentance, justification, and sanctification. The "extraordinary means" are those God sovereignly uses to convey grace, such as the voice from heaven in Paul's conversion. Sometimes God may act without any means, especially for those unable to hear or read. The "outward and ordinary means" are God's ordinances, like the word, sacraments, prayer, fellowship, church government, discipline, fasting, psalm-singing, and swearing by God's name when appropriately called.

The word, sacraments, and prayer are the most significant outward and ordinary means. The word preached or read is a powerful means of grace, leading many to salvation (Acts 2:41). The sacraments—baptism and the Lord's Supper—do not convert sinners but seal the grace already received through the word (Acts 8:39; 1 Cor 10:16). Prayer—whether public, private, or secret—is a vital means of communion between Christ and believers, allowing divine influences to flow into the soul.

Boston explains that an ordinance must have a "divine institution or warrant" to be a valid means of grace. Human-made ordinances—like "crossing in baptism, kissing the book in swearing"—are not spiritually beneficial and can even lead to sin. The efficacy of any ordinance depends on God's blessing and sanction, without which the use of such ordinances is in vain (Matt 15:9). God condemns human inventions in religion (Jer 32:35) and warns that their use can lead to self-made worship that provokes God's wrath (Col 2:20–23). True ordinances of grace are those instituted by God (Isa 8:20), and they are the only means of grace through which God communicates salvation to the soul.

The Lord's ordinances, argues Boston, are not effectual for everyone who partakes in them. Although many may come to the ordinances, not all will experience salvation. While God's purpose is salvation, those who reject or misuse the ordinances may face damnation. The ordinances are effectual only for the elect (Acts 13:48), where only those ordained to eternal life receive salvation through them. Moreover, the ordinances' efficacy comes not from their inherent virtue or the one administering them but from the Spirit of the Lord working through them (1 Cor 3:7).

TEA WITH THOMAS BOSTON

1. How can you grow in your appreciation of God's ordinances (word, sacraments, prayer) as means of grace? (Acts 2:41; 1 Cor 10:16; Eph 6:18)

2. How do God's ordained means of grace differ from human-made rituals in salvation? (Matt 15:9; Jer 32:35; Col 2:20–23)

3. Why is it important to understand that the efficacy of ordinances depends on God's blessing, not the rituals themselves? (1 Cor 3:7; Gal 3:3; Isa 8:20)

4. How can you incorporate the means of grace (word, sacraments, prayer) into your daily life for spiritual growth? (Acts 2:42; Rom 12:1; Col 3:16)

5. How can you teach young believers or children to value God's word for salvation and spiritual nourishment? (Matt 4:4; Deut 6:6–7; 2 Tim 3:15)

 Red raspberry leaf tea is a soothing, earthy tea, representing trust in God's salvation symbolized by the ordinances.

 Heavenly Father, thank you for the grace flowing through your means of salvation; may I faithfully receive your word, sacraments, and prayer by your Spirit. Amen.

 "Great is the sin and loss of those who come to the wells, but never draw of the water nor taste it: who are never bettered by ordinances, but remain as dead and unconcerned about their souls as if the means of salvation were not vouchsafed to them."[1]

---

1. Boston, *Works*, 2:421 (2:416–21).

Day 73

How the Word Is Made Effectual to Salvation

> Q89. *How is the word made effectual to salvation?*
>
> A. The Spirit of God makes the reading, but especially the preaching, of the word an effectual means of convincing and converting sinners, and of building them up in holiness and comfort through faith unto salvation.

. . . and take the helmet of salvation, and the sword of the Spirit, which is the word of God.

EPHESIANS 6:17

EPHESIANS 6:17 DESCRIBES GOD'S word as the sword of the Spirit, emphasizing its role in the Christian's spiritual armor. As God's revelation, the Bible is essential for every believer striving for heaven. Paul calls it the sword of the Spirit because the Holy Spirit uses it to win souls for Christ and lead them through spiritual warfare against the devil, the world, and the flesh. While the word is the weapon, the Spirit, claims Thomas Boston, is the one who wields it effectively.

God's word is both an ordinance of God and a means of salvation through its reading and preaching. Public reading in congregations (Neh 8:8) and private reading in families (Deut 6:6–9) are essential practices. Personal reading is also necessary for every believer (John 5:39), and Scripture should be accessible in common languages. Though all may read Scripture, Boston claims that only those qualified and called should preach it (2 Cor 3:6; Rom 10:15)—preaching is the primary means of grace (1 Cor 1:21). While reading benefits the soul, preaching remains the chief means of salvation. Preaching predates written Scripture, as seen in the ministries of Noah (2 Pet 2:5) and Enoch (Jude 14), and was central to Jesus' ministry. Preaching illuminates Scripture, like snuffing a lamp to make it shine brighter, and should be attentively received by all who seek salvation.

For unbelievers, the word convicts and converts sinners. It awakens them from spiritual slumber, convicting their specific sins and the heinous nature of sin, revealing their condition before God (1 Cor 14:24–25; Heb 4:12). The word also shows them their misery, unveiling their guilt and lost state (Acts 2:37). The word is the means God uses to convert sinners to himself (Ps 19:7; Acts 26:18). It drives sinners out of themselves to trust in Christ by faith (Acts 2:37–38) and urges them to turn from their sin to God, embracing obedience and repentance (Acts 20:21).

For believers, God appoints the reading and preaching of the word for their holiness and comfort. Boston likens the church and each believer's life to unfinished buildings, and the word continues to support them, much like scaffolding, until they are complete (Eph 4:11–13). Upon the foundation of conversion, the word builds believers up in holiness (Acts 20:32) by establishing them in the good they have attained to withstand temptations (Eph 4:14), cleansing them from remaining sin (Ps 119:9), pressing them forward to maturity (2 Cor 3:18). Moreover, the word provides comfort (Rom 15:4) by offering a proper perspective on their struggles (Ps 73:17) and offering suitable promises and doctrines to address their griefs (Isa 40:1–2). However, Boston states that the word's efficacy does not come from the word itself or the preacher but from the Spirit's operation (1 Cor 3:5–6). The inward means by which the Spirit makes the word effective is faith resting on God's faithful word (Heb 4:2).

TEA WITH THOMAS BOSTON

1. How has God's word convicted you of sin and led to repentance? (1 Cor 14:24–25; Heb 4:12; Acts 2:37)

2. When has God's word comforted you during struggles and strengthened your faith? (Rom 15:4; Ps 73:17; Isa 40:1–2)

3. Why is preaching considered the primary means of grace, even though personal Bible reading is important? (1 Cor 1:21; Rom 10:15; 2 Cor 3:6)

4. How does the word's power to convict and convert distinguish Christianity from other religions? (Acts 2:37; Heb 4:12; Ps 19:7)

5. How can you help young believers develop a habit of reading and hearing God's word? (John 5:39; Rom 10:17; 2 Tim 2:2)

 Dandelion leaf tea has a slightly bitter flavor, symbolizing the conviction and edification of God's word.

 Heavenly Father, thank you for your word. Empower me through your Spirit to receive and live by it, convicting, transforming, and strengthening me for your glory. Amen.

 "Those who do not make a practice of daily reading the scripture, are none of the Lord's people, whatever otherwise they may profess . . . . The dust of many people's Bibles will be a heavy witness against them at the great day."[1]

---

1. Boston, *Works*, 2:423, 426 (2:421–26).

Day 74

How the Word Is to Be Read and Heard

> Q90. *How is the word to be read and heard, that it may become effectual to salvation?*
>
> A. That the word may become effectual to salvation, we must attend thereunto with diligence, preparation, and prayer; receive it with faith and love, lay it up in our hearts, and practice it in our lives.

Take care then how you hear, for to the one who has, more will be given, and from the one who has not, even what he thinks that he has will be taken away.

LUKE 8:18

IN LUKE 8:18, JESUS warns, "Take care then how you hear," stressing that how one receives God's word determines its effect. Drawing from the parable of the sower, Thomas Boston shows that while some benefit from hearing, many do not. Genuine spiritual growth depends not merely on exposure to the word but on receiving it rightly, which, Boston claims, requires attention before, during, and after hearing God's word.

Before hearing the word, preparation and prayer are essential. Drawing from Jacob's example (Gen 35:2–3), preparation is the ordinary means of receiving divine blessing (Isa 64:5), even though God can work sovereignly in the unprepared (Isa 65:1). Preparation involves recognizing God's holiness, setting aside distractions (Matt 13:7), applying Christ's atonement, purging sinful lusts (1 Pet 2:1–2), and stirring spiritual desires. Preparation is vital due to God's greatness (Heb 12:28–29) and the eternal stakes of hearing the word (2 Cor 2:16). Prayer—both personal and corporate—should seek God's guidance for the preacher (2 Thess 3:1), personal transformation (Ps 119:18), and the Spirit's outpouring (Prov 1:23). Yet, Boston warns that success depends on the Spirit's sovereign work (John 3:8), requiring continual dependence on God.

While hearing the word, Boston teaches that we need diligence, proper reception, and retention. Diligence means seizing every opportunity to hear it (Prov 8:34) and giving it undivided attention, showing reverence (Luke 4:20), discerning truth as the Bereans did (Acts 17:11), and seeking understanding as Lydia did (Acts 16:14). This is vital, as hearing concerns eternity—distractions, sin, and spiritual dullness hinder our understanding (Isa 59:2). Proper reception is to believe its truth (Ps 119:160), applying it to our lives (Job 5:27), embracing it for conviction (Acts 2:37), conversion (1 Pet 1:23), holiness (1 Pet 2:2), and comfort (Rom 15:4). We should also receive the word with love (2 Thess 2:10), as Boston states: "Faith receives the word as true, love receives it as good." Loving the word means prizing it above all (Job 23:12), longing for it (1 Pet 2:2), and delighting in it (Ps 119:162). Retention means we store the word in our hearts (Ps 119:11), treating it as treasure (Col 3:16), safeguarding it against loss (Matt 13:4), and recalling it for future guidance (Isa 42:23). Deeply imprinting the word in our souls and seeking God's help to retain it (Ps 119:93) ensure its lasting impact.

After hearing the word, meditation helps it take root in the heart (Ps 1:2), prevents it from slipping away, and strengthens memory (Luke 9:44). Discussing Scripture in conversation reinforces its impact and deepens understanding (Luke 24:14), as Moses commanded Israel (Deut 6:6–7). Proper hearing leads to transformed lives, bearing fruit in obedience (Luke 8:15; Jas 1:25), for hearing alone is in vain without application.

TEA WITH THOMAS BOSTON

1. How has the word taken root and borne fruit in your life? (Matt 13:23; Ps 119:162; Jas 1:25)
2. How does Christianity's focus on hearing and applying Scripture set it apart from other religions? (Isa 42:23; Acts 17:11; Luke 8:18)
3. How can we build a habit of meditating on Scripture? (Ps 1:2; Luke 9:44; 119:93)
4. What steps can you take to share Scripture with others? (Deut 6:6-7; Luke 24:14; Acts 17:11)
5. How can we help young Christians apply and practice God's word? (Luke 8:15; Josh 1:8; Job 5:27)

Nettle tea has a grassy, slightly bitter flavor, symbolizing strength and nourishment from God's word.

Heavenly Father, grant me a heart that diligently prepares to receive your word, listens with faith and love, and treasures it deeply to bear fruit for your glory. Amen.

"The word heard, but not practised, will sink men deeper in damnation; but heard and practised too, will bring them into eternal salvation."[1]

---

1. Boston, *Works*, 2:434, 426 (2:427-34).

Day 75

How the Sacraments Become Effectual Means of Salvation

> Q91. *How do the sacraments become effectual means of salvation?*
>
> A. The sacraments become effectual means of salvation not from any virtue in them, or in him that does administer them; but only by the blessing of Christ, and the working of his Spirit in them that by faith receive them.

For in one Spirit we were all baptized into one body—Jews or Greeks, slaves or free—and all were made to drink of one Spirit.

1 CORINTHIANS 12:13

FIRST CORINTHIANS 12:13 HIGHLIGHTS the unity of all believers in Christ through the work of the Holy Spirit, signified by baptism and the Lord's Supper. The sacraments of the New Testament—baptism, signifying initiation into Christ and union with Christ, and the Lord's Supper, signifying ongoing nourishment and communion with Christ—are effectual only for believers through their participation in the Spirit. Sacraments' power, Thomas Boston insists, comes neither from the sacraments themselves nor their administrators but from the Holy Spirit, working through the sacraments by Christ's blessing.

The sacraments are "means of salvation," contributing to the salvation purchased by Christ, which includes deliverance from the guilt and power

HOW THE SACRAMENTS BECOME EFFECTUAL MEANS OF SALVATION

of sin (Matt 1:21) and from God's wrath (1 Thess 1:10). A means of salvation is anything God appoints to bring about this end, with the word serving as the "means of conversion" (1 Cor 3:5) and the sacraments as "means of confirmation" (Rom 4:11). The sacraments are effectual because God ordained them for this purpose (Acts 2:37–38; 1 Cor 10:16) and because they produce "saving effects" in believers who use them rightly (Acts 8:39; 2:42).

The sacraments' efficacy lies in their ability to "represent, seal, and apply" Christ and his benefits to the soul (Rom 4:11; 1 Cor 12:13; 1 Pet 3:21). When they accomplish this, they are effectual means of salvation; when they do not, they are ineffectual. Sometimes, their effects are clearly perceived, as with the eunuch in Acts 8:38, while at other times, they are real but unnoticed, like the disciples on the road to Emmaus (Luke 24). Signs of their efficacy include a stronger reliance on Christ and his righteousness (Phil 3:3) and an increased longing for holiness and deliverance from sin (Rom 6:4; 8:23).

The efficacy of the sacraments does not come from the physical elements (water, bread, wine) or the piety of the administrator. The sacraments do not have inherent power to confer grace (John 6:63), nor can a minister—however holy—make them effectual (1 Cor 3:6–7). Instead, their efficacy depends on Christ's blessing and the working of the Holy Spirit. Christ has authorized the sacraments through his command and promise (Matt 28:19–20), and the Spirit makes them effectual for the recipients (1 Cor 12:13).

The sacraments are not effectual for all who partake of them. Some, like Simon the sorcerer (Acts 8:13, 23), receive them without true faith, and others partake unworthily (1 Cor 10:1–5). However, they are effectual for believers, as seen in the Ethiopian eunuch (Acts 8:37, 39) and affirmed in Mark 16:16. Like the word (Heb 4:2), the sacraments must be received with faith. Nevertheless, Boston states that baptism does not exclude infants despite their "not capable of actual believing," as it can still be effective for them through the Spirit's work.

TEA WITH THOMAS BOSTON

1. How has participating in the sacraments deepened your relationship with Christ? (1 Cor 12:13; Matt 28:19–20; Acts 8:39)

2. Why is it crucial to understand that the sacraments derive their efficacy from Christ's blessing and the Spirit's work, rather than from any power inherent in them? (1 Pet 2:21; 1 Cor 3:6–7; John 6:63)

3. What distinguishes Christian sacraments from rituals in other religions? (Acts 8:37–39; Matt 26:26–28; 1 Thess 1:10)

4. How can a proper appreciation of the sacraments encourage you to pursue holiness and spiritual growth? (Rom 6:4; 8:23; 1 Pet 3:21)

5. How can we help children or young believers understand the significance of the sacraments? (Deut 6:6–7; Mark 16:16; Acts 2:38)

 Orange blossom tea has a gentle citrus fragrance, reflecting the joy and peace that flow from the Spirit's work in those who receive the sacraments by faith.

 Heavenly Father, may the sacraments truly seal and apply Christ and his benefits to my soul, deepening my union with him and strengthening my faith. Amen.

 "God has put a power of nourishment in our meat, and of warming in our clothes; but no power of working grace either in the water of baptism, or bread and wine in the Lord's Supper."[1]

---

1. Boston, *Works*, 2:463, 426 (2:460–65).

Day 76

The Nature and Number of the Sacraments

Q92. *What is a sacrament?*

A. A sacrament is a holy ordinance instituted by Christ; wherein, by sensible signs, Christ and the benefits of the new covenant are represented, sealed, and applied to believers.

Q93. *Which are the sacraments of the New Testament?*

A. The sacraments of the New Testament are baptism and the Lord's Supper.

He received the sign of circumcision as a seal of the righteousness that he had by faith while he was still uncircumcised. The purpose was to make him the father of all who believe without being circumcised, so that righteousness would be counted to them as well.

ROMANS 4:11

CIRCUMCISION, AS A SACRAMENT, was a sign and seal of the Old Testament covenant, now replaced by baptism in the New Testament. God instituted circumcision and intended it as both a sign and a seal—signifying and applying spiritual blessings, with the external act representing the righteousness of faith. The sacrament signifies the covenant between God and Abraham's descendants. Jesus' circumcision also served as a seal of God's promises and connection to the covenant community.

Thomas Boston states that "sacrament" originally referred to a military oath where soldiers pledged loyalty to their leader. Through the sacraments, believers pledge allegiance to Christ, waging spiritual warfare under him, "the Captain of our salvation," while Christ, in turn, commits to our salvation. While "sacrament" is not a biblical term, its concepts—spiritual commitment and God's promises—are biblical. The church has adopted it to represent ordinances that are signs and seals of the covenant of grace. Jesus, as the King and Head of the church, is the author of the sacraments. The sacraments are part of religious worship, which only God can appoint. The sacraments become valid by Christ's word of institution (Matt 28:19-20; 1 Cor 11:23), which includes the command to perform the rite and the promise of grace for its proper use.

The two parts of a sacrament are outward sensible signs and inward spiritual grace. The outward signs—including physical elements (water, bread, and wine) and actions (like sprinkling water or breaking bread)—are visible. These signs are only valid when used according to Christ's institution. The inward grace signified by the outward signs refers to Christ's heavenly benefits, perceived only by faith (Rom 2:28-29). The sacraments represent Christ himself and his saving benefits, which include wisdom, righteousness, sanctification, and redemption (1 Cor 1:30). Unbelievers cannot receive these benefits, as the essence of the sacraments lies in partaking of Christ, and through him, all the blessings of salvation (Rom 8:32).

The "sacramental union," explains Boston, is the connection between the outward signs and the inward grace they signify, whereby the signs "represent, seal, and exhibit" spiritual benefits to worthy recipients (Gen 17:10; 1 Cor 11:24-25). This union is not a natural or physical one but a spiritual relationship established by Christ's institution. The sacraments are only for those within God's covenant (Rom 15:8), including believers and their children, who have the right to baptism. However, only those who have made a credible profession of faith are entitled to partake in the Lord's Supper (Exod 12:48; 1 Cor 11:28). The sacraments are holy signs representing Christ and strengthening faith (Rom 4:11). They act as public seals, confirming the covenant and obligating obedience (Rom 6:3). They also apply and exhibit Christ and his benefits to the believer (1 Cor 11:24). Moreover, they are "badges of our Christian profession," distinguishing believers from non-believers (Eph 2:11-12).

TEA WITH THOMAS BOSTON

1. How do the sacraments, as signs and seals, deepen your appreciation of God's grace? (Rom 6:3; 1 Cor 1:30; Eph 2:8–9)
2. Why are baptism and the Lord's Supper the only sacraments instituted in the New Testament? (Matt 28:19–20; 1 Cor 11:23–26; Luke 22:19–20)
3. How would you respond to someone who believes that sacraments grant grace apart from faith? (1 Cor 11:27–29; Rom 4:11; Gal 2:16)
4. How do the sacraments encourage obedience to God's covenant? (Ezek 36:25–27; 1 Cor 10:16–17; 2 Pet 1:5–8)
5. How can we teach children the importance of the sacraments? (Deut 6:6–7; Acts 2:39; 16:31–33)

Lemongrass and ginger tea has a bold, warming flavor, reflecting how the sacraments visibly seal and apply Christ's covenant blessings.

Heavenly Father, thank you for the sacraments as signs and seals of your covenant and Christ's saving work. Strengthen my faith and devotion to you. Amen.

"The signs are earthly, to be perceived with the bodily eyes; the thing signified heavenly, to be perceived only by faith. The former tends to the body, the latter to the soul. The one is received corporeally, the other spiritually."[1]

---

1. Boston, *Works*, 2:463, 468 (2:465–70).

Day 77

The Nature of Baptism

Q94. *What is baptism?*

A. Baptism is a sacrament, wherein the washing with water, in the name of the Father, and of the Son, and of the Holy Ghost, does signify and seal our ingrafting into Christ, and partaking of the benefits of the covenant of grace, and our engagement to be the Lord's.

Q95. *To whom is baptism to be administered?*

A. Baptism is not to be administered to any that are out of the visible Church, till they profess their faith in Christ and obedience to him; but the infants of such as are members of the visible Church are to be baptized.

Go therefore and make disciples of all nations, baptizing them in the name of the Father and of the Son and of the Holy Spirit.
MATTHEW 28:19

MATTHEW 28:19 RECORDS CHRIST'S institution of baptism, emphasizing baptism in the name of the Trinity, its administration by the apostles and their successors through teaching, and its recipients as those from all nations who first become disciples before being baptized. Thomas Boston identifies four types of baptism in Scripture: the baptism of light—doctrine

(Acts 18:25); blood—martyrdom (Matt 20:22-23); the Spirit—the outpouring of the Spirit (Matt 3:11); and water—the proper sacrament (Acts 8:38-39). The signifying element in baptism is pure water, regardless of its source, while the Catholic practice of adding oil, salt, and spittle is condemned (Heb 10:22).

Water signifies both the blood and the Spirit of Christ in baptism. The resemblance between water and Christ's blood and Spirit highlights the grace in baptism: water is freely accessible to all, symbolizing the free offer of Christ's blood and Spirit (Isa 55:1). Water cleanses, just as Christ's blood cleanses the defiled conscience (Heb 9:14) and the Spirit purifies the soul (Titus 3:5). Water refreshes, as Christ's blood and Spirit refresh the thirsty soul (John 6:35). Water has a "fructifying" power, just as Christ's blood and Spirit bring forth fruits of holiness (Isa 44:3-4). Water is necessary for life, and so is Christ's blood and Spirit for salvation (Heb 9:23). Lastly, just as water must be applied to have an effect, we must partake of Christ's blood and Spirit for transformation (1 Cor 1:30).

Boston argues that baptism does not require complete immersion; it is rightly administered by "pouring or sprinkling water," as evidenced by the apostles who baptized three thousand in one day (Acts 2:41) and the Philippian jailor and his family at night (Acts 16:33). While immersion may have been practiced in some cases, sprinkling adequately represents the symbolism of baptism, such as cleansing and burial (Heb 12:24; 1 Pet 1:2). The person administering baptism should be a lawfully called minister, as Scripture ties the authority to baptize to the preaching of the word (Matt 28:19; 1 Cor 4:1). The words used in baptism—baptizing in the name (not names) of the Father, and the Son, and the Holy Spirit—emphasize the unity of God's nature (Matt 28:19). The words highlight the authority of the triune God and signify the individual's commitment to the "profession, faith, and obedience" of the Holy Trinity.

Baptism acts as a "solemn admission to the visible church," acknowledging those already within the covenant, including infants of believing parents. It also signifies and seals saving benefits for salvation, including union with Christ and the benefits of the covenant of grace—regeneration, remission of sins, adoption into God's family, sanctification, and resurrection. Finally, baptism is a "dedicating ordinance," symbolizing a person's commitment to live for God, renounce sin and Satan, and engage in spiritual warfare under Christ's banner. It is an outward declaration of acceptance of God's covenant.

TEA WITH THOMAS BOSTON

1. How has your understanding of baptism deepened regarding its role in our union with Christ and participation in the covenant? (Gal 3:27; Rom 6:4; Col 2:12)

2. How does baptism symbolize our commitment to the Lord and reflect the covenant of grace? (Eph 4:5; Titus 3:5; Jer 31:33)

3. How does baptism in the name of the Trinity distinguish Christianity from other religions? (2 Cor 13:14; John 14:6; Acts 10:48)

4. How can baptism inspire you to live under Christ's banner and engage in spiritual warfare? (Rom 6:4; Eph 6:10–11; 1 Pet 5:8)

5. How can you explain the significance of baptism and its connection to God's covenant to a young believer or child? (Acts 2:38; 1 Pet 3:21; Gen 17:7)

Strawberry hibiscus tea has a vibrant, refreshing flavor, reflecting the cleansing, covenantal grace, and joy of being united to Christ through baptism.

Heavenly Father, may I embrace baptism's call to union with Christ, purification through Christ's blood and Spirit, and a life dedicated to your covenant. Amen.

"What more is there for God's elect to expect in this world, but these two things, that they receive life and nourishment, that they be taken into the covenant, and kept in it? Baptism is the sign of the one, and the Lord's Supper of the other. The one is the sacrament of our ingrafting into Christ, and the other of our nourishment in him."[1]

---

1. Boston, *Works*, 2:471 (2:471–81).

Day 78

The Nature of the Lord's Supper

Q96. *What is the Lord's Supper?*

A. The Lord's Supper is a sacrament, wherein, by giving and receiving bread and wine, according to Christ's appointment, his death is showed forth; and the worthy receivers are, not after a corporal and carnal manner, but by faith, made partakers of his body and blood, with all his benefits, to their spiritual nourishment and growth in grace.

For I received from the Lord what I also delivered to you, that the Lord Jesus on the night when he was betrayed took bread, and when he had given thanks, he broke it, and said, "This is my body, which is for you. Do this in remembrance of me." In the same way also he took the cup, after supper, saying, "This cup is the new covenant in my blood. Do this, as often as you drink it, in remembrance of me."

1 CORINTHIANS 11:23–25

CHRIST INSTITUTED THE SACRAMENT of the Lord's Supper on the night he was betrayed, giving it divine authority and holiness. The elements of bread and wine are ordinary but sacred, as they "represent, seal, and apply" Christ and his benefits—what Thomas Boston calls the "whole Christ." This sacrament will continue until Christ returns, serving as a memorial of him. The "words of institution" include a command to observe it and a promise of spiritual blessing for worthy recipients of Christ's body and blood.

The bread symbolizes Christ's body, which nourishes the soul (John 6:56) and was prepared through suffering, like grain ground and baked (Ps 22:14). Bread is commonly available, reflecting the "common salvation" (Jude 3) and the invitation to receive life (Rev 22:17). Bread is essential for physical life, so eating Christ's body is essential for spiritual life (John 6:53). The wine represents Christ's blood, poured out under God's wrath like grapes pressed in a winepress (Isa 63:3). Even as wine has a healing power to strengthen the body (Luke 10:34), Christ's blood heals and refreshes the soul (John 6:55) and brings joy (Prov 31:6; 1 Pet 1:8). Together, the bread and wine provide a "full feast for our souls" (John 6:56). The separation of bread and wine in the sacrament reflects the separation of Christ's blood from his body on the cross. We must receive them by faith to nourish the soul, highlighting the necessity of union with Christ for salvation.

Boston explains the signifying actions in the Lord's Supper as follows. The administrator begins by taking the bread and cup, symbolizing the Father's choosing the Son to be the Mediator (Ps 89:19; Isa 42:1). This action speaks of humanity's spiritual starvation, God's provision of Christ as heavenly bread, and the divine initiative in redemption. Then, consecrating the elements through "the word of institution, thanksgiving, and prayer" signified the Father's consecrating the Son to the "Mediatory office" to be sealed and sent (John 10:36). The breaking of bread vividly portrays Christ's body broken and blood shed through his sufferings, from circumcision to crucifixion. Finally, giving bread and wine to the communicants signifies Christ offering himself and all his benefits to believers. The communicants' taking the elements by hand shows receiving Christ by faith, and eating and drinking signify spiritual nourishment and union with Christ. However, without true faith, these outward acts mock God, rendering unworthy communion a grievous sin.

The Lord's Supper—a signifying, sealing, and exhibiting sign of Christ and his benefits—is "children's bread." Its purposes include remembering Christ's death (1 Cor 11:24, 26), confirming our union and communion with Christ (1 Cor 10:16), spiritually nourishing believers through faith, and testifying to our communion with all saints as members of Christ's body (1 Cor 10:17).

TEA WITH THOMAS BOSTON

1. How can the Lord's Supper deepen your relationship with Christ through faith and remembrance? (1 Cor 11:26; Matt 26:29; John 6:56)
2. How does the Lord's Supper highlight the uniqueness of Christianity? (John 14:6; Acts 4:12; 1 Cor 10:16)
3. How does the Lord's Supper reflect the unity of the Church? (1 Cor 10:17; Eph 4:4–6; Col 3:15)
4. How can the Lord's Supper encourage you in your daily walk with Christ and motivate you to live out the gospel? (Luke 22:19–20; Phil 1:27; 2 Cor 5:15)
5. How can we teach younger believers reverence and gratitude in the Lord's Supper? (1 Cor 11:28–29; Heb 12:28–29; Rev 19:9)

Licorice root and fennel tea is sweet and aromatic, symbolizing the spiritual nourishment and grace believers receive through the Lord's Supper.

Lord Jesus, as we partake of your body and blood, strengthen our faith and unite us to you deeply until you return. Amen.

"Hence we may see the unparalleled goodness and bounty of a gracious God to his people, in covering a rich table for them in this wilderness, stored with the best meat and drink for their refreshment and nourishment in their pilgrimage-state, till they arrive at their father's house in the heavenly Canaan."[1]

---

1. Boston, *Works*, 2:487 (2:481–88).

Day 79

The Worthy Receiving of the Lord's Supper

> Q97. *What is required to the worthy receiving of the Lord's Supper?*
>
> A. It is required of them that would worthily partake of the Lord's Supper, that they examine themselves, of their knowledge to discern the Lord's body, of their faith to feed upon him, of their repentance, love, and new obedience; lest, coming unworthily, they eat and drink judgment to themselves.

Let a person examine himself, then, and so eat of the bread and drink of the cup.
1 CORINTHIANS 11:28

THE WORTHINESS TO PARTAKE in the Lord's Supper, Thomas Boston teaches, is not about "legal worthiness" or deserving it based on our own actions, as we remain unworthy servants (Luke 17:10). Worthiness, instead, is about being "gospel-fitness," coming to the sacrament with a deep sense of "utter vileness" and spiritual emptiness (Isa 55:1). This worthiness consists of "habitual meetness"—meaning one is in a "gracious state," spiritually alive and made fit for the Lord's table—and "actual meetness," which requires a spiritually alert and fruitful life, as one must not approach the table lethargically, even if one is a true believer. Like the virgins who not only have oil but also have their lamps burning, a person must have a spiritual life and maintain it to be fit for communion.

The goal of self-examination for worthy participation in the Lord's Supper is to discern whether one is truly in Christ and possesses saving grace (2 Cor 13:5) since the Supper is a "confirming ordinance" (Rom 4:11), not a "converting ordinance" like the word (Rom 10:17). God appoints the sacrament "for nourishment, which presupposes life." Boston asks participants to examine the presence of five key graces: knowledge—which must be competent and saving (1 Cor 11:29), with understanding of essential doctrines and the nature of the sacrament; faith—which is necessary to receive Christ and spiritually feed on him (John 1:12; Heb 11:6) and is marked by a "superlative desire of Christ and his grace" (Matt 5:6) and a total dependence on Christ for righteousness; repentance—without which one cannot rightly remember Christ's death or receive a "sealed pardon" (Acts 2:38) and which is evidenced by a turning from sin to God (Acts 26:18); love—both to God as our "supreme love," and to our neighbor, shown in forgiveness, unity, and affection for fellow believers (1 John 3:14); and, lastly, new obedience—which flows from love for God (Heb 6:10), seeking to glorify him (1 Cor 10:31), and is marked by loving all his commands (Ps 119:6) and loving consistently (Matt 24:13), always leading believers back to Christ for cleansing when one failed.

Self-examination is essential to avoid partaking unworthily and to prevent divine judgment, which affects both soul and body (1 Cor 11:29–30). Therefore, believers must engage in serious self-examination despite challenges such as ignorance, hidden sins, fear, and opposition from Satan, who seeks to hinder this vital practice. The examination must be impartial, seeking an honest understanding of one's spiritual state, because self-deception only brings harm (1 Cor 11:31). Boston warns that while those who "sincerely desire Christ and his grace" may come even amid doubts (1 John 3:20–21), those whose conscience is not confident of a genuine turning to Christ should refrain. One must carefully discern one's spiritual condition before approaching the Lord's table, lest one incurs the guilt of "trampling on the body and blood of Christ."

TEA WITH THOMAS BOSTON

1. How do you hunger and thirst for Christ in the Lord's Supper? (Isa 55:1; Matt 5:6; Ps 42:1–2)
2. What sins or spiritual laziness do you see when you examine your heart before communion? (1 Cor 11:28; Ps 139:23–24; 1 John 1:9)
3. How do knowledge, faith, repentance, love, and obedience help prepare you for the Lord's Supper? (1 Cor 11:29; John 1:12; Heb 6:10)
4. How does self-examination help you grow in holiness? (1 Cor 11:31; 2 Tim 2:21; Ps 26:2)
5. How can the Lord's Supper strengthen discipleship and growth in your church? (Acts 2:42; 1 Cor 10:16–17; Heb 10:24–25)

 Tulsi basil tea is a calming herbal infusion, symbolizing the self-examination and spiritual readiness needed to partake worthily of the Lord's Supper.

 Heavenly Father, make me fit by your grace to come to your table with repentance, faith, and love, that I may partake worthily in Christ. Amen.

 "Faith is the hand and mouth of the soul. An unbeliever may feed on the bread of the Lord, as the beasts drank of the water of the rock in the wilderness; but they cannot feed on that bread which is the Lord."[1]

---

1. Boston, *Works*, 2:493 (2:489–97).

Day 80

The Necessity of Self-Examination Considered

> Q97. *What is required to the worthy receiving of the Lord's Supper?*
>
> A. It is required of them that would worthily partake of the Lord's Supper, that they examine themselves, of their knowledge to discern the Lord's body, of their faith to feed upon him, of their repentance, love, and new obedience; lest, coming unworthily, they eat and drink judgment to themselves.

Examine yourselves, to see whether you are in the faith. Test yourselves. Or do you not realize this about yourselves, that Jesus Christ is in you?—unless indeed you fail to meet the test!

2 CORINTHIANS 13:5

TO BE "IN THE faith," Thomas Boston explains, means to possess true, saving faith—a personal, living trust in Christ that unites one to Christ and marks one as God's elect (Titus 1:1). This faith is not merely intellectual, based on miracles, or temporary but a divine gift given only to those ordained to eternal life (Acts 13:48). It is how a sinner embraces Christ as Savior and relies entirely on him for salvation. This faith transforms believers' lives, leading them away from the life of gratifying the flesh and into a life "lived by faith in the Son of God" (Gal 2:20), bringing about genuine holiness and obedience. True faith is never dormant; it expresses itself through love (Gal

5:6), sanctifying the whole person and producing fruits consistent with repentance and grace (Mic 6:8).

Possessing genuine faith is of the highest importance because everything else depends on it: our union with Christ (John 15:5), our justification and peace with God (Rom 5:1), our ability to please God (Heb 11:6), and our eternal salvation (John 3:36). Therefore, believers need to examine themselves honestly to see whether they are genuinely in the faith (2 Cor 13:5), for their eternal destiny depends on it. Faith comes through hearing the word (Rom 10:17), so we must diligently attend preaching, use the sacraments, and pray fervently for it.

Believers must seriously examine whether they are "in the faith" (2 Cor 13:5), which, explains Boston, involves understanding both the doctrine and grace of faith since self-examination is impossible without knowledge (1 John 2:11). Many profess faith may still be unbelievers—"foolish virgins" (Matt 25:1–12), making this examination essential. Boston assures that true self-knowledge is attainable through ordinary means—primarily through God's word, which serves as our rule and mirror (2 Pet 1:10; 1 John 5:13). We also have a God-given ability to judge ourselves, using conscience and reason enlightened by Scripture (Prov 20:27). Therefore, we must diligently and honestly apply this inward examination, rousing ourselves from spiritual laziness (Matt 6:23) and testing our hearts against God's word as the psalmist did (Ps 77:6), with a view toward Christ's promise of self-revelation to those who obey him (John 14:21).

Boston explains that self-probation—"prove yourselves"—is equally essential for truly discerning whether one is in the faith (2 Cor 13:5). Believers must not merely assume their gracious state without clear biblical evidence (Isa 44:20; Rev 3:17); such groundless hope is dangerous. Careful self-examination can, through Scripture, reveal the actual state of one's soul (Job 8:13–14). Believers must persevere in this work, seeking God's help and light until we reach a decisive understanding. Finally, once the truth of our condition is known, we must respond appropriately—either by urgently seeking Christ if we are not in the faith or by giving thanks and living for God's glory if we are.

TEA WITH THOMAS BOSTON

1. In what areas of your life do you need more self-examination to grow in Christ? (2 Cor 13:5; Ps 77:6; Matt 6:23)

2. How does knowledge of the gospel relate to self-examination in the faith? (1 John 2:11; 2 Pet 1:10; Heb 4:12)

3. What is the danger of false assurance in the faith, and how can you avoid it? (Matt 25:1–12; Isa 44:20; Rev 3:17)

4. How does regular self-examination foster holiness and obedience, and what role do the sacraments play? (2 Pet 1:10; Rom 10:17; 1 Cor 11:28)

5. How can believers practice self-examination without falling into legalism or self-condemnation? (Gal 6:4; 1 John 5:13; Rom 8:1)

Rosehip tea has a tangy, refreshing flavor, symbolizing the vitality of repentance and the beauty of self-examination in approaching the Lord's Supper.

Heavenly Father, grant me the honesty to examine my heart, the light to see my true condition, and the grace to trust in Christ alone. Amen.

"Satan has a mighty influence to the hinderance of it, both in saints and sinners. In the former he mars the comfort of the clear view of their state: in the latter he keeps them from waking out of their natural security."[1]

---

1. Boston, *Works*, 2:508 (2:497–510).

Day 81

The Nature of Prayer

Q98. *What is prayer?*

A. Prayer is an offering up of our desires unto God, for things agreeable to his will, in the name of Christ, with confession of our sins and thankful acknowledgment of his mercies.

Praying at all times in the Spirit, with all prayer and supplication. To that end, keep alert with all perseverance, making supplication for all the saints.

EPHESIANS 6:18

PRAYER IS "THE OFFERING of our desires to God," where we lift our hearts toward him and present our needs. Thomas Boston states that prayer can be without words, as "the desires of the heart offered to God" constitute true prayer if there is sincere affection and intention. Prayer is to be directed exclusively to God—Father, Son, and Holy Spirit—since worship is due to God alone, not to saints, angels, or any created beings (Matt 4:10). God is the only one capable of hearing prayer, searching the heart (1 Kgs 8:39), being omnipresent, and fulfilling the desires of his people (Ps 145:18–19). He is the only one qualified to respond to our prayers, as he alone can pardon sins and meet our needs. We pray to God alone because "the object of prayer and of faith are the very same" (Rom 10:14).

We must pray in the name of Christ, not through saints or angels (John 14:13). It is not "a faithless mentioning of his name" but an intentional, heartfelt petition to God through Jesus as our Mediator (Heb 7:25).

It involves going to God at Christ's command, depending on his merit and intercession (John 16:24). We rely on Christ for access, acceptance, and gracious response to our petitions (1 John 5:14). We pray in Christ's name because sin has separated us from God. Only Christ, the appointed Mediator, can bridge that gap (1 Tim 2:5). Christ alone can satisfy God's justice and intercede for us (1 John 2:1). Moreover, prayer is acceptable only through the Holy Spirit's assistance (Gal 4:6; Rom 8:26). The Spirit helps us by teaching, guiding, and inspiring us to pray according to God's will, infusing our prayers with "faith, fervency, and humility" (Zech 12:10; Jas 5:16). Without the Spirit, our prayers lack the power and direction to reach God's throne.

Boston teaches that we should pray for all living Christians and non-Christians, including those in authority and people of all backgrounds (1 Tim 2:1–2). However, we should neither pray for the dead nor those who have committed the unpardonable sin against the Holy Spirit (1 John 5:16). We should pray for future generations as Christ did for future believers (John 17:20), for the church (Eph 6:18), magistrates (1 Tim 2:2), ministers (Col 4:3), Christian acquaintances (Jas 5:16), our communities (Jer 29:7), families (Job 1:5), and even our enemies, following Christ's example (Matt 5:44).

In our prayers, we seek things that align with God's will in Scripture and avoid asking for sinful desires or things contrary to God's holiness (Jas 4:3). Our prayers should seek what is pleasing to God, for his glory (Matt 6:9), the welfare of the church, and our "temporal, spiritual, and eternal good" (Ps 122:6). Finally, we must pray "understandingly, reverently, humbly, feelingly, believingly, sincerely, fervently, watchfully, perseveringly, and dependingly."

TEA WITH THOMAS BOSTON

1. How can you ensure that your prayers align with God's will? (Eph 6:18; Ps 145:18–19; 1 John 5:14)
2. How does Christian prayer differ from prayer in other religions? (John 14:13; Heb 7:25; Phil 4:6–7)
3. How can you grow in praying with greater humility and fervency? (Luke 18:13; Col 4:3; Jas 5:16)
4. How can praying for others—including enemies and those in authority—foster spiritual growth? (Rom 12:14; 1 Tim 2:1–2; Eph 4:2–3)
5. What habits can you encourage in children and young believers to help them grow in prayer and rely on the Holy Spirit? (Rom 8:26; Gal 4:6; Luke 11:1–2)

 Birch leaf tea is an earthy, slightly bitter tea, symbolizing the honest confession, cleansing, and renewal found in heartfelt prayer.

 Heavenly Father, grant me understanding, humility, and faith as I pray, seeking your glory, trusting in your goodness, and waiting for your answer. Amen.

 "Cold, lifeless, and formal prayers, are not of the right stamp. We should, as in a most weighty matter, be boiling hot."[1]

---

1. Boston, *Works*, 2:535 (2:526–39).

Day 82

A Discourse on Secret Prayer

> Q98. *What is prayer?*
> A. Prayer is an offering up of our desires unto God, for things agreeable to his will, in the name of Christ, with confession of our sins and thankful acknowledgment of his mercies.

But when you pray, go into your room and shut the door and pray to your Father who is in secret. And your Father who sees in secret will reward you.
MATTHEW 6:6

IN MATTHEW 6:6, JESUS teaches the importance of secret prayer, cautioning against praying for public attention (v. 5). Jesus directs us to choose a private place for prayer, ensure secrecy by closing the door, and pray to God as our Father in Christ, who will reward the private, sincere prayers made in faith and fervency. Jesus frequently retreats to solitary places to pray (Matt 14:23). Secret prayer is vital for spiritual growth.

Thomas Boston argues that secret prayer is necessary—not to earn merit or salvation—but because God commands it. It acknowledges God's omniscience and omnipresence, declaring that God sees and knows everything. Secret prayer also demonstrates sincerity, showing that our devotion is not for outward display but flows from genuine obedience and desire to serve God. Since no one knows our personal needs, struggles, and sins as well as we do, we must come privately before God to confess and seek mercy in ways that are not fitting in public. Moreover, because our needs constantly arise and temptations are ever-present, we must continually draw strength and grace from God in prayer beyond what family or public prayer can provide.

Secret prayer is a vital spiritual discipline that believers should frequently practice, as Scripture exhorts us to "pray always" (Eph 6:18) and "without ceasing" (1 Thess 5:17), maintaining a prayerful spirit throughout the day and responding to God's promptings (Ps 27:8). Scripture shows varied examples of frequency—David prayed multiple times daily (Ps 55:17); Daniel maintained his practice even in danger (Dan 6:10). At minimum, saints should pray morning and evening, reflecting biblical patterns and the natural rhythm of life. The proper place for secret prayer is any secluded location, even if not literally a closet, as Jesus withdrew to solitary places. Various bodily postures are found in Scripture—standing (Mark 11:25), kneeling (Eph 3:14), lying prostrate (Matt 26:39), or sitting (2 Sam 7:18)—but all should express reverence (1 Cor 6:20) and suit the heart's condition while aiding devotion. Prayer may be silent, as with Moses (Exod 14:15), or spoken when appropriate, since using the voice can stir the heart and focus the mind (Ps 57:8), provided it is not for show. While secret prayer is not an infallible sign of sincerity—since even hypocrites may engage in it (cf. Judas)—when practiced consistently with communion, answered prayer, and delight in God, it becomes strong evidence of true faith.

Those who neglect secret prayers have strong reason to doubt the sincerity of their faith. Even many hypocrites pray privately, though falsely trusting it will earn them favor with God—how much worse to neglect it entirely. Neglect suggests a lack of self-awareness, as those who feel their sin and need will naturally turn to God in secret prayers. Public worship alone, argues Boston, is not true religion—sincere faith must entail hidden, heartfelt devotion.

TEA WITH THOMAS BOSTON

1. What role does secret prayer play in your life, and how does it reflect your walk with God? (Matt 6:6; Ps 139:1-2; 2 Cor 13:5)
2. What barriers hinder you from praying in secret more often, and how can you overcome them? (Rom 7:18-19; Luke 22:40; Heb 4:16)
3. How is Christian secret prayer distinct from meditation or prayer in other religions? (Matt 6:7-8; John 14:6; Phil 4:6)
4. How does secret prayer guard against hypocrisy in public and family worship? (Matt 6:1-4; Gal 1:10; Col 3:23-24)
5. How can you help children or young believers develop the habit of secret prayer without it becoming mechanical? (Deut 6:6-7; Ps 119:9; Prov 3:5-6)

Hibiscus mint tea has a refreshing tang, symbolizing the quiet renewal and spiritual refreshment in secret prayer.

Heavenly Father, draw me deeper into communion with you in secret so that I may know your presence, depend on your grace, and walk sincerely before you. Amen.

"The neglect of secret prayer is an incontestible evidence of one's being a stranger to Christ."[1]

---

1. Boston, *Works*, 2:541 (2:539-54).

Day 83

The Rule of Direction in Prayer

> Q99. *What rule has God given for our direction in prayer?*
>
> A. The whole word of God is of use to direct us in prayer, but the special rule of direction is that form of prayer which Christ taught his disciples, commonly called the Lord's Prayer.

Pray then like this: Our Father in heaven, hallowed be your name.

MATTHEW 6:9

IN THE SERMON ON the Mount, Jesus addresses hypocritical showiness (Matt 6:5) and meaningless repetition (Matt 6:7–8) in prayer. As a remedy, he offers "the Lord's Prayer" as a model prayer, though not necessarily to be repeated verbatim. Thomas Boston teaches that believers need direction in prayer because we approach a holy God, and careless prayer dishonors God (Eccl 5:2). As guilty sinners—like rebels before a king—we must come humbly and cautiously (Luke 18:13). Prayer is weighty, involving worship and eternal concerns, and only God can meet our true needs (Mic 6:6). Yet we are weak and prone to errors, often asking wrongly or praying insincerely (Jas 4:3). Wrong prayer can provoke God, bring harm, or be rejected (Ps 106:15). Therefore, we need God's guidance to pray rightly.

God has graciously given us the general rule of the whole Scripture and the special rule of the Lord's Prayer to guide our prayer. The Bible is a complete guide for prayer, furnishing us with the parts (petition, confession, thanksgiving—Ps 51:4–5; Phil 4:6), and the manner (sincerity—Heb 10:22;

humility—Ps 10:17; faith—Jas 1:6; fervency—Jas 5:16), and even "the most fit words" (Hos 14:2). We are to pray according to God's will as revealed in his word (1 John 5:14). In addition, Jesus gave us a "special rule" in the Lord's Prayer (Matt 6:9–13; Luke 11:2–4), which serves as a model rather than a "set form," which is evident from the variations between Matthew and Luke's versions.

Boston points out that in Luke, the fourth petition is "give us day by day our daily bread," while in Matthew, it appears, "Give us this day our daily bread." The Matthew version focuses on asking for present needs, whereas the Luke version emphasizes ongoing provision. Moreover, Christ did not use the Lord's Prayer in his prayer at Lazarus's tomb (John 11:41) or in his high priestly prayer (John 17), and neither did his apostles (Acts 1:24) or the early church (Acts 4:24). While the Lord's Prayer may be used with "understanding, faith, reverence"—especially by those who struggle to form their own prayers—it is not the only acceptable way to pray. The Lord's Prayer teaches us to approach God with reverence, dependence, and a desire for his glory, and it stands as a concise and rich directory for all true prayer.

Although the rules for prayer in Scripture provide sufficient external guidance, the Holy Spirit's assistance is essential for effective prayer (Rom 8:26). We should be thankful for God's direction and study the Bible for a deeper understanding of how to pray. Neglecting prayer or relying only on a set form is wrong, as Scripture offers ample guidance. Prayer is essential to the Christian life, and we must rely on the Holy Spirit to help us pray— bringing our needs, confessing our sins, and interceding for others.

TEA WITH THOMAS BOSTON

1. Why must Scripture guide our prayers? (2 Tim 3:16–17; Ps 119:105; John 17:17)
2. How is the Lord's Prayer a model, not a fixed formula? (Matt 6:9–13; Luke 11:2–4; John 11:41)
3. How is Christian prayer different from other religions' prayers? (Matt 6:7–8; 1 Thess 5:17; Acts 17:24–25)
4. What are the dangers of careless prayer, and how can we avoid them? (Jas 4:3; Ps 106:15; Eccl 5:1–2)
5. What prayer habits should we teach new believers? (Luke 11:1; Ps 1:2; Col 4:2)

Sarsaparilla tea is an earthy, slightly sweet beverage, symbolizing the restorative guidance of God's word in shaping our prayers.

Heavenly Father, teach us to pray humbly and sincerely by your Spirit and word, seeking your will and trusting you for all we need. Amen.

"Our Saviour chiefly intended this prayer as a directory, respecting the matter of our petitions, rather than a form; because it does not explicitly contain all the parts of prayer, particularly confession of sin, and thankful acknowledgement of mercies."[1]

---

1. Boston, *Works*, 2:559 (2:555–60).

Day 84

The Preface of the Lord's Prayer

> Q100. *What does the preface of the Lord's Prayer teach us?*
>
> A. The preface of the Lord's Prayer, which is, "Our Father which art in heaven," teaches us to draw near to God with all holy reverence and confidence, as children to a father, able and ready to help us; and that we should pray with and for others.

Pray then like this: Our Father in heaven, hallowed be your name.
MATTHEW 6:9

MATTHEW 6:9 OPENS THE Lord's Prayer with a preface—"Our Father which art in heaven"—which identifies God as the object of our worship. Thomas Boston states that in prayer, believers should approach God as a *Father, our* Father, and our Father *in heaven.*

Calling God "Father" in prayer teaches several foundational truths about our relationship with him. It reminds us that only those born again and adopted into God's family can pray acceptably—true, saving prayer is the privilege of God's children (John 9:31). However, unbelievers are still duty-bound to pray. It also points to our access to God through Christ, whose mediation secures our adoption. We approach the Father in prayer through Christ's name and merit (Eph 2:18). Calling God "Father" shows that we pray in the Spirit, who, as the Spirit of adoption, is "the principle of all acceptable praying to God." The Spirit enables us to "call God Father" (Gal 4:6), stirs our hearts to pray, and gives us the right words and affections

(Rom 8:26). This address also shapes the posture of our prayer—we come with "childlike dispositions and affections," honoring God's holiness while depending on his tender care (Matt 7:11). In all these ways, calling God "Father" reflects the new relationship we have through Christ, the Spirit's transforming work in our hearts, and the reverent confidence that should mark every believer's approach to God in prayer.

Calling God "*our* Father" in prayer teaches us to pray privately and with others, emphasizing the importance of public and family prayer. It also encourages praying for ourselves and others, following biblical examples (Acts 12:5; 1 Tim 2:1–2). Boston states that praying with and for others reflects the communion of saints and the shared blessings of being part of God's family.

Addressing God as "our Father *in heaven*" teaches us to recognize his sovereign power and dominion, trusting that he can help us in any situation and do whatever he wills (Ps 115:3). Unlike earthly fathers, our heavenly Father is almighty. Our prayers should be filled with "heavenly affections," acknowledging God's greatness and approaching him with awe (Ps 123:1; Eccl 5:2). We are to marvel at God's condescension as he looks down from his heavenly throne to us—"poor worms on earth" (Isa 66:1–2). Finally, we approach God as "strangers on this earth," viewing this world as a pilgrimage and longing for our true home in heaven—"our Father's house"—where we will join the angels and the spirits of the righteous (1 Pet 1:17).

True prayer requires faith, as only by faith can we call God our Father and have fellowship with him. The saints are blessed to be in communion with the Trinity, and being adopted into God's family brings great joy. God's children have hope, as they can always turn to their Father in heaven for support, whether in life or death, ultimately leading to eternal joy with him.

TEA WITH THOMAS BOSTON

1. How does knowing that God is your "Father" shape your prayer life? (Matt 6:9; Gal 4:6; Rom 8:15)
2. How does the confidence that God is willing and able to help influence your trust in him? (Matt 7:11; Ps 115:3; Heb 4:16)
3. How does praying with and for others enrich your prayer life and strengthen relationships within the church? (Acts 12:5; Rom 15:30; Jas 5:16)
4. How does the idea of God as "Father" distinguish Christianity from other religions? (Matt 6:9; John 1:12–13; 1 John 3:1)
5. How can you make interceding for others a more regular part of your daily prayers? (Phil 1:3–4; 1 Tim 2:1–2; Col 4:12)

 Moringa tea is rich and nourishing, symbolizing the confidence and reverence we approach our heavenly Father, who graciously provides for his children.

 Heavenly Father, thank you for adopting us into your family, and may your Spirit guide our prayers with faith, reverence, and confidence in your love and care. Amen.

 "Being married to the Son, we call God Father, and make bold in his house, by virtue of our relation to him, through our Lord and Husband."[1]

---

1. Boston, *Works*, 2:562 (2:561–65).

Day 85

The First Petition

Q101. *What do we pray for in the first petition?*

A. In the first petition, which is, "Hallowed be thy name," we pray that God would enable us, and others, to glorify him in all that whereby he makes himself known, and that he would dispose all things to his own glory.

Pray then like this: Our Father in heaven, hallowed be your name.

MATTHEW 6:9

"HALLOWED BE THY NAME" is the first of six petitions in the Lord's Prayer. The first three focus on God's honor, while the last three concern our needs, rightly placing God's glory above our interests. This opening petition emphasizes the sanctifying, or glorifying, of God's name and is listed first because it should be our highest priority. Thomas Boston explains that God's name refers to God himself, encompassing everything by which he reveals himself to his creatures (Ps 8:1)—his names, such as YHWH; his titles, like "God of peace" or "God of patience"; his attributes and perfections; his word and ordinances; his mighty works; and especially Jesus Christ, through whom God is most clearly revealed (John 1:18).

Boston explains that to hallow God's name does not mean making God "more holy," for he is already perfectly holy (1 John 1:5). Rather, it means acknowledging and manifesting his holiness—bringing it to light where it has been hidden or unrecognized. God's name is said to be "hallowed" instead of simply "glorified" because his holiness is the crown of all his attributes; it is the beauty and glory of his "wisdom, power, mercy," and every perfection. Scripture repeatedly calls God "the Holy One." When angels worship, they highlight his holiness above all (Isa 6:3). God's greatest glory is when he communicates his holiness to his people—when they bear his image and reflect his character. A "holy poor man," argues Boston, glorifies God more than an "unholy monarch" because only the holy can actively glorify God. Thus, God is most glorified when his holiness shines through his people.

This petition asks that God's name be glorified in two ways. First, by God himself, as he reveals his holiness and glory through all his works and providence (John 12:28). Despite opposition from sin and Satan, we pray that God would cause his name to shine—breaking through obstacles, using even evil for his glory, and ultimately removing all hindrances to his honor. Second, we pray that God would enable us and others, by his grace, to glorify his name. Since we must live for his glory (1 Cor 10:31) and cannot do this in our strength (2 Cor 3:5), we ask God to empower us to hallow his name. This includes internal reverence—"esteeming him, his names, titles, attributes, ordinances, words, and works"—and external honoring through words and actions that praise him (Phil 1:11).

True believers grieve over sin because it dishonors God (Ps 119:136). Those who habitually profane God's name show that they are not his children. Holiness is our true glory, and God's people desire to see his name honored by all. They submit to God's will so that Christ may be magnified (Phil 1:20) and live to glorify him in heart, word, and deed.

TEA WITH THOMAS BOSTON

1. How does God's holiness as his "crown" deepen your awe when praying "hallowed be thy name"? (Isa 6:3; Ps 8:1; Rev 4:8)
2. How does the sin of dishonoring God's name move you to grieve and repent as David did? (Ps 51:4; 119:136; Jer 3:13)
3. How can you honor God's name in word and deed through your daily interactions this week? (1 Cor 10:31; Col 3:17; Matt 5:16)
4. If holiness is our glory, what steps can you take now to pursue sanctification? (1 Pet 1:15–16; Phil 1:20; 2 Cor 3:18)
5. What habit can you encourage in young Christians to help them esteem God's name, and how can you model it? (Ps 34:3; Col 3:16; Deut 6:6–7)

 Red clover blossom tea is gently sweet and earthy, symbolizing the pursuit of God's glory and the growth of holiness through his grace.

 Heavenly Father, may your name be hallowed—revealed in your glory, honored by your people, and magnified through our lives by your grace. Amen.

 "None are fit to glorify him but those who are holy."[1]

---

1. Boston, *Works*, 2:567 (2:565–70).

Day 86

The Second Petition

> Q102. *What do we pray for in the second petition?*
>
> A. In the second petition, which is, "Thy kingdom come," we pray that Satan's kingdom may be destroyed; and that the kingdom of grace may be advanced, ourselves and others brought into it, and kept in it; and that the kingdom of glory may be hastened.

Your kingdom come, your will be done, on earth as it is in heaven.
MATTHEW 6:10

THE SECOND PETITION OF the Lord's Prayer, "thy kingdom come," calls for the advancement of God's kingdom, which is the means of glorifying his name. Thomas Boston identifies a "fourfold kingdom of God": the "Kingdom of his power"—God's universal rule over all creation, where every being submits to him as the "universal Monarch" (Ps 103:19; Rom 14:11); the "Kingdom of his gospel"—the visible church within the first kingdom where Christ reigns, governed by his word and ordinances (Matt 21:43; Eph 1:22–23); the "Kingdom of his grace"—a subset of the second kingdom, the invisible church where Christ reigns in the hearts of true believers, empowered by the Holy Spirit to overcome spiritual enemies (Luke 17:21; Eph 3:17); and the "Kingdom of his glory"—the eternal, perfected state in heaven after Christ's return, where the elect are ruled by the triune God and worship eternally (1 Cor 15:50; Rom 8:29–30).

The kingdom of glory is not yet fully realized (1 John 3:2), as God's full glory is veiled and many of the elect remain in sin, pilgrimage, or the grave. It will, however, come at Christ's return, offering eternal happiness and freedom from sin and death. Believers long for its arrival, desiring Christ's return and the destruction of death (1 Cor 15:26). If Christ's return terrifies, it may reflect a worldly heart (Phil 3:18–20) or lack of assurance. The kingdom of grace involves a transformative process where individuals are brought out of Satan's dominion and into God's grace, with the recognition that only God can bring this about (John 6:44). God calls believers to pray for the advancement of this kingdom, including the conversion of sinners and the preservation of those already in it. The kingdom of the gospel is crucial for bringing people into the kingdom of grace, but numerous hindrances, such as Satan and human resistance, block the gospel's spread. Believers must desire the removal of these obstacles, the spread of the gospel, and its compelling power to transform hearts. Lastly, the kingdom of power emphasizes the need for God's omnipotent intervention to accomplish these goals, with believers praying for God's active involvement in bringing his kingdom to fruition (Isa 64:1–2).

God's children are concerned for the coming of his kingdom because their new nature draws them toward heaven and the kingdom of Christ (Phil 3:20). As children of God, they care for their Father's kingdom and honor (Matt 6:9–10). Their eternal welfare is tied to the kingdom's success, as they are subjects of both the kingdom of grace and glory (Jer 29:7). The advancement of the kingdom benefits all saints and the salvation of the elect (Ps 122:8). Their betterment rises and falls with the kingdom's advancement. Finally, the kingdom of Christ's victory over the devil's kingdom is sure—"the perfection of Christ's kingdom will be the destruction of the other"—and believers long for the defeat of evil (Gen 3:15).

TEA WITH THOMAS BOSTON

1. What do you long for when you pray "thy kingdom come"? (Phil 3:20; Rev 22:20; Ps 73:25)
2. Does Christ's return give you joy or fear? Why? (1 John 3:2; 1 Cor 15:26; Phil 3:18–20)
3. How does God's kingdom challenge the world's values? (Dan 7:27; Matt 6:33; Rom 14:17)
4. How should God's kingdom shape your prayers and priorities? (Matt 6:10; Col 3:2–4; Rom 12:2)
5. How can we show children and new believers their place in God's kingdom? (Eph 2:4–7; Rom 8:29–30; 1 Thess 2:12)

Elderflower tea has a delicate floral fragrance, symbolizing the advance of grace and the hope of God's coming kingdom.

Heavenly Father, let thy kingdom come in power, gospel, grace, and glory—overthrow every enemy and hasten the day when Christ reigns visibly and eternally. Amen.

"Let our royal Master have your hearts for his throne, and set up his kingdom of grace there."[1]

---

1. Boston, *Works*, 2:575 (2:571–86).

Day 87

The Third Petition

Q103. *What do we pray for in the third petition?*

A. In the third petition, which is "thy will be done in earth as it is in heaven," we pray that God, by his grace, would make us able and willing to know, obey, and submit to his will in all things, as the angels do in heaven.

Your kingdom come, your will be done, on earth as it is in heaven.
MATTHEW 6:10

THE THIRD PETITION—"THY WILL be done"—is about advancing God's kingdom by doing his will, which ultimately glorifies him. Thomas Boston points out that, despite the plurality of Persons within the Trinity, the Lord's Prayer uses singular pronouns like "thy" since plural forms such as "your" or "ye" might wrongly imply belief in multiple gods.

Boston differentiates God's will of command and providence. The will of command is God's law revealed in Scripture, calling all to obedience—especially in faith in Christ and holiness. Faith is the first and final duty under the covenant of grace, where the call is no longer "do and live" but "believe and be saved" (John 3:16). Holiness is God's will for his people, reflecting his nature. God's will of command is perfectly obeyed in heaven, wholly rejected in hell, and imperfectly followed on earth, where sincere believers strive to keep it (Acts 13:22). God's will of providence is his sovereign rule over all creation (Ps 135:6), by which he orders every detail of life (Matt

10:29–30) and guides our responsibilities through various circumstances. This includes both blessings and afflictions—what Boston calls "smiling providences" (Rom 2:4) and "frowning providences" (Mic 6:9)—all under God's wise and sovereign hand. Believers should spiritually discern them and not be "idle spectators of Providence" (Ps 107). To pray "thy will be done" is to seek joyful obedience to God's commands and humble submission to his providence, as found in heaven.

Boston explains that praying this petition involves confession, profession, and desire. Regarding God's will of command, this prayer confesses that even the godly struggle to fulfill his will (Gal 5:17), and all are naturally indisposed to obey—lacking ability (1 Cor 2:14), willingness (Ps 110:3), and inclination (Ps 14:1). It professes the saints' grief over such disobedience (Ps 119:136) and their faith in divine grace to renew their hearts (Ezek 36:26). It desires God to remove their "spiritual blindness" (Eph 1:17–18) and empower them to overcome "weakness, indisposition, and perverseness," aspiring to do God's will "evenly, unweariedly, universally, humbly, cheerfully, readily, and constantly," like that in heaven. Though perfection in this life remains out of reach, the prayer reflects the believer's duty, longing, and effort to grow toward it (Phil 3:13–14).

Concerning God's will of providence, the petition similarly confesses the human tendency to murmur (Num 14:2), envy others (Matt 20:15), resist affliction (Job 2:10), and spurn providence's lessons (Rom 2:4). It professes sorrow for such resistance (Jer 31:18), trusting God's grace to bring conformity to his will. It desires grace to submit to "afflicting providences" (Ps 39:9), to receive "merciful and kind providences" with gratitude (Luke 1:38), to fulfill one's providential calling (Acts 13:36), and to consent fully and freely to God's purposes in all things, echoing Christ's own submission (Matt 26:42).

TEA WITH THOMAS BOSTON

1. What areas of your life are you reluctant to surrender to God's will, and how can you grow in submission? (Gal 5:17; Ps 110:3; Jas 4:7)

2. How does the distinction between God's will of command and providence highlight his sovereignty and our obedience? (Dan 4:35; John 3:16; 14:15)

3. How does God's will of providence set Christianity apart from atheism or other worldviews? (Acts 17:28; Job 12:10; Prov 16:9)

4. How does spiritual discernment help you recognize God's will in daily life, and how can you grow in it? (Eph 1:17–18; Rom 12:2; Phil 1:9–10)

5. How can you model joyful submission to God's will to encourage others in their faith? (Ps 40:8; 2 Tim 2:1–2; 1 Cor 11:1)

 Jasmine mint tea is aromatic and refreshing, symbolizing the joyful submission and renewal found in doing God's will.

 Heavenly Father, help us to joyfully obey your will and humbly submit to your sovereign rule for your glory and our sanctification. Amen.

 "But which of the commandments do we not break on earth? What part of God's will is done by us in every point as is required? None at all. But the saints hope and long for the day, when they shall be able to know and do the whole of it in every point."[1]

---

1. Boston, *Works*, 2:596 (2:586–601).

Day 88

The Fourth Petition

> Q104. *What do we pray for in the fourth petition?*
>
> A. In the fourth petition, which is, "Give us this day our daily bread," we pray that of God's free gift we may receive a competent portion of the good things of this life and enjoy his blessing with them.

Give us this day our daily bread.
MATTHEW 6:11

THE LORD'S PRAYER SHIFTS from God's glory in the first three petitions to human welfare in the last three. Thomas Boston teaches that this transition reflects a divine order—God's children must prioritize God's honor above their temporal and spiritual welfare. Temporally, saints prefer God's glory over their daily provision (Acts 21:13), rejecting bread gained unlawfully against God's name, kingdom, or will (Heb 11:25), and trust God to supply their needs while pursuing God's ends (Ps 37:3). Spiritually, they submit even their "spiritual comforts" to God's glory, as seen in David (2 Sam 15:25–26) and Christ (Ps 22:1–3), willingly yielding all to God's sovereign will as Mary did (John 20:17). This prioritization stems from God being man's chief end and good (Rev 4:11), reversing it would be a prideful perversion.

"Bread," states Boston, refers to the physical sustenance necessary for our bodies, not "spiritual bread," signifying Jesus Christ in the second petition, or "sacramental bread," representing forgiveness in the fifth petition.

While we are encouraged to care for our bodies, as they are temples of the Holy Spirit, the fourth petition emphasizes that our primary concern should be for our souls, which are immortal and of far greater importance than our mortal bodies—"the body is of the earth, the soul is from heaven." The soul, being eternal, should receive more care than the body, as it determines our eternal destiny. "Bread" here encompasses "good things of this life"— not only the necessities like food and clothing but also conveniences that provide comfort—which God provides according to each person's circumstances. Thus, while we must care for our bodies, God calls us to prioritize the well-being of our souls, as they ultimately determine both our earthly and eternal welfare (Matt 6:33).

The phrase "give bread" reminds us that God is the ultimate provider. Everything we receive is a gift (Ps 145:16). Even when we have bread, we must pray for God's blessing upon it, as it can only nourish us through the providence of God, who is our "Creator, Preserver, Proprietor, Provisor, and Friend." "Give *us* bread" extends to our families and others, showing our duty to care for those in need (Jas 2:15–16). The words "give us *our* bread" imply that we should possess the things of life lawfully, acknowledging our "covenant-right" through Christ (1 Cor 3:22) and "civil-right" through our efforts (2 Thess 3:12). The phrase "*daily* bread" teaches contentment with sufficient provision for each day, guarding against the pursuit of wealth and worrying about the future (Prov 30:8). Finally, "give us *this day* our daily bread" emphasizes living day by day, trusting that God will provide for our needs and reminding us of the uncertainty of tomorrow (Matt 6:34; Jas 4:14). This petition encourages us to trust God's daily provision and remain content with what he gives us.

TEA WITH THOMAS BOSTON

1. How has trusting God for "daily bread" changed your view of provision and contentment? (Matt 6:11; Ps 37:3; Prov 30:8)
2. How does this petition highlight the biblical balance between prayer and lawful labor? (2 Thess 3:12; Prov 14:23; Eph 4:28)
3. In what ways does Christianity uniquely affirm both the spiritual and physical aspects of life? (Gen 1:31; 1 Tim 4:4–5; Rom 12:1)
4. What steps can you take to avoid anxiety about future needs and trust in God's daily provision? (Matt 6:34; Jas 4:14; Luke 12:24)
5. How can you model generosity and care for others' "daily bread" in your home or church community? (Jas 2:15–16; Gal 6:10; Acts 2:45)

White tea is light and soothing, symbolizing dependence on God's daily provision and the quiet trust that flows from his care.

Heavenly Father, help us prioritize your glory and trust in your daily provision for our bodies and souls, seeking to honor you in all things. Amen.

"We are to pray for daily, not weekly and yearly bread. Riches are a snare to our corrupt hearts."[1]

---

1. Boston, *Works*, 2:610 (2:601–12).

Day 89

The Fifth Petition

Q105. *What do we pray for in the fifth petition?*

A. In the fifth petition, which is, "and forgive us our debts, as we forgive our debtors," we pray that God, for Christ's sake, would freely pardon all our sins, which we are the rather encouraged to ask, because by his grace we are enabled from the heart to forgive others.

. . . and forgive us our debts, as we also have forgiven our debtors.
MATTHEW 6:12

THOMAS BOSTON STATES THAT the fifth petition—"forgive us our debts"—follows the request for daily bread not because bread is more important than pardon but because "this life" is the only opportunity to receive forgiveness (Heb 9:27). Forgiveness is the first of the spiritual blessings as unpardoned sin blocks communion with God (Ps 66:18). The petition is connected to the previous one by the word "and," indicating that earthly provision without forgiveness is ultimately empty and meaningless (Ps 17:14). Without pardon, even life's blessings are joyless, like a meal under the shadow of divine judgment (Luke 12:19–20). Thus, forgiveness gives genuine sweetness to all other gifts.

In this petition, "debts" refer to sins—the sinner is the debtor, unable to repay the debt; God is the creditor, holding the sinner accountable; the sinner has taken, by abuse, God's honor; and the sinner owes God the reparation of that honor. Every sin is a spiritual debt: a "drowning debt" unpayable by human strength (Matt 18:24–25), often downplayed by the sinner (Luke 16:6) yet fully remembered by God (Amos 8:7) and inevitably pursued (Matt 5:25). These debts are "ours," contends Boston, by imputation (Rom 5:19), by inborn corruption (Ps 51:5), by commission or omission (Jer 16:10), and by association with others' sins (1 Tim 5:22). The "us" in the petition includes not only ourselves but others as well, even unbelievers (Luke 23:34).

Forgiveness is the removal of guilt—eternal (Rom 8:1), temporal (Ps 89:30–33), or experiential (Luke 7:47–48). In this petition, we confess sin (Dan 9:5), admit our helplessness (Ps 130:3–4), and plead for free forgiveness through Christ (Rom 3:24). For the unconverted, it seeks deliverance from wrath; for believers, it seeks restoration from the Father's displeasure and renewed assurance (Ps 4:6). Though Christ paid the cost, we receive pardon freely by grace.

The phrase "as we forgive our debtors," argues Boston, serves not to "move God to forgive us" but to strengthen our faith that God will hear our prayer. Our "debtors" are those who have wronged us (1 Sam 2:25), and forgiving them means sincerely releasing the injury, harboring no hatred or malice, but showing goodwill and readiness to do them well (Matt 5:44–45), though not necessarily delighting in their character if there is no cause (Ps 26:4). "As we forgive" does not imply our forgiveness equals God's—ours is imperfect—but it must be "real and sincere" (Matt 18:35). It precedes our request for forgiveness (Luke 11:4). This shows that the prayer seeks not pardon from eternal wrath, which belongs to the unconverted. However, the removal of fatherly displeasure and the assurance of pardon, which believers can seek (Luke 7:47). The encouragement we draw is this: if we, by God's grace, can forgive others, then surely the gracious God can forgive us. Our willingness to forgive confirms that we belong to God and can confidently hope for renewed cleansing.

TEA WITH THOMAS BOSTON

1. When you have struggled to forgive, how has seeking God's forgiveness helped you extend forgiveness to others? (Matt 18:35; Luke 11:4; 1 John 1:9)

2. What does the word "debts" mean in the context of the Lord's Prayer? (Matt 6:12; Luke 7:47–48; Col 2:13)

3. What makes Christian forgiveness distinct from concepts of forgiveness in atheism or other religions? (Eph 1:7; 2 Cor 5:18–19; Isa 55:7)

4. How can you practically forgive those who wrong you, just as God forgives you in Christ? (Matt 5:44–45; 1 Pet 3:9; Col 3:13)

5. How can you teach children or new believers about forgiveness in light of the gospel? (Eph 4:32; Mark 11:25; Matt 18:21–22)

Licorice and fennel tea is a sweet, soothing blend, symbolizing the grace of forgiveness and the healing it brings through Christ.

Heavenly Father, we confess our sins and ask for your forgiveness. Strengthen us to forgive others as you have forgiven us, restoring our communion with you. Amen.

"See your debts, and mourn over them, and apply to the blood of Christ for the pardon of them all, your imputed, your inherent, and your actual sins."[1]

---

1. Boston, *Works*, 2:619 (2:612–19).

Day 90

The Sixth Petition

Q106. *What do we pray for in the sixth petition?*

A. In the sixth petition, which is "and lead us not into temptation, but deliver us from evil," we pray that God would either keep us from being tempted to sin or support and deliver us when we are tempted.

And lead us not into temptation, but deliver us from evil.

MATTHEW 6:13

THOMAS BOSTON ARGUES THAT the term "and" in "forgive us our debts *and* lead us not into temptation" shows that true repentance seeks both pardon for past sins and strength to resist future ones. We cannot sincerely ask for pardon while planning to continue in sin (Ps 66:18). A genuine believer desires both justification and sanctification. Forgiveness alone does not remove danger—believers remain vulnerable to relapse and spiritual attack. Even pardoned sinners must pray for protection, knowing that Satan is "most apt to bait the pardoned sinner" (Acts 13:8).

"Lead us not into temptation" is a plea for "preventing grace." Temptation refers specifically to enticements to sin, which, according to Boston, involve four components: the one being tempted—ourselves; the tempters—Satan (Matt 4:3), others (Acts 26:11), and our sinful desires (Jas 1:14); the bait—such as worldly gain (Matt 16:26); and the destructive aim—our spiritual ruin (1 Cor 10:12). God, in his providence, may allow us to enter situations where our hearts might be drawn into sin (cf. 2 Sam 24:1; 1 Chr 21:1), but God remains holy and just in doing so (Ps 81:11–12). God can restrain temptation or use it for our good, such as humbling us. This petition also reflects that spiritual danger constantly surrounds us (1 Pet 5:8), and, apart from God's grace, we cannot stand (Rom 7:23–24). Thus, God's people earnestly pray to be kept from temptation (Matt 26:41), for Satan to be restrained (2 Cor 12:8), for their hearts to be purified (Ps 119:133), and for protection from the evil of the world (John 17:15). Since our spiritual enemies are strong and persistent, we need both vigilance and constant dependence on Christ's grace to stand firm.

"But deliver us from evil" is a plea for "assisting grace." It expresses the believer's desire to be rescued from sin and its enticements. "Evil" here refers primarily to sin—which Boston deems "the greatest of evils, the worst of evils, and the cause of all other evils" (Amos 5:15)—as well as to temptation to sin, which includes anything that draws the soul away from God. Deliverance from evil includes recovery from temptation when one has fallen into sin (Ps 51:12) and protection from falling again (Jude 24). This petition acknowledges that as long as we live in this world, we are never free from the danger of temptation—whether in prosperity or adversity, solitude or company (Ps 119:107). God's children, therefore, earnestly long for deliverance in three ways: "in temptation" that God would empower them to resist (2 Cor 12:8); "under temptation" that God would lift them when they fall (Ps 51:8); and from all temptation, through final deliverance into a sinless state in heaven (Rom 7:24). Ultimately, this petition is offered in faith, trusting that only God has the power and mercy to deliver his people from evil.

TEA WITH THOMAS BOSTON

1. What temptations do you face, and how does God's deliverance encourage you? (Matt 6:13; Ps 119:133; John 17:15)

2. How have you experienced God's grace in temptation, and how has it deepened your dependence on him? (2 Cor 12:8; Ps 51:12; 1 Cor 10:13)

3. How does God's holiness and justice relate to his allowing temptation? (Ps 81:11-12; 1 Cor 10:13; 2 Sam 24:1)

4. How can we guard our hearts from temptation daily? (Matt 26:41; Ps 119:107; 1 Pet 5:8)

5. How can you help a new believer rely on God's strength to resist temptation? (1 Cor 10:13; Ps 51:8; Jude 24)

 White tea with ginger is a light, invigorating blend, symbolizing spiritual alertness and God's protection in times of temptation.

 Heavenly Father, forgive my sins and strengthen me to resist temptation, that by your grace I may be kept from evil and brought safely to glory. Amen.

 "Praying without watching is a tempting of God: watching without praying is a contempt of God and his grace."[1]

---

1. Boston, *Works*, 2:636 (2:619-38).

Day 91

The Conclusion of the Lord's Prayer

> Q107. *What does the conclusion of the Lord's Prayer teach us?*
>
> A. The conclusion of the Lord's Prayer, which is "for thine is the kingdom, and the power, and the glory, for ever. Amen," teaches us to take our encouragement in prayer from God only, and in our prayers to praise him, ascribing kingdom, power, and glory to him, and in testimony of our desire and assurance to be heard, we say, Amen.

For thine is the kingdom, and the power, and the glory, for ever. Amen.
MATTHEW 6:13

THOMAS BOSTON EXPLAINS HOW the concluding doxology, linked by the particle "for," serves as a set of arguments to reinforce the petitions, urging God to hear them based on God's kingdom, power, and glory. This structure teaches believers to plead and press their prayers with reason, enhancing their effectiveness. Pleading in prayer is not to change God's mind, as God is unchangeable and cannot be persuaded (Jas 1:17; Job 23:13). Instead, pleading strengthens our "praying graces, faith, and fervency." While pleading may result in God's answering our prayer, it is not to move God but to express the necessity and reasonableness of our requests. Pleading deepens our earnestness, similar to how a child pleads with a parent—not to persuade the parent but to emphasize the urgency and need of the request.

Boston teaches that the "kingdom" represents God's universal reign over all creation, not just his kingdom of grace or glory. The "power" is not just authority but the ability to accomplish his will in his kingdom. The "glory" is the honor God receives from his actions in his kingdom, which will shine forever. This conclusion serves as both praise and pleading arguments. In praise, we exalt God as the universal Monarch, omnipotent and the ultimate purpose of all creation (1 Chr 29:11). We acknowledge him as the sole Sovereign and "the chief end of all things." God is for his own glory (Isa 48:11). It teaches us that we should both praise and petition God in our prayers. Praise is essential to worship, directly honoring God and enduring eternally. The Lord's Prayer begins and ends with praise to remind us to focus on God's glory when we begin and conclude our prayers.

In prayer, our arguments are drawn solely from God's nature—his kingdom, power, and glory. This teaches us to find our encouragement in God alone when praying, relying on what he is rather than any worthiness in ourselves. We should not base our pleas on our merits but on God's attributes. While we may mention both our sins and virtues, the force of the plea, Boston claims, lies in God's qualities, such as his mercy, faithfulness, and name. For instance, David pleads for forgiveness not based on his sin but for God's name's sake (Ps 25:11), and Hezekiah pleads for life extension based on God's promise (Isa 38:3). The plea for hearing, therefore, is threefold. The kingdom is God's, so he has the authority to grant our requests (Matt 20:15). The power is God's, so he can accomplish what we ask, even "over the belly of all opposition" (Eph 3:20). The glory is God's, so he will act to preserve his glory, which is tied to answering our prayers (Josh 7:9). Finally, the word "amen" expresses our desire to be heard—saying "even so" (Rev 22:20)—and shows our confidence that God will fulfill our requests, reflecting faith and assurance in God's promise to answer prayer (2 Chr 14:11).

TEA WITH THOMAS BOSTON

1. How does ending prayer with God's kingdom, power, and glory grow your confidence in prayer? (Matt 6:13; 2 Chr 14:11; Ps 25:11)
2. How is Christian prayer unique in focusing on God's unchanging nature? (Jas 1:17; Job 23:13; Num 23:19)
3. How does ending prayer with praise and confidence deepen your faith? (Ps 145:1–3; Heb 13:15; Col 4:2)
4. How can we teach others to pray confidently by focusing on God's kingdom, power, and glory? (Matt 6:13; Ps 145:11–13; Rom 8:15)
5. Why should we teach that "Amen" expresses both desire and faith? (Rev 1:7; 2 Cor 1:20; Mark 11:24)

 Golden flower tea is a fragrant, floral blend, symbolizing the glory, assurance, and eternal truth of God's promises, reminding us to praise him with confidence in prayer.

 Heavenly Father, since thine is the kingdom, and the power, and the glory forever, we rest in faith that you will hear and answer for your name's sake. Amen.

 "Never bow a knee unto God for supplicating a mercy from him, without praising him for what mercies ye enjoy."[1]

---

1. Boston, *Works*, 2:643 (2:638–45).

Appendix
Thomas Boston's Personal Covenants

A FIRST PERSONAL COVENANT[1]

I, MR. THOMAS BOSTON, preacher of the gospel of Christ, being by nature an apostate from God, an enemy to the great JEHOVAH, and so an heir of hell and wrath, in myself utterly lost and undone, because of my original and actual sins, and misery thereby; and being, in some measure, made sensible of this my lost and undone state, and sensible of my need, my absolute need of a Saviour, without whom I must perish eternally; and believing that the Lord Jesus Christ, the eternal Son of the eternal God, is not only able to save me, by virtue of his death and sufferings, but willing also to save me (though most vile and ugly, and one who has given him many repulses), both from my sins, and from the load of wrath due to me for them, upon condition that I believe, come to him for salvation, and cordially receive him in all his offices; consenting to the terms of the covenant: therefore, as I have at several opportunities before given an express and solemn consent to the terms of the covenant, and have entered into a personal covenant with Christ; so now, being called to undertake the great and weighty work of the ministry of the gospel, for which I am altogether insufficient, I do by this declare, That I stand to and own all my former engagements, whether sacramental, or any other way whatsoever; and now again do RENEW my covenant with God; and hereby, at this present time, do solemnly COVENANT and ENGAGE to be the Lord's and MAKE a solemn resignation and upgiving of myself, my soul, body, spiritual and temporal concerns, unto the Lord Jesus Christ, without any reservation whatsoever; and do hereby give my voluntary consent to the terms of the covenant laid down in the holy scriptures, the word of truth; and with my heart and soul I TAKE and

---

1. Boston, *Works*, 2:671–72. Boston wrote this covenant on August 14, 1699, before his ordination to the ministry.

RECEIVE Christ in all his offices, as my PROPHET to teach me, resolving and engaging in his strength to follow, that is, to endeavour to follow his instructions: I TAKE him as my PRIEST, to be saved by his death and merits alone; and renouncing my own righteousness as filthy rags and menstruous cloths, I am content to be clothed with his righteousness alone; and live entirely upon free p 672 grace; likewise I TAKE him for my ADVOCATE and INTERCESSOR with the Father: and finally, I TAKE him as my KING, to reign in me, and to rule over me, renouncing all other lords, whether sin or self, and in particular my predominant idol; and in the strength of the Lord, do resolve and hereby engage, to cleave to Christ as my Sovereign Lord and King, in death and in life, in prosperity and in adversity, even for ever, and to strive and wrestle in his strength against all known sin; protesting, that whatever sin may be lying hid in my heart out of my view, I disown it, and abhor it, and shall in the Lord's strength, endeavour the mortification of it, when the Lord shall be pleased to let me see it. And this solemn covenant I make as in the presence of the ever-living, heart-searching God, and subscribe it with my hand, in my chamber, at Dunse, about one o'clock in the afternoon, the fourteenth day of August, one thousand six hundred and ninety-nine years.

T. Boston

A SECOND PERSONAL COVENANT[2]

O LORD, the God and Father of our Lord Jesus Christ, I confess from my heart, that I am by nature a lost and undone sinner, wholly corrupted, and laid under the curse, in Adam, through the breach of the covenant of works; and have ruined myself more and more by my innumerable actual transactions, whereby my whole life appears in mine eyes this day a heap of vanity, sin, and foolishness. I am fully convinced, and do from my heart acknowledge, that I am utterly unable to help myself, in whole or in part, out of this gulf of sin and misery, into which I am plunged; and that it is beyond the reach of the whole creation to help me out of it; so that I must inevitably perish for ever, if thine own strong hand do not make help to me. But forasmuch as there is a covenant of grace, for life and salvation to lost sinners, established between THEE and thine own SON, the Lord Jesus Christ, as second Adam; wherein, upon condition of his fulfilling all righteousness, which is now performed, in his having been born perfectly holy, lived altogether righteously, and made perfect satisfaction to justice by his death and

---

2. Boston, *Works*, 2:672-74. Boston wrote it on December 2, 1729, roughly two years and five months before his death.

sufferings, thou hast promised that thou wilt be their God, and they shall be thy people, to the making of them holy and p 673 happy for ever; and that this covenant is, in Christ the head thereof, offered and exhibited to me in thy gospel, and thou callest me into the fellowship thereof, in him: Therefore (adhering to my former acceptings, and taking hold of it, declared whether by word or writ before thee, without wilful mistaking of it, or known guile), upon the warrant of, and in obedience to, thy command and call, I, in myself a poor perishing sinner, and worthy to perish, do now again TAKE HOLD of that COVENANT, for life and salvation to ME; believing on the name of Christ crucified the head thereof, offered and exhibited to me, as the great High Priest, who, by the sacrifice of himself, hath made atonement, paid the ransom, and brought in everlasting righteousness for poor sinners. I CREDIT his word of grace to me, and accordingly TRUST on him, that he with his righteousness will be mine, and that, in and through him, God will be my God, and I shall be one of his people, to the making of me holy and happy for ever. O my God, I do by thy grace acquiesce in that covenant, as all my salvation, and all my desire. With my whole heart and soul, the Son incarnate is my only PRIEST, my surety, my Intercessor, and my Redeemer; and, in him, the FATHER my FATHER, the HOLY GHOST my SANCTIFIER; GOD in CHRIST my God. I resign my self, soul and body, to him, to be saved by his blood alone; renouncing all confidence in mine own righteousness, doings, and sufferings. With my whole heart and soul he is my HEAD and HUSBAND: and I am his only, wholly, and for ever; to live by him, to him, and for him. I take him for my alone PROPHET, Oracle, and Guide; give up myself wholly to him, to be taught, guided, and directed, in all things, by his word and Spirit; and renounce mine own wisdom, and the wisdom of this world. He is, with my heart's content, my alone KING and Lord. And I resign myself wholly, soul and body, unto him, to be rescued, by the strength of his mighty hand, from sin, death, the devil, and this present evil world, for to serve him for ever, and to be ruled by the will of his command as my duty, and the will of his providence as to my lot. I am, with my whole heart, content (Lord, thou knowest) to part with, and do renounce, every known sin, lust, or idol, and particularly that sin which most easily besets me; together with my own foolish will, and other lords besides him; without reservation, and without exception against his cross: Protesting in thy sight, O Lord, that I am, through grace, willing to have discovered unto me, and upon discovery to part with, every sin in me that I know not: and that the doubtings and averseness of heart, mixed with this my accepting of thy covenant, are what I allow not: and that, notwithstanding thereof, I look to be accepted of thee herein, in the Beloved, thine only Son and my Saviour, purging away these, with all my other sins, by his precious blood.

Let it be recorded in heaven, O Lord, and let the bed on which I leaned, the timber, and the stones, and all other things about me here, in my closet, bear witness, That I, though most unworthy, have this second day of December, One thousand seven hundred and twenty-nine years, here taken hold of, and come into thy covenant of grace, offered and exhibited to me in thy gospel, for time and eternity; and that thou art my God in the tenor of that covenant, and I am one of thy people, from henceforth and for ever.

T. Boston

Bibliography

Beeke, Joel, and Randall Pederson. *Meet the Puritans: With a Guide to Modern Reprints.* Grand Rapids: Reformation Heritage, 2007.

Boston, Thomas. *Scattered and Kept: Twenty-Eight Lost Sermons of Rev. Thomas Boston.* Brighton: Ettrick Press, 2022.

———. *The Whole Works of Thomas Boston.* Edited by Samuel M'Millan. 12 volumes. Aberdeen: George and Robert King, 1848–52.

Ferguson, Sinclair B. *The Whole Christ: Legalism, Antinomianism, and Gospel Assurance—Why the Marrow Controversy Still Matters.* Wheaton, IL: Crossway, 2016.

Fesko, J. V. *The Theology of the Westminster Standards: Historical Context and Theological Insights.* Wheaton, IL: Crossway, 2014.

Gerstner, John H., et al. *A Guide to the Westminster Confession of Faith: Commentary.* Signal Mountain, TN: Summertown, 1992.

Goldberg, Nathan. *Passover Haggadah.* Rev ed. Hoboken, NJ: Ktav, 1993.

Greenwald, Randall. "'Written for Children': The Westminster Shorter Catechism's Unhelpful Reputation." *Reformed Faith & Practice* 2 (2022) 73–77.

Hamilton, Ian. "Thomas Boston's Memorable Last Words." *Banner of Truth Magazine* 698 (2021).

Kapic, Kelly M., and Wesley Vander Lugt. *Pocket Dictionary of the Reformed Tradition.* Downers Grove, IL: IVP Academic, 2013.

Lachman, David C. *The Marrow Controversy, 1718–1723: An Historical and Theological Analysis.* Edinburgh: Rutherford House, 1988.

Macleod, Donald. *From the Marrow Men to the Moderates: Scottish Theology 1700–1800.* Fearn: Mentor, 2023.

McGowan, A. T. B. *The Federal Theology of Thomas Boston.* Edinburgh: Rutherford House, 1997.

Packer, James Innell. *Puritan Portraits: J. I. Packer on Selected Classic Pastors and Pastoral Classics.* Fearn: Christian Focus, 2012.

Riddlebarger, Kim. *The Lion of Princeton: B. B. Warfield as Apologist and Theologian.* Bellingham, WA: Lexham, 2015.

Ryken, Philip. *Thomas Boston as Preacher of the Fourfold State.* Edinburgh: Rutherford House, 1999.

Torrance, James B. "Strengths and Weaknesses of the Westminster Theology." In *The Westminster Confession in the Church Today: Papers Prepared for the Church of Scotland Panel on Doctrine*, edited by Alasdair I. C. Heron, 40–54. Edinburgh: Saint Andrew Press, 1982.

Torrance, Thomas F. *Scottish Theology from John Knox to John McLeod Campbell*. Edinburgh: T&T Clark, 1996.

Trueman, Carl. *The Creedal Imperative*. Wheaton, IL: Crossway, 2012.

Tse, Chun. *The Marrow of Certainty: Thomas Boston's Theology of Assurance*. Göttingen: Vandenhoeck & Ruprecht, 2023.

Watson, Jean L. *The Pastor of Ettrick: Thomas Boston*. Edinburgh: James Gemmell, 1883.